PRAISE FOR *TELL ME MORE ABOUT THAT*

"In *Tell Me More About That*, Rob Volpe illuminates not just the why, but the how, of empathy. With clarity, honesty, and deep insight, Rob shows how every interaction offers us the opportunity to build more connection and understanding—and ultimately a better world for us all."

RISHAD TOBACCOWALA, author of *Restoring the Soul of Business: Staying Human in the Age of Data*

"*Tell Me More About That* is a must-read for anyone who cares about how we live and lead into the future. Rob Volpe has poured his wisdom, heart, vulnerability, and experience walking in other people's shoes into this thoughtful, funny, informative book. There's no one better to be our guide for seeing more of ourselves in others and why we should do it than Rob and his empathy superpower."

ANDREW BLOTKY, founder and CEO, Azure Leadership Group; author of *Honestly Speaking: How the Way We Communicate Transforms Leadership, Love, and Life*

"Empathy has become the new catchphrase of leadership. However, knowing what it really is and applying it to become a spectacular leader that your talent becomes deeply connected to is rare. Rob Volpe is a master and his '5 Steps to Empathy' brilliantly lay out exactly how to do just that. This book is a must-read-and-apply for you to lead in the new world of business!"

DOV BARON, The World's Leading Meaning Authority, bestselling author, Top 30 Global Leadership Guru, and host of the *Leadership and Loyalty* podcast; DovBaron.com

"In a world dominated by digital technology, the success of a brand, venture, or leader isn't determined by the quality of their product or the efficiency of their operations. To truly succeed and stand out from the crowd, you need to understand and respond to the needs, wants, and desires of your customers, employees, and colleagues. You need empathy. Rob Volpe's *Tell Me More About That* guides the way."

MARK ACHLER, managing director, MATH Venture Partners; entrepreneurship and innovation lecturer, Northwestern University's Kellogg School of Management

PAGE TWO

Tell Me More About That

Solving the **EMPATHY CRISIS** One Conversation at a Time

ROB VOLPE

Cataloguing in publication information is available from Library and Archives Canada.
ISBN 978-1-77458-089-9 (hardcover)
ISBN 978-1-77458-090-5 (ebook)
ISBN 978-1-77458-197-1 (audiobook)

Page Two
pagetwo.com

Edited by Emily Schultz
Copyedited by Christine Savage
Proofread by Alison Strobel
Jacket and interior design by Jennifer Lum
Author's headshot by Lori Eanes (photo),
Steven Kamla (hair), Charles LaBrecque (styling)
Printed and bound in Canada by Friesens
Distributed in Canada by Raincoast Books
Distributed in the US and internationally by Macmillan

22 23 24 25 26   5 4 3 2 1

5stepstoempathy.com

For those curious to understand...

and courageous enough to try.

For my husband, Charles, who both inspires me

and keeps me grounded every day.

Contents

Introduction

We must support each other and empathize
with each other because each of us is more alike
than we are unalike. I think we all have empathy.
We may not have enough courage to display it.
MAYA ANGELOU

I WAS NOT BORN an empathy guru, but just like every human being, I was born empathetic. Through a combination of genetics, parenting, and lived experiences, I have developed a strong ability for cognitive empathy—to see the world from another person's perspective, and to walk a mile in their shoes. I also have a gift for insight into human behavior, including my own, which allows me to decipher problems and make the solutions relatable.

By trade, I am a market researcher. That means I get to listen to people and their stories. It's a job where empathy skills are critical to success. Over the course of my career, I've met thousands of individuals. These are everyday people. The ones you interact with every day. The people behind us in line at the store, or next to us at the stoplight, or in front of us at the movie theater. The people we don't necessarily give a second thought to when we pass them on the street. They aren't influencers on social media with millions or even thousands of followers. They haven't been on a reality show, nor have they been on the news. For what it's worth, these are "normal" people. And I am one of those people. I'm sure when I'm standing in line, no one gives me a second thought, just as I don't always give them a second thought. And there are over 332 million of us in the United States. Each one of us is someone else's overlooked person on the street. We are our own counterparts—neighbors and coworkers, residents of the same communities. And we all have our own story to tell—if only we took the time to ask each other the questions, listen to the stories, and see each other for who we are.

And that's what makes me love what I do—I get to be that person. I get to build empathy with people by asking questions, listening to their stories, and seeing them for who they are and their perspective on the world. And then, for some "icing on the cake," I get to share those stories with my clients to get them inspired to take action on that "One Big Idea" that will move their business forward.

The projects that my firm, Ignite 360, handles involve what may, to an outsider, seem like the more mundane, everyday parts of our lives, like snacks. Yes, snacks! Our clients are fascinated with why you buy what you buy or what needs you may have that will inform future new products. It's serious work with high stakes. The impact of our thinking, finding insights by building empathy with consumers and turning it into strategy, can mean hundreds of millions of dollars in additional revenue for our clients. The bonus is that, in the course of interviewing someone to find out how they think and feel about snacks, we are also getting to know them, who they are as a person and what motivates them in life. Will the nation heal its wounds and come together through a shared love of a salty snack or a breakfast cereal? Probably not, but when any two people get in a room together and talk, we do get to know each other better, and that understanding is what will help us come together again. One conversation at a time.

Empathy, and a knack for storytelling, is my superpower. It's how I'm able to connect with people and understand where they are coming from. It provides me with the vision to see the world through someone else's eyes. Everyone has their own worldview made up of individual, unique combinations of factors that create their perspective. By listening and adapting a shift in my own perspective to temporarily align with someone else's, I'm able to reach cognitive empathy with another person, which forges that connection through understanding.

Unfortunately, empathy skills are at an all-time low in the United States and have been since the start of the twenty-first century. A study from the University of Michigan Institute for Social Research published in May 2010 found, through a meta-analysis of student life surveys from 1979 to 2009, that there was a 40 percent decline in the ability of students to see the point of view of their classmates in 2001 compared to previous decades. In a study that Ignite 360 conducted in March 2021, nearly one-third of American adults over the age of eighteen had no strong feelings toward, or *disagreed with*, the statement, "It's easy for me to see the point of view of others." These numbers, while disappointing, should come as no surprise when you consider the state of our discourse—in person as well as on social media—on almost any topic, including politics, religion, gender identity, racism, immigration, policing, welfare, and other social equity issues. The evidence of our decline in empathy surrounds us 24/7. Lack of empathy is generating tension as each side digs in their heels instead of working together toward solutions. This breakdown is "the empathy crisis."

The empathy crisis is wearing away at the gears of society, grinding us down to nubs, inhibiting our ability to enjoy life. The range of a person's ability to empathize is increasingly limited to the bubbles of their individual lives and belief systems. This breakdown shows up in our resorting to trolling, bullying, and cruelty toward others in order to feel safe and justified in our own attitudes or beliefs rather than expressing compassion. And forget about finding forgiveness; that's another action that's hindered when there is no empathy.

The breakdown is happening both at work and at home. In the workplace, empathy helps with collaboration among teams, improved leadership ability, understanding and relationships with employees, and decision-making. The "EQ" (emotional intelligence) expectation of employees and leaders has increased precisely because empathy skills have declined. At home, in the midst of an increasingly diverse population, there is also an increasingly divided culture. We are cheering on division instead of celebrating diversity. Whether we're divided by race or religion, political affiliation, income, privilege, or any other difference, we've lost touch with the ability to be good neighbors. Instead, people disregard the diversity that makes us strong as a nation and have reverted to segregated factions aligned with the different sides in the culture wars. Segregating us further and hastening the decline of our empathy skills are our technological advances, which haven't truly shrunk the world but actually have shrunk us, creating greater distance between us than ever. Ironically, the biggest divide is with the people we used to be most connected to—those people around us in our community. Our neighbors. The ones walking past us on the street. The everyday humans.

Compounding the effect of this segregation is the desire of many Americans to be seen as being noteworthy. Perhaps this is a revised "American Dream," where having greater value than your parents or prior generations is now defined by followers and "likes" rather than moving up the socioeconomic ladder? Collectively, many Americans have convinced themselves that they must be showcasing an always-on-the-go, "fabulous" life on social media in order to be legitimized, receive validation from others, and therefore have that greater value. The validation is coming in the form of little blue thumbs-up icons or hearts signifying likes. The more likes, the more validation, which releases dopamine in the brain, creating a desire for even more likes the next time. This forms a habit of living life in pursuit of likes.

This addiction to validation has squandered the available time that was previously used to form connections casually, like over the fence with the neighbor, or with the adjacent table in a restaurant, or the neighboring pew in church. How often do you now look at your phone instead of striking up a conversation? We've squandered opportunities to build empathy with each other, and, as a result, our ability to empathize has atrophied. Now, people bump into one another. Instead of expressing understanding, we're raging at each other, all because we aren't taking the time to pay attention, listen, and see another's point of view.

AND THEN, a virus came along and upended everything. The COVID-19 pandemic forced many of us to live life full-time inside our own homes. The exciting adventures once posted and validated in the past were replaced, in my feed, by pictures of sourdough bread, sunsets from the backyard, and, finally, people getting vaccinated. Since many of our lives had become so routine and similar to each other, our FOMO (fear of missing out) and quest for validation dissipated. Amid the illness, death, and disruption of the pandemic, people were given an opportunity to reflect on their lives and who they wanted to be when the pandemic was over.

I was surprised to find, in another Ignite 360 study called *Navigating to a New Normal*, which gathered data from more than thirty-seven thousand adults between April 2020 to March 2021, that 72 percent of American adults wanted some form of change in their life instead of going back to life as it was pre-pandemic.

But what type of change are they wanting? Diving into that data, I was surprised when we found that, of those people looking for change, 74 percent were looking to have more gratitude and appreciation for the things that they have. A major insight coming out of the data was people's desire for connection and community and to do so in a more meaningful way. That includes 65 percent of people who said they wanted to make an effort to understand the point of view of other people. They identified empathy as an area they wanted to change or had changed already! That's a lot of interest in building empathy skills. Perhaps you are one of those people, and that's why you picked up this book?

The more time I've spent thinking about empathy—what it is, how we give it and get it, and why—I've realized that empathy really is like a muscle to be trained and exercised until it's toned and in shape, fit, and firm. Currently, many of us have empathy muscles that are flabby and atrophied. Isn't it time to get them back in shape?

TELL ME MORE ABOUT THAT is based on my personal journey toward understanding my own empathy superpower and making my empathy muscle stronger. In the course of this journey, I've gone from being a victim, where I felt people didn't have empathy with me, to learning to dismantle my own judgment and biases so I could truly hear the stories being told to me and achieve empathy with others. Many of these realizations came about in my adventures meeting everyday people while I was doing marketing research projects. In these pages, I will share a selection of these adventures and the lessons that I learned.

Meanwhile, I recognized, and grew frustrated, that more and more leaders and commentators were calling for us as a society to have more empathy. At the same time, clients were asking my firm, in increasing numbers, for empathy engagements so they could get closer to their clients and "get some empathy." If empathy is an atrophied muscle, then we need a training plan—a way to strengthen a skill gone soft. But no one had stepped forward with instructions on *how* to do that.

At Ignite 360, we're big on the application of insights—how to put knowledge into action. Without that, our insights are just data sitting around gathering dust. Similarly, I didn't see the value in creating an empathy engagement between a client and their consumer if they weren't going to actually reach empathy. The experience wouldn't turn into something of lasting value. What I recognized was missing was the knowledge on *how* to reach empathy in the moment of engagement that could be taught to others.

Due to my personal experiences growing up, the thousands of people I've interviewed, and being insightful about how my clients and I respond to those people, as well as conversations with a psychologist to help inform my thinking, I've been able to identify the five steps that get us to cognitive empathy. My goal is to help you understand The 5 Steps to Empathy™ and how to apply them to your own life, whether at work, at home, or at play.

I start with a few stories from before I was as well versed in empathy as I am now, and the near disasters that created. Then, I share the 5 Steps to Empathy. Each step is brought to life in the context of some of my most memorable moments interviewing people, where barriers to empathy came up relevant to that particular step and how I overcame the obstacles. As you read these stories, consider how you would react if you were there and how you might respond to get to a place of empathy incorporating the focus step of the story and your own instincts.

Like so much of life, I've found that learning and practicing the 5 Steps has been a circuitous journey. I am not perfect. I am human. Even today I will catch myself being judgmental, which will prevent me from having empathy with someone. Fortunately, I now have the skills to dismantle my judgment.

Every person I have written about is real. I've changed names and some identifying characteristics to protect their identities. I share their stories, and mine, for learning and inspiration. You may easily imagine who these people are in your own life. They could be your family, your friends, your coworkers, or your neighbors. They are you and me. Together, we can reverse course on the empathy crisis and make all of our lives better in the process.

PART 1

When Empathy Eludes Us

1

It's Like Christmas Morning

There are so many ways of being despicable it quite
makes one's head spin. But the way to be really
despicable is to be contemptuous of other people's pain.
JAMES BALDWIN

THE WELCOME CHILL of the air as we entered David's apartment brought relief from the steamy, Chicago-in-July morning heat and humidity. It was going to be another scorcher. The type of day that makes me uncomfortable—where tempers flare and fuses are short, not unlike the state of the world we live in today. My preferred environment is an air-conditioned harmony of collaboration and working together, enabled by taking the perspective of one another. That cools the air, dries the sweat off our brows, and lets us see the person in front of us. Unfortunately, that type of "air-conditioning" is in short supply due to the decline in empathy skills. Fortunately, inside David's apartment, I found a fellow soul who was naturally curious and able to extend that curiosity to achieve empathy.

David was a respondent on a research project that I was moderating for clients about the snacking habits of young adults. Joining me for the day were two clients and a videographer who would record the session to be used as part of a short summary video. David, in his mid-twenties, lived with a roommate in a large apartment just north of downtown.

As we cooled off and made small talk in his kitchen while the video equipment was being set up, David turned to me and said, "You must have some good stories." I paused for a moment. His question was "out of turn." I was there to ask *him* the questions. About his life, his shopping habits, his eating habits, and anything else he wanted to share. I had several typed pages of questions for him, in fact. Instead, David was turning the tables on me. I was on the spot and had to answer some questions before I could do the asking. There, in his kitchen, I found myself admitting for the first time, out loud in front of strangers, that I was writing a book about empathy and how these conversations, like the one we were about to have, helped inform my understanding of empathy.

"Have you ever felt unsafe?" he asked me. David's curiosity was healthy, and I appreciated that, although it was unusual for the moderator to be asked so many questions. I suppose he could have been trying to build empathy with me and see the world from my perspective. It also crossed my mind that he could be a good moderator himself someday.

I answered his question: "Have I felt uncomfortable doing this type of work? Definitely. Unsafe? Not really." I'd be lying if I said it didn't feel a little uncomfortable going into a stranger's home in a strange town. I'd call it nervous anticipation. To help allay those feelings, either on the side of the respondent or the moderator and clients, at Ignite 360 we do something we call "screendowns," which resemble an audition process. The screendowns are designed to help ensure both quality and safety. Our respondents are found locally through recruiters from nearby research facilities. When we come to the facility with a project, we give them some specs that form a behavior profile and the demographics of the people we're hoping to meet. The recruiters then reach out to their database and within their community to find people that fit, and they share a short list of candidates with us. Then one of the moderators from my company does a screendown with those people to hear directly from them, evaluating their comfort in sharing their stories, and confirming that their behaviors match what we are looking for and that they have some sense of what they are getting themselves into. Once we find the people we want to meet, there are several more conversations for scheduling, confirmation calls, and the like. Our moderator ends up creating a short bio of the respondent we're about to see, and hopefully the respondent has some sense of what to expect. It also helps create rapport when we first get to the person's house. When I reference my colleague who they had talked to in the screendown, the respondent instantly relaxes.

As to David's safety question, due to the screendowns it's never been a concern, with only the rarest of exceptions, like one time in Memphis when I wasn't sure if my rental car would be in the spot where I left it, or the time in Lexington, Kentucky, when someone let the air out of the tires of my rental car in the parking lot of the Walmart where I was conducting research. (Thank goodness for the Walmart store's tire center coming to my rescue!) Other than that, no fear for my safety.

Any anxiety that I have is really anticipation. Who is this person? What's their house going to be like? Having done hundreds of in-homes, I'm usually comfortable heading in. A client, however, particularly one that doesn't get to do in-homes regularly, can experience an *Alice Through the Looking Glass* moment. It's like going down the rabbit hole, where the only thing you can expect is the unexpected. Even though we as humans have so much in common, individual people are very different in how they live their lives. I've found that flexibility and comfort with the unknown are keys to success in research. That uncertainty can make some people nervous. I don't blame them. While there are many basic human values that we all share, there are also those values that aren't shared, or at least the expression of them is subjective. For example, a standard level of cleanliness in a home. Often, clients have preconceived notions or a stereotype of the consumer they are going to meet. It's often a loyal "champion" user of their product or service that they've built up in their mind. This creates a good amount of dissonance and discomfort starting just minutes after entering someone's home, as clients come to terms with what they are seeing versus their idealized notion. Then the "champion" starts to open up and share their story, and instead of sounding familiar, it can get even stranger! If this is in contradiction to what was expected, it can make it really difficult to try to see the point of view of another person. This is true in my research situations as well as in daily personal life. Accepting the diversity in society comes easier for the moderator, who is trained, experienced, and looks for it, than it is for some clients. That means, as the moderator, I pull double duty, having to establish my own empathy with the respondent while also being empathetic with the clients, how they are processing the situation, and what I can do to help them reach empathy like I have built with the respondent. It's through this process, repeated hundreds upon hundreds of times, that I was finally able to understand the 5 Steps to Empathy and what is required to successfully climb those steps.

For me, the unknown, which can make the clients feel nervous, is part of the joy of what I do. When I walk up to knock on the respondent's door, I don't know what I am going to experience. The session could be pretty straightforward, very functional and practical, which has its place. Or it could be that unicorn of a respondent, someone whose story personally touches me and might even inspire me to make changes in my own life. And in between those two extremes are many, many other people who are willing to pull back the curtain and share a glimpse into their life.

"This job, it's like Christmas morning every time I'm in the field," I told David. "You know you are going to be given a gift, but you don't know what that gift will be."

"But I always know I'm going to like what I'm going to get at Christmas," he replied.

"Yes, sometimes you get that toy that you always wanted, and other times you get a piece of clothing that you need. There's a difference," I told him. I got the signal the videographer was ready so I transitioned my conversation with David to start the actual interview I was there to conduct.

I GOT a green sweater at Christmas one year. Nice, but I really wanted something else. So I was disappointed by that. It was a functional/practical gift that I "needed" rather than what I "wanted." My relative who gave me that gift didn't really know me well enough to put themselves in my shoes and get me something that I could use. To be fair, I was probably about twelve, and that can be a hard age to shop for, as I've learned with my own nephews. But being a good gift-giver is about having empathy. Putting yourself in the shoes of the recipient and imagining what they would like to receive. I find in-homes are just like this. The respondent is giving me a gift that I want, which is their stories on the topic we're studying.

Since it's socially awkward to receive a gift and not have anything to give back in return, what I strive to give back is the gift of empathy. I do that by listening to people without judgment. In turn, that lets me truly hear someone and see their point of view. Empathy is about sitting together rather than one person standing over another. There's a difference in having sympathy *for* someone and having empathy *with* them. Sympathy has a power dynamic, one person superior to the other. Empathy is experiencing and understanding on equal footing. That's where the connection comes in. We are starving in today's society to feel recognized and understood, to have someone sit with us, rather than be judged and minimized, someone standing over us. Taking the time to listen and see someone's point of view, even if only for a few moments in a single day, can make all the difference. I know the respondent I'm talking with is looking to be seen. To know that their story is being heard. My job is to be present for them to share that story while feeling safe, secure, and seen. It's the power of the gift of empathy that leaves someone with a feeling of being valued and of self-worth. That's more durable and enduring than a "like" on a social media post. This is about real human connection. Face to face. In real time. No filters.

We're often so quick to judge people and shut down those voices that don't align perfectly with our worldview. I cringe when I hear people being judgmental toward others. What makes one person think they are "better" than another? Every person has a right to be heard and to tell their story. They have a right to exist and be treated with kindness, compassion, and understanding, just like you want to be treated yourself. I have always held that as my core belief. It comes from my own experiences back in the 1970s and '80s, growing up in small-town Indiana. My spirit went from carefree to crushed in a matter of months. I was the victim of judgment from classmates. My truth and the path that I had been headed on ran smack into a brick wall in the form of a heterogeneous Hoosier community that was as hard to navigate and as alien to me as I was to them.

We moved to Indiana when I was three. Before that, my parents and I were living in New York City with my paternal grandparents. I believe, and am told, that I was in heaven with that living arrangement. And I loved the NYC subway to the point of obsession. An elevated line was just a few blocks from my grandma's house. On visits later in my life, I would lie in bed at night and hear the trains pulling in and out of the station. The exhale of pneumatic brakes transported me to the platform and a journey across the cityscape. But my dream life was interrupted when my dad got a job offer in the Midwest. And so off we went. My grandma still recounts how her heart broke when we left. Loaded into the car, my parents and I were about to drive away. I turned and waved and said, "Bye, grandma, see you soon!" Little did I know how much my world was about to change and how much it would change me.

In the first Indiana small town we lived in, life was good. I was either too young to know better or I got lucky in that early experience. I made friends along my street, explored the dry creek bed behind our house, often role-playing with the other kids. I had a best friend, Joey, who lived nearby. We were inseparable, except for the inconvenience of his going to Catholic school each day. For me, elementary school came easily, and I enjoyed it. Miss Welch, my fourth-grade teacher, even changed my name. Until then, I had gone by Robbie. She decided I was "too mature" for Robbie and started calling me Rob. Except for a few relatives who kept calling me Robbie as a term of endearment, the shortened name stuck.

Even at that young age, the idea of being judged by others bothered me. Joey and I were happy and had our own fun, fueled by a passion for DC Comics and the action heroines on TV in the mid- to late '70s. Our role-playing tended to be more Wonder Woman, Bionic Woman, Isis, and Charlie's Angels than *Adam-12* or *Dukes of Hazzard*. In the creek bed behind my house, while the other boys were playing Army and trying to impress the girls by peeing in front of them on a large rock, Joey and I would pretend we were Amazons, captured by Nazis and forced to mine "Feminum," the fictitious rare metal that makes the Amazons' bulletproof bracelets. It was literally straight out of a two-part episode of the *Wonder Woman* TV series, and we had a blast role-playing in our own little world. Spinning around to change into our superhero outfits, catching bad guys, and stopping the forces of evil. It was my childhood, and I was very happy.

In this small town, Joey and I never got teased by the other kids, at least not then. But our choices of games to play informed choices that others made about us playing their games with them—notably on the T-ball "field," which was the cul-de-sac right in front of my house. T-ball was our neighborhood version of baseball, played with tennis balls so we wouldn't break any windows. There were regular pickup games when the weather was nice, and most of the kids on the street would play, as best I can remember. Until one day, when Joey and I were excluded from one of the games. No reason given; they just didn't want us to play. And they wouldn't listen to us when we asked to be included. We were shut out, and that didn't seem right to me, especially since my mailbox was home plate! The kids also threw their personal crap in my yard while they played. It seemed mighty unfair that they would exclude us from playing when they were taking over part of my front yard.

Rejected but not defeated, Joey and I went inside my house. My mom was home at the time. We grumbled and complained. She listened but clearly wasn't going to intervene on our behalf. We needed to solve this ourselves, she encouraged. So, since they weren't listening to "reason," we decided that we should protest. We found some cardboard in the garage, made a few signs that we could carry, and started to muster up the courage for our first protest march. I remember being really nervous. Scared is probably the better word for it. Knowing my best friend was there with me gave me that little dose of extra courage to get me over the hump of hesitation. Except, it turns out, he was more scared than I was. He didn't want to go. But I couldn't go out there by myself. I had a brainstorm and told him that if we did it together, perhaps the local newspaper would come out and take some pictures and write a story about how the kids were being unfair.

The promise of publicity and the importance of our cause bonded us together and forged our commitment to stand up for our rights. We took our signs and stepped out into the bright sun. We "marched" around the cul-de-sac, basically right along the bases but in reverse order. The other kids were staring at us incredulously. Joey stayed right behind me, repeatedly asking me, "When is the reporter going to come?" and "When is the newspaper going to get here?" I was so uncomfortable, but we needed to keep going to get our point across. When they listened to us, that's when we'd stop.

Or... the combination of summer heat and feelings of awkwardness would get to us first. We only made it around a couple of times before we retreated into the safety and air-conditioning of my house. We didn't extract an apology from the kids, nor did we get to play, but we certainly made some kind of point with our protest.

Sadly, the newspaper reporter never showed up. In hindsight, that might have been for the best. The headline "Kids Are Cruel" wouldn't have won the Pulitzer despite its truth. And if I thought being excluded from a T-ball game was cruel, I had a lot to learn.

At the end of fourth grade, when I was ten, we moved from one small town to an even smaller small town in Indiana. Being the newcomer and not just like all the other kids, who were the product of multiple generations living out life in this county filled with small towns and farmland, I became an easy target. I also didn't have Joey, or anyone remotely like Joey, that I could pal around with and be myself. Learning how to exist in this new environment required learning a whole new language of being. Instead of just being me, like I always had, I quickly learned that I had to mind what I said and how I said it. Basically, I had to monitor my every movement through this new world. Of course, no one shared the rules of this game with me; it was all trial and error. And every error was subject to ridicule. So, I got teased and bullied. A lot. I was judged. Put into a box marked "other" and continually derided. *Gay* and *faggot* became the preferred terms to use behind my back and to my face.

The "teasing" started shortly after we arrived in that smaller small town. That was just months before I started fifth grade. From the moment I tried playing with some of the other kids in the neighborhood, I had trouble fitting in. I didn't understand why these kids weren't like Joey. Nobody in this town was interested in playing Wonder Woman, Charlie's Angels, or Bionic Woman. Where was I? What strange planet had I landed on?

Fifth and sixth grade were my living hell. This was 1980. Small-town Indiana in 1980. The words hurled at me were really derogatory and beyond the language I knew at the time. The boys would sling vulgarities at one another while the girls opted for a different approach, making comments about appearance, clothes, hair, overall looks. I noticed that the kids who had older siblings seemed to have the more "advanced" vocabulary when it came to insults and put-downs, which they had obviously learned from older brothers and sisters. They had a leg up on the firstborns like me. Even though they may not have fully understood what the words meant, they could hurl insults my way so casually, it was like they'd been doing it for years. I often had to hold back the tears all day long. Lingering to leave one class to avoid some, bolting out of another class to evade others. I made excuses about having hay fever and other allergies on the rare occasion a teacher noticed my eyes were red. I remember more than once riding the bus home, biting my lower lip to keep it from quivering, stung by the insults of the day. As soon as I'd step off the bus into my front yard, the tears would break free and roll down my cheeks as I made a beeline for my front door.

I didn't even understand what "gay" was until one day I came home and asked my mom. I can't imagine what that was like for my mom or any parent. Kids may say the craziest things, but the initial ideas come from somewhere outside their brains. Instead of me coming home and asking about the birds and the bees, I'm wondering out loud about a topic that was still widely considered deviant behavior back then, especially in Indiana.

Friends were few and far between those first couple years as I was regularly being pummeled by rumor, innuendo, taunts, and threats. It was crushing to my spirit, and I was lonely. When I look at the annual school portraits that are now arranged in a large frame at my parents' house—the "Wall of Rob," as we call it—I can see the difference in the pictures of "Robbie" in the small town and the pictures of "Rob" in the smaller small town. Rob's eyes completely lost their spark in those years after the move. The joy was gone. Back then, I didn't understand why the kids were rejecting me. I hadn't done anything wrong that I was aware of. I was just being me.

The pictures reveal that I retreated so far inside myself to try to save myself, my light was shining inward instead of out through my eyes. Those "Wall of Rob" pictures, to this day, remain a visible reflection of what I went through and what I had lost in my childhood.

At home I tried to keep things happy by being a good son. At least I could have a refuge at home. My family loved me, and I could rely on that. Home became my safe harbor from the storms in every other aspect of my life.

I almost gave up the fight in sixth grade. I remember coming home one day, another of the countless days of being taunted or teased or pushed around or all of the above. I'd had enough. I couldn't take it anymore. I was being told by adults to fight back physically. Land a single punch on my tormentors and it would all be over, they counseled me. But physical violence runs counter to who I am. It feels so wrong to me, deep down. Intellectually I knew if I threw a punch or two, it could change things. But it goes against who I am as a person. In spite of the suffering, I wasn't willing or able to overcome that guiding principle, even though it might have brought me emotional relief. I just wouldn't fight with my fists. I remained so lonely and miserable; I couldn't take it. I reached the point where killing myself seemed like an acceptable alternative. A release from this suffering. I remember thinking at the time that at least the torment I was living through would be over.

I gave some thought to how I might do it. I knew I would need a knife but didn't know how to cut myself. I'm grateful there was no Internet available back then. The lack of information slowed me down. What also slowed me down was that safe harbor in my house. I was upset and seeking relief from the suffering, but I wasn't at the point where I could ignore the reality of what I'd put my family through if I went ahead with killing myself. I also knew, deep down, that I wouldn't be in this smaller small town forever. It's hard, at age twelve, to imagine that in only six years—a span of time that is half of the life I'd already lived; in other words, an eternity—I'd be able to escape, move away, and live a happier life somewhere else for a much longer period of time than that seeming eternity of suffering I'd had to endure. All of those thoughts, for me, won out over my intense desire to escape the pain.

I resolved to myself to stick it out. This wouldn't be forever. I also knew that there were other places far away from these small towns, and I'd be able to leave someday. The worst of my torment was those last two years of elementary school. With each passing year after that, as the kids either matured or got used to me, or I learned how to assimilate and manage the rumors, life gradually got better. Year by year, the light slowly returned to my eyes. I still had to keep my guard constantly up, and I had to always mind my behavior and what I said in case the gay taunts or rumors would kick in again. By watching my classmates' behavior, I learned how rumors spread, and I became especially mindful to watch myself in the early part of the week. If a rumor broke out on Thursday or Friday, it'd be forgotten by Monday, and I'd be away from everyone over the weekend. But the weeks where a rumor started on Monday or Tuesday, those ended up being some of the longest weeks of my life.

AS I mentioned, in the first small town in Indiana, I had felt like the kids knew me and accepted me for who I was. Maybe I was just lucky because I was so young. And I was also fortunate to have Joey, my best friend down the street who also liked to role-play female action heroes and never gave it a moment's hesitation. We were who we were, and we never gave a thought to the idea that life wasn't going to continue this way forever—at least until I moved and learned otherwise.

After my family's move, Joey and I drifted apart. Occasional letters, one or two visits, a phone call. It didn't feel the same. Maybe because I was getting teased for exactly what and how Joey and I used to play together. And when he did visit, I remember not wanting to introduce him to the other kids in my neighborhood for us all to play together. It was hard enough for me on my own. So we drifted further and further away from each other. We completely lost touch by the time I went off to college. It was only through social media that we were able to reconnect some thirty years later. Turns out Joey went through his own personal hell a few years after I started my journey. The kids in his high school were just as cruel as the kids I had to deal with. So maybe I wouldn't have escaped the teasing had we not moved. Or maybe Joey and I would have faced it together. Safety in numbers.

People today ask me when I knew I was gay. Once we arrived in that smaller small town, I knew *something* was up. I definitely wasn't like all the other boys. I wouldn't have gone to the word *gay*, largely because I didn't know what it meant, and I was still a couple years away from puberty. The label isolated me, as I didn't understand what I had done wrong in their eyes or what I should do to fix it. Yet deep down, somewhere inside, I knew there was something different about me. Perhaps *gay* wasn't just something random the kids picked up. Perhaps that's who I really was. And that created another problem for me. How could I complain in sixth grade about kids teasing me for being gay? Even that phrase— *being gay*—felt like it acknowledged a truth. So, if the taunts were true, were they right in being so cruel to me? What administrator or teacher would stand up for me? What if the principal asked me if it was true? If I *was* gay, the kids were just calling it like it was, years before I was able to understand and come to terms with it myself. If the kids were telling the truth, was I a liar for denying it? How could I ask the principal to protect me or punish the other kids if I'm the liar? Best not to do anything, then. Swallow it and deal. Day by day. So goes the mind of a sixth-grader, caught up in the spin cycle of childhood.

In the smaller small town, I never felt like my elementary school classmates took the time to get to really know me. To hear my story, my interests and passions. I was different, and that threatened the status quo of the school and the town. I was an infection, and the kids were the town's antibodies trying to drive me out. Like so many kids who have experienced similar situations, whether gay, Black, physically or mentally disabled, or different in their own unique and wonderful way, there was no empathy gift exchange for me in that smaller town.

I now know that my experience was not unlike that of so many kids, whether or not they fall into the "other" category. It could be based on race, ethnicity, religion, sexual orientation, smarts or looks, choices of clothes or hairstyles, or anything else that the student antibodies judged was an infection to be eradicated. Like so many other kids before and after me, those years were a time filled with pain, confusion, and isolation. Sometimes I marvel that I survived it. I had a stable home life, so that certainly helped. I also had the inner resources to see that this wasn't a permanent situation. We had moved in, and we (or I) could move out. And deep down I knew that the future, my future, would not always involve living in that small town.

Not everyone is so lucky; some kids are driven past the brink, pummeled senseless by the weight of endless hurtful comments and actions. And so even though my experience is similar to that of so many others, maybe including yours, it is dissimilar as well. I certainly had privilege, being white and male. The people who teased me may not have been as vicious as what you experienced, or maybe they were worse. It was my experience, the only one I know. What happened to me contributed significantly toward molding me into the adult that I am today. Out of this wound, my empathy superpower started to kick in. When I felt that no one could see my perspective and take my side, I turned it on and used empathy as a survival skill, to blend in and get along, keeping the rumor mill at bay.

Ironically, even though my classmates weren't listening to me, I still loved to talk to people. And I was pretty adept at it. The age of the person I was talking with didn't matter; I just liked to talk and hear people tell their stories, connecting *with* them rather than having sympathy for or being judgmental toward them.

In junior high school, I started my first job as a paperboy. Every week or two, I'd go door-to-door and collect payment for subscriptions. What should have taken no more than two hours often took me six because I'd spend hours chatting with the various adults whose homes were on my route. It was supposed to be a quick transactional conversation where I asked for the balance due, then gave them their proof of payment when I collected the cash. That takes minutes. But sometimes, with some houses, not all of them, I'd get invited inside and we'd talk about whatever was on their mind. World events, local politics, work, family traditions. Those conversations opened up new worlds for me. It was the first time I got to peek into other people's lives. See how they lived compared to my own home. Learn what rituals and celebrations were important to them. Understand how these adults viewed the world. I was highly curious and had lots of questions. I also liked to share my own thoughts, young and formative though they might have been. I often came home eager to share the stories I'd heard that day. I didn't realize it at the time, but I was doing my own version of ethnographic research. Those experiences gabbing with the people on my paper route taught me how enjoyable it is to listen to others, and how to be open to differences when I encounter them. And because these good people listened to me in return, I finally experienced the empathy gift exchange. And I liked it.

From my earliest memories, I've always had a good degree of compassion and empathy for others. I couldn't imagine being cruel toward others the way I felt the kids were cruel to me. I always believed in emotions as a strength, inspired and modeled by my Uncle Ted and my paternal grandpa, who were both willing to show their emotions and even shed a tear out of compassion or empathy with others. They helped me learn to be me and see the world as a place where everyone has their story and each person's experience is as important as the next.

The story of a working-class, Black single mother struggling to make ends meet is no more or less worthy of being heard than the most adored celebrity of the moment. The jock's story is no more or less worthy than the nerd's. Or even my own story. Within our everyday lives, among the mass non-influencer populous lie the stories of compassion, resilience, and inspiration that are the true story of our collective humanity. These tales are meaningful, and they have the ability to inspire when they deal with the shared experiences that we all relate to, regardless of who the stories come from. Revealing true emotion and feeling that is universal to our common existence, and being able to have empathy, is when we truly connect with each other. The rest of it is artifice. I believe each and every one of us has a story to share, and we deserve to be heard.

You don't need to be a market researcher like me to develop and practice empathy skills. Humans, as a species, are born with the ability to be empathetic. Right now it's like an atrophied muscle that needs to be trained back into shape. My journey to developing and practicing empathy wasn't like flipping on a light switch. It took years of awareness and focus, reflecting on what I was noticing within myself and exploring the barriers that came up. Practice and patience were plentiful. So were cringe-inducing moments where I was being judgmental and having to check myself to come back in line. Empathy isn't achieved in a day, and the skill isn't developed in a linear fashion. Mastering these skills is an iterative process, more like a loop-de-loop with curlicues, taking two steps forward, one step back. And that's okay. Even today, I'm nowhere near perfect. How can I be? I'm human, just like everyone else. I check in with how I'm doing and where I am today. Like developing any skill, you need a combination of awareness, forgiveness, and resilience to keep going. I don't measure myself against where I've been or where I want to be, and you shouldn't either. It's today that matters, having empathy in the moment.

This is why I want to introduce you to the 5 Steps to Empathy that I've uncovered in my work building empathy between myself and clients and consumers—and the amazing people along the way who helped me gain the awareness to identify the steps. Could I just give you a quick chart or list and send you on your way? Yes, of course. But then you would miss the heart of the matter, the whole story. And I suspect you picked up this book because you want to have a personal experience and know more. The next stories are examples of when I was still fumbling in the dark, less empathetic in the moment than I am now. Then, I'll tell you about the "light-bulb moment" that turned me around in a direction to uncovering the 5 Steps and my experiences learning about each one of them.

EMPATHETIC REFLECTIONS

- Looking back on your childhood or another point in your life, when did you feel misunderstood by others? How did that feel? What comforted you during that time? How did you get through it?

- How would you rate your current ability to have empathy? Where do you think you need to focus your training?

2

The Hazards
of the Job

*Don't criticize them; they are just what
we would be under similar circumstances.*
ABRAHAM LINCOLN

O NE JUNE MORNING I woke up on the floor of Washington, DC's Dulles International Airport with a cocktail of anxiety-induced adrenaline and cortisol coursing through my veins. I moved the T-shirt that was covering my eyes, revealing the rosy, red sky of dawn giving way to the brighter light of day. The concourse was becoming illuminated by natural daylight. I reached for my phone, which was, fortunately, still plugged into the industrial outlet at the base of the concrete column beside me. It was 5:30 a.m., a little more than three hours after I had last checked the time. I had managed to spread myself out so that I was touching every personal possession while I slept. Dirty clothes were stuffed into my backpack to form a pillow for my head. My arm was still resting on my carry-on suitcase in a casual embrace usually reserved for a lover. From my horizontal perspective I could see other people walking past. Still others were seated around me. This was embarrassing. I had become "that person" who sleeps in the airport. I had become that person that I have always been judgmental about.

Before this incident, I would think to myself, *Who does that?* as I moved past people-shaped lumps strewn on airport floors and seating areas. How could anyone sleep with an armrest pressing on their ribs? And the floors: they may get vacuumed daily, but they are still dirty. *Ick*. My judgment was so strong that I couldn't muster any empathy or even find some sympathy, let alone have compassion.

I know now that I was being judgmental because I couldn't understand why these airport sleepers allowed themselves to get into this situation instead of being resourceful like me. Didn't they have a friend or family they could stay with? What about getting a hotel room for the night? Surely that would be more comfortable than bivouacking it in the airport gate area. My judgment stopped me cold in my tracks from having *cognitive empathy*—seeing the other person's point of view; *emotional empathy*—feeling what others are feeling as they are feeling it; and even *sympathy*—feeling for another person and their misfortune.

Yes, even sympathy. One mistake people make is confusing sympathy for empathy when they are actually two different things. I describe the difference as the discrepancy between the words *for* and *with*. Empathy is a more powerful tool in our communication and relationship skill set because it can be used in good times and in bad—you can have empathy *with* someone who got a promotion, bought a car, or fell in love just as easily as you can have empathy *with* someone who lost their job, got into a car accident, or ended a relationship. (For more on the difference between the two and how to respond to someone empathetically, I love the YouTube video "Brené Brown on Empathy vs Sympathy.")

Until it happened to me, I was having none of the above with people sleeping overnight in airports. I was being judgmental of them, and that got in the way of me having any feelings that would take me toward compassion. Until I was, literally, in the same situation myself.

I found myself in this supine position thanks to severe thunderstorms up and down the East Coast the night before. I had been traveling between New York City and Atlanta for a project I was working on about teenagers and bubble gum. We had a "travel day," and since it was a relatively short distance between the two cities on our study, I thought I'd connect in Washington, DC, in order to spend the afternoon with relatives and reap the reward of more frequent-flier points, as that routing let me fly my preferred airline. Great idea and fun visit, but bad idea in the summer when thunderstorms regularly upset the delicate apple cart of airline schedules.

This trip was turning into *The Amazing Race*. I had to get to Atlanta to start a day in the field. The clients' flight from Newark to Atlanta miraculously made it, despite the storms the night before. And to make matters worse, my fellow moderator was stuck in New York City and couldn't get a flight to Atlanta for two days! Fortunately, we knew of an Atlanta-based moderator who happened to be available and could pinch-hit for us. Hooray! Except I was now the only continuity on the project. Allison, the new moderator, had barely been briefed and hadn't even met the clients. I felt the pressure of responsibility to make sure I was there.

Since I would be hitting the ground running in Atlanta, I needed to figure out how to use the resources at Dulles Airport to get myself dressed and presentable before my flight. There weren't many options. No showers in lounges were available at Dulles back in 2007. There wasn't even a private lounge nearby that I could buy my way into. I decided my only real option was to figure out some sort of sponge bath situation in the public restroom.

This was like a challenge straight out of *MacGyver*. How do you get yourself clean using nothing but the clothes in your suitcase, paper towels, and the soap dispenser in an airport bathroom? And on three hours of sleep?

Intrepid is a word that's been used to describe me over the years, and this was a moment that required a dose of intrepid ingenuity. I set my suitcase down, unzipped it, and took a look. I spotted a clean athletic sock and realized that if I turned it inside out, the nubby fabric resembled the texture of a washcloth, which would work to cleanse my skin. I selected a sink toward the end of a row of sinks so as to be less conspicuous. I bent over the sink, waving my sock under the motion sensor to activate the water, got it wet, applied a little soap from the dispenser, and began bathing myself. I didn't fully lather up and clean my entire body, just the parts that can get a little funky smelling. And yes, other passengers were walking in and out of the bathroom as I stood in front of a public sink, nearly naked, legs spread, trying to clean myself. They'd give me the side-eye and walk quickly to another part of the bathroom, where they could avoid making direct eye contact. A couple brave souls quickly splashed water on their fingers at the other end of the row of sinks. I was definitely feeling their judgment, just like I had judged other airport sleepers.

Of course, once I was wet, I needed to get dry. Paper towel from the dispenser fell apart quickly, having not been designed for maximum absorbency. Looking in my suitcase, I selected an undershirt to be my makeshift towel. Fortunately, I had facial soap in my carry-on, along with a toothbrush, razor, and hairstyling product, so I was able to get myself looking somewhat close to "normal."

Let's just say I'm *not* eager to repeat this experience. Ever. But if you find yourself needing to bathe in an airport restroom, look to your athletic socks.

Freshly "clean," I returned to the gate area to wait for my flight to whisk me to Atlanta.

TRAFFIC IN Atlanta was relatively light. An omen for a good day? I arrived at the hotel only forty-five minutes late to meet everyone. Allison and I had never met, so there was a faux-familiar greeting, and then we excused ourselves for a couple of minutes to coordinate. She had already briefed the clients using the materials I had sent the night before. We were scheduled to do three interviews each, so it would be a full day. We agreed to meet up for drinks at the bar afterward. That put drinks about twelve hours away from this moment. It sounded like an eternity, but I was pretty sure I'd already earned a round or two, and a proper shower followed by a blissful sleep in a clean bed was just on the other side of this already action-packed day.

The first two sessions must have been fine. I don't really remember them because the third session was so memorable. It was late afternoon/early evening when we arrived. The weather that day, like the day before in DC, had been hot and humid. Mid-nineties on both measures, or so it felt. Air-conditioning, when we were in it, was like a gift from the gods.

The "house" we were to visit was actually in an apartment complex from the '60s. It resembled an early version of townhomes. Each unit was side by side and comprised multiple floors. It reminded me of row houses in a contemporary subdivision.

We pulled up and started to get out of the car when the respondent's mom looked out the door and stepped outside. As we headed toward the front steps, she pointed to a small hill across the road. "That," she said, "is the community recreational area." Mom said she thought we could sit over there. I indicated that, given the oppressive weather and the fact that there were four of us, we would be better off inside the house. She refused and said she'd told the recruiter we needed to stay outside. That was news to me. Sit outside? In this heat and humidity?

That morning I was judging myself in the airport—but now I was about to judge this woman, let me tell you.

There's no way I'd agree to an outside interview in the summer in Atlanta. But we had no choice. There was no alternate respondent booked. And we had specific age and gender quotas to meet. Bailey was our seventeen-year-old male teenager; we had to talk to him. And that meant playing by his mom's rules. The spot that Bailey's mom had picked out for us was a poured concrete, molded round picnic table and benches. Any tall trees in this area were all to the east of us, so they offered little protection from the sun. There was an enclosed "community room," but it was locked. We were stuck outside, in the sun. The one saving grace was a very occasional light breeze to cool us down, but we were all quickly glistening in the summer heat.

Looking over Bailey's head, I could see storm clouds punching up higher and higher into the sky. On the one hand, the idea of an afternoon thunderstorm sounded refreshing to offset the sticky heat. On the other hand, a thunderstorm could make things challenging given our paperwork, electronics, and gentle selves, if we weren't able to get inside Bailey's house.

I started the interview. The first question is typically an ask to introduce yourself, how old you are, and who lives at home. And wouldn't you know it, right out of the gate, Bailey's answers were at a mumble. He was speaking really softly—like his lips weren't moving. I was straining to hear every word. I asked him to speak up. That worked for a sentence or two, but then he quieted down again. And the four of us were beginning to wilt in the heat. And I'd had three hours of sleep. Only an hour and forty-five minutes of this to go. No sweat, except for the beads of it rolling down my temples.

About halfway through the session, two things happened. First, one of the clients was really curious to get into the house. While Bailey was talking to the rest of us, the client slipped over and whispered to me that she was going to ask the mom if she could use the restroom. She was using that as an excuse to get inside. I nodded in agreement, a fellow intrepid spirit.

When the client returned from her trip to the bathroom, she gave me a nod, but it lacked any real indication of what she'd experienced. No foreshadowing *at all* of what we would witness inside the house. A few minutes later, the second thing happened. Bailey's parents emerged, jumped in their pickup truck, and headed out. The house was empty! And ... it was air-conditioned!

My desire to get into the house was driven by a few factors: to escape the heat even for a few minutes, to get a better picture of Bailey's life and see some of his personal possessions, and to give us a chance to use the restroom. We already had a motive, and now, with the parents' departure, we had the opportunity. I just had to make it happen in an organic way that would give us plausible deniability should the parents come back.

Bailey had been telling us about hip-hop dance videos that he had made with some friends and posted on YouTube. Today these videos would be posted on TikTok, and he'd be able to show us on his phone, but smartphones were not yet ubiquitous back in 2007, so we would need to see it on a computer. For all of his mumbling, I was growing to like Bailey. He was a big, gentle giant of a kid, easily over six feet and over two hundred pounds. A solid guy but soft in the middle. With blond hair and blue eyes, he was the furthest thing I could think of from a hip-hop dancer, which made me want to see his videos even more.

And then, in my head, a lightbulb went off. I knew how I could bring up going inside the house without derailing the conversation. Three hours of sleep hadn't turned my brain completely to mush. Bailey could show us his hip-hop videos on YouTube on his computer. Inside his house. Inside his air-conditioned house!

He said yes. Relieved, we picked up our stuff and headed for the house, eagerly anticipating that blast of cooler, drier air when we opened the front door.

WHEN I learned to moderate, I was taught that you need to pay attention to both the verbal and nonverbal cues. It's like listening with all of your senses. One of those senses walloped us after we opened the front door, striking like the knockout punch of a heavyweight. At first, the mingled smells were hard to tease apart. Putridly sweet is one way to describe it. Turns out we were in for a real awakening inside Bailey's house.

The first smell that I was able to decipher was of a freshly baked yellow cake. How delicious. Bailey's mom must have just made the cake for the family to enjoy later that evening. But wait, what's that pungent, slightly acidic scent that's coming through alongside the yellow cake smell? Why yes, it's urine. Cat *and* dog urine. Lots of it. In our nostrils, the urine smell was mixing with the sweet aroma of a Betty Crocker Super Moist yellow cake. Or was it Duncan Hines Moist Deluxe? Who could tell? It was an all-out assault on our olfactory nerves.

Visually, we were overwhelmed as well. Straight ahead of us were stairs leading up to the bedrooms. Turning to the right as you walked in the door, you entered the living room. It was unlike any living room I had seen before. I could make out the cushions and backs of a sofa and maybe an armchair or two. But almost every other surface was covered by something. Anything. Everything. There was so much stuff, it was impossible to process what it all was. The TV was visible, or at least the screen was. The other thing that stood out to me in the living room was the dozen or so pieces of vintage 1950s Coca-Cola memorabilia. Holiday ornaments, a Santa Claus with the classic bottle, and signs from sixty years ago hung on the walls. Being in Atlanta, I wondered if there was a family connection or just a love of the brand and a particular attraction to that era in the brand's history.

Single file, we stepped gingerly along a path that cut through the piles and piles of clutter. Stacks upon stacks of papers and magazines and books were the most recognizable objects. I'm tempted to call it crap, but the family had placed it there, so it must have had some meaning for them. But it was seriously disgusting how messy the house was. And that smell! What type of conditions are these for people to live in? My mind was racing with lots of judgment and questions, but also with a degree of bewildered fascination. I'd never been in a house like this before. Like an intrepid reporter, I continued on, in search of the story. I was trying hard not to be judgmental… but I was also trying not to touch anything or let anything touch me.

Bailey led the way along the path into the next room. It would have been a dining room if the dining table wasn't piled high with parts from a bicycle, a bike tire pump, the rubber tube from inside a bike tire, an old PC tower and monitor, computer speakers, wires, a keyboard, and other random objects. The chairs were nowhere to be found at the dining table. Perhaps they were lost in the living room? One was at a computer desk that was in the room; it was the only cleared surface in the lower floor of the house. As we reassembled in the dining room, Bailey sat down at the desk and pulled up his videos. The mumble that he was using outside was gone. Bailey was talking in a more regular voice. I believe this was because he was engaged and excited to show us his videos rather than answer questions about gum.

While he described the videos and his interest in hip-hop dancing, I started scanning around to see what other surprises awaited us. The dining room was in the back of the townhouse. Out the sliding glass door in the rear of the room, I saw a small backyard. A concrete patio was packed with more bicycles. An overturned outdoor dining set resided there near a gas grill.

Back inside the dining room, the stench was becoming overwhelming. Looking down at our feet, I could see patches of old, stained carpet that was matted down from too many years of use and not enough shampooing. Back toward the living room was the bathroom, with the door open. Inside the bathroom I spotted the litter box next to an old, stained toilet. I could see uncovered cat feces atop the litter. It was in need of a scooping, but the permeating stench was so pervasive, the problem wasn't just the litter box. That strong of a smell meant urine had to be indelibly inked into the carpet like a pungent scratch-and-sniff tattoo.

I was so shocked, disgusted, and uncomfortable. My jaw must have been on the urine-soaked carpet. Moving my eyes a little to the left, I spotted the kitchen. Close to us, sitting on the stove's heating coils, was a thirteen-inch glass casserole dish with the freshly baked yellow cake cooling off. I realized what Bailey's mom had been up to. It's like that realtor's trick. Bake something like cookies or a cake to create a warm, inviting smell when doing an open house. The house is then filled with a pleasant aroma. "Can't you," possible buyer, "see yourself comfortable and at home in this house, baking a cake for your family?" Now, spritz cat pee generously and allow it to hang in the air like a noxious chemical agent, and you'll get the experience we were having.

The sky outside continued to darken as the thunderstorms drew closer. Inside, Bailey continued playing his dance videos for us, seemingly oblivious to the looks of shock and disgust that were passing among his four visitors. Ever the optimist, I looked for the bright side. At least it was cooler inside than out. I continued looking. Across from the stove with the cooling cake, on the other side of the kitchen, was the sink. It was a traditional double-sided sink. Each side was piled to overflowing, forming a mound extending at least six to eight inches above the edge of the sink. It was a true mountain of dirty dishes. And the dish rack next to it was also piled high, I presumed with clean dishes. At least, I hoped some of the dishes were clean. *What type of house is this?* I thought to myself as I processed everything I was seeing, my eyes still focused on the sink. *Wait, is that a cockroach?*

Oh yes, it was a cockroach. And once you see one, you can't help but notice the others. Like the one about to saunter across the Betty Crocker Super Moist. There were bugs scampering all over the place.

I'M PRETTY laid back. I strive to be casual and comfortable when I'm in people's homes, even stranger's homes, but I was standing upright, ramrod straight, with my back stiff, arms folded, elbows tucked against my ribs. I whispered to one of the clients, who was pointing toward the cockroach, "touch nothing." The sights, the smells, it was overwhelming. Sensory overload—and not in a July 4th, too many people, too much food, and lots of fireworks kind of way.

And yet, most importantly, to honor and respect Bailey, we acted as though there was nothing wrong. This wasn't his fault. He was seventeen. Poor kid. What must he have been thinking about this? He was excited about having us in to look at his videos, but he must have known his house wasn't like other houses. Or did he? We tried very hard to visibly hide our discomfort with the conditions in his house. We didn't want him to feel uncomfortable or that we were judging him. I wasn't judging him. I was judging his parents. This situation was beyond Bailey's control. He was just a seventeen-year-old kid giving us the gift of his story. We were having to deal with all of our biases and stereotypes and worries while Bailey was trying to share his life. Our judgment was getting in the way, however. I now know that dismantling judgment is the first step toward empathy. It's the first step and the hardest of all the steps because it is damn difficult. Back then, in Bailey's house, what must have been the dirtiest house in America, there was a deluge of judgment to rival the fiercest of summer storms.

What makes his parents think living in squalor is acceptable for their family? This place is disgusting. And they baked a cake to help mask the smell?! Gross! My brain was becoming preoccupied with judging. Once I started down that path, I kept noticing how different Bailey's parents were from what I consider to be "normal." And with all the Coke memorabilia too. That just made it seem even more bizarre. I was so blinded by my judgment that all I could see was piles of junk, dirty dishes, and cockroaches skittering atop a freshly baked sheet cake.

We did our best to keep our focus on Bailey and his answers to our questions about chewing gum and hip-hop dancing. Ultimately, we wrapped the interview on time. While the surroundings were repulsive, this was Bailey's life and part of his experience. He was giving us a gift by sharing it with us. It was our struggle to listen to him and build empathy. We said our goodbyes to Bailey and got into the car, just as the rain was starting to fall. Thunder and lightning crackled in the sky. Bailey's parents passed us at the entrance to the complex as we were heading out.

Inside the car, it was silent the first ten minutes of our ride back. We each admitted that we were in shock with what we saw. Our brains were still trying to process what we had experienced inside the house. We did our best to stay focused and honor what Bailey had to say rather than let our judgment get in the way. It was not easy for any of us.

I believe that with wisdom comes empathy. In the moment of that interview, I didn't know enough to recognize that Bailey's parents were hoarders. It was two years before the *Hoarders* reality series would launch and popularize the term. I also didn't know enough about how to get to empathy to recognize that my judgment was in the way and that was keeping me from seeing Bailey's point of view. I think I had *sympathy*, feeling for Bailey and his living situation, but I didn't go to *empathy* and imagine what it must be like to see the world through his eyes.

Back at the hotel, after the clients had all gone to bed, Allison and I had a much-needed cocktail. I was physically and mentally exhausted, but it was good to download and share what I had experienced at Bailey's house. Allison then expressed empathy with me and my experience. That was a relief, and it felt good to have someone understand where I was coming from. She told me a few stories of her own experiences on in-homes where the houses and bathrooms were dirtier than "normal." It's not as uncommon as you might think, which leads me to my other lesson from that day. Standards of cleanliness are entirely subjective. One man's filthy is another man's fine. Especially if you bake a cake just before your guests arrive to create a pleasant aroma...

ONE LESSON I learned that day, besides how to MacGyver a sponge bath in an airport bathroom, was that I would need to figure out how to get to empathy in the future, as this wouldn't be the only time I was in an unfamiliar setting that I would find unsettling. In Bailey's case, the physical surroundings were unsettling. At other times, it's the words or the reaction of the person you are talking to.

Having a conversation where you might be trying to build empathy is like walking through a minefield. Blindfolded. You might have in your mind's eye a sense of what the physical minefield looks like, but you never know exactly where the mines are buried across the terrain. And these mines are psychological, and they are set off by words. Specifically, words in the form of questions that touch a sensitive subject. *Boom!* Without warning, an explosion of emotion comes hurtling toward you. It can leave you trying to comfort while not fully understanding what it was that set off the eruption. Rather than risk navigating the emotional minefield, fear of the possible explosion leaves some people avoiding the conversations they need to have—in both their personal and work lives. If the conversation doesn't happen and the questions aren't asked, it is impossible for empathy to be established.

Navigating the minefield is unavoidable when I'm doing an in-depth interview. It's a hazard of the job. When you are talking with someone for the first time, you don't really know them, and so you don't know which question will set off which psychological land mine. You also have no idea what the resulting "explosion" will look like. It can show up as anger or defensiveness. I've had respondents shut down and retreat rather than engage in conversation. The explosion can also express itself in tears. So I have to be ready to respond at a moment's notice.

Of course, I know this now. Back when I was a "baby moderator" and before I had started to increase my understanding of empathy, I stumbled through the minefields wearing the thickest of blindfolds.

A few months after I met Bailey, I was on a project exploring the role of breakfast and how parents (really just moms in the less gender-role-enlightened years of the mid-aughts) approach and prepare breakfast for their kids. For this project we got up really early in the morning, went to people's homes, and joined them while they made breakfast. Nothing reveals the truth better than an eyewitness. The opportunity to gloss over a detail or embellish a fact is removed when you have witnesses to your very behavior. Being able to see what was happening was really important for this project. Back in the early 2000s, the breakfast "occasion" (marketing speak) had been a particularly challenging "meal occasion" (more marketing speak) for clients to understand. People's habits had changed over the decades, from the 1950s family sitting down to breakfast with Dad reading the paper and Mom at the stove to the 2000s, where everyone is on their own, grabbing something and eating it—or skipping breakfast altogether—while they race around the house or head out the door. To understand people who were still making breakfast at home, we wanted to see them in action. That would give us a sense of what else was happening in the house as the day was getting going. And being in their home, we could see what other items they had on hand for breakfast. Do they make pancakes all the time or would we find breakfast bars and cold cereal too? That knowledge would help inform marketing campaigns and new product development that is appealing to a contemporary consumer.

One of the respondents on our early morning crusades was Rebecca, a married mom of three young kids. Rebecca homeschooled her children, and she described her days as having a schizophrenic feel to them, jumping from mom to teacher and back to mom again. She also tried to cook a hot breakfast for the kids several times a week. Often, she chose to make pancakes, a breakfast staple in many American households.

Nutrition aside, pancakes are quite possibly a perfect breakfast food. Not only are they warm and filling, but there is the intense sweetness in the accompanying moat of syrup on the plate. That allows fun for kids who may dip, dunk, or mop up the sticky sweet liquid. For parents, there's the nostalgia and carrying on of tradition as they re-create what they experienced in their own childhood with their parents and grandparents. These everyday activities evolve over the years to become rituals that take on meaning beyond the "occasion" they are serving, like "breakfast." They come to represent expressions of love, locked in our memories.

The shape of love isn't limited to the round fluffy disc of a pancake, either. Think about your own family. Which foods were special? What comes to mind for me were the egg, cheese, and sausage breakfast sandwiches my dad would make on Sunday mornings. Pancakes, really light and fluffy, were on the menu on Saturday mornings, along with bacon cooked to order. My mom would make French toast on our days off from school, both federal government holidays and snow days. All three of these foods are now fortified in my memory so that I can't have them without thinking of my parents.

Endless cycles of repetition and reward, combined with the right emotional context, can make food a land mine, triggered by the powder keg of memory meeting a spark of emotional electricity. That ignites in feelings—sometimes in a burst of visible joy on a person's face, sometimes in a shower of tears. Will I step on a trigger? What reaction will I get?

We started the interview in Rebecca's kitchen. She was at the counter, making pancakes for her kids, who were scurrying in and out of the hallway leading to their bedrooms. I was asking Rebecca questions while she was trying to cook and keep her kids progressing toward getting ready for their day. And there was a video camera recording the whole thing.

After grilling Rebecca with questions while she was making breakfast and getting the kids fed, we sat down at her dining room table so we could be more comfortable as we continued the interview. There was also a prework assignment Rebecca had completed, to make a collage about what breakfast meant to her.

On the collage she had put a sunrise and a representation of her kids, as well as a picture of some sunny-side up eggs. I asked her, "Why eggs?" and she replied that her dad used to make eggs for her. I asked a follow-up question: "Tell me more about your dad making eggs for you; what was special about that?"

The next thing I knew, Rebecca was crying. Like, really crying, not just a tear rolling down her cheek; this was crying sobs. I was totally taken by surprise. I just "made" someone cry. I felt bad, but I didn't know how to respond. Totally frozen, a deer in the headlights. Rebecca's daughter, about age four, came by and looked at her, then looked at us. She appeared to be trying to understand why her mom was crying, why we weren't, and what did that mean? What did we do to her mom? Wanting to help but still unsure how, I suggested that maybe her mom could use a hug from her right now? The daughter looked at me like I was an alien, still trying to understand what was going on and why her mom was crying in front of these strangers.

Inadvertently, I had stepped on one of Rebecca's hidden land mines, buried deep within her heart. With Rebecca, the detonation resulted in tears.

I was caught off guard. How did we get to tears? This project was all about seeking understanding of pancakes at breakfast. What brought on tears? Rebecca was the first person to cry during one of my interviews. No one had prepped me during my moderator training for how to handle respondents in tears. Before this, in my personal life, when I would see someone crying and not understand why, I would have sympathy and want to comfort them. Or, if I knew them, I might be able to have empathy with why they were crying and try to comfort them.

Fortunately, one of the clients who was at the session with me, and happened to be sitting next to Rebecca, reached in and gave her a reassuring touch. She then soothingly asked her what had brought up the tears. Rebecca composed herself a bit and recalled her father, who had recently passed away, making her eggs. He loved eggs and made them daily. And when she was in college, she'd come home for the weekend, and he'd make eggs for the two of them.

Those mornings were special for both of them. It was when they could connect, father to daughter. The type of eggs that he made or that she preferred didn't matter. Eggs for breakfast were the vehicle to get them to connection. It became a treasured ritual during Rebecca's college years. And now that her father had died, eggs for breakfast became a trigger, the memory bringing up the pain of her father being gone and that she had lost connection to him. My question was innocent enough. I just had no idea it was linked to buried emotions that would surge forward into tears. That's what made it the trigger on the "land mine."

And then, Rebecca gave a loving look at her little girl, who was still bewildered. She instinctively reached out to comfort her daughter with a smile and a caress.

After Rebecca explained the connection to her father and the fact that he had passed away, I was able to have cognitive empathy with her and why she'd started crying. I wasn't strong enough in my empathy skills at the time to offer her any comfort, however. I froze in the moment, as I didn't have the information on why she was crying to know what to say. Part of the problem in this situation was that, if I'm being self-critical, I wasn't as present in the interview as I needed to be in order to engage in active listening (Step 3). As a result, I wasn't able to understand (Step 4) what was happening and how to use my imagination (Step 5) to figure out what Rebecca needed from me in the moment. I volunteered a hug from her daughter instead of my own comforting words. My client got it, though. She knew what to do and modeled a response for me, which I've been able to use in other cases when a respondent (or any person) starts crying. "What brought up the tears?"

A crying burst in front of colleagues or complete strangers isn't typically the norm. However, I think we'd all benefit from exposing a bit more of our emotional selves, daring to show vulnerability, and opening ourselves up to being treated with kindness and compassion in return. We may be able to express emotions and to feel, yet we're socialized to bottle it up and keep it in. Some of us suppress it "better" than others but all that really does is create a pressure cooker that leads to an unhealthy outburst instead of releasing the pressure gradually before it builds up to an explosion.

I'm really grateful for the client who was there with us during the interview, a mom herself, who knew instinctively to reach out and provide a reassuring touch. Her actions showed me a better way to hold space and let the person get their emotion out. I've also learned over the years that it's okay to show a little emotion yourself in that situation, as long as it's from a place of empathy.

My interviews with Bailey and Rebecca are just two examples of where full empathy was elusive for me. Instead of listening and understanding, I was being judgmental of Bailey and insensitive with Rebecca. I had much to learn.

EMPATHETIC REFLECTIONS

• When have you been really uncomfortable in a situation, and you then became judgmental? What made you judgmental? How did it help you? How did it hinder you?

• Think of a time when you set off an emotional "land mine" with someone. How did you respond? What worked well? What would you do differently? How would you want someone to respond if it was you who had the emotional outburst?

• What would it look like if you were to show a little more vulnerability at work? In your personal life? What holds you back? How might you overcome it?

3

Turning Perspective Around

It's not what you look at that matters, it's what you see.
HENRY DAVID THOREAU

MY HUSBAND, CHARLES, and I often walk down the street together, side by side, and we will comment to one another about what we see. I usually note the buildings, stores, and signs, while he notices the people. He picks up on what they are wearing, who's cute, who we might want to avoid. I'll notice an ad for an exhibit we might want to check out or observe the pace of construction on a building if it's on a well-worn route of ours. Even though we are together, walking in the same direction, what we each see is pretty different from the other. We have the same viewpoint, but our points of view are not identical.

And so it is with understanding perspective. Two people standing in the same spot and looking at the same vista will end up seeing completely different things. Through our eyes, our brains are both registering the same visuals, but our mind selects what we focus on. In some ways, we are "listening" with our eyes. And what we focus on is informed by our own biases and past experiences. Even though I talk with people for a living, I find it dizzying to focus on every person coming at me on a crowded street. I think that's why my eye wanders toward the inanimate objects that remain static, and it informs how I end up seeing the world around me. If Charles wants me to see what he sees, I have to look at what's in front of me differently. Similarly, if I hope to understand someone else's point of view, to have empathy with them, then I'll need to change my mental perspective.

In addition to seeing the world from someone else's viewpoint, I also love changing my physical perspective in order to see things differently—whether that's getting down on the ground and looking at the world at the eye level of my cats, looking at the world upside down while in a yoga position, or observing the world from an airplane at thirty-five thousand feet. You see and understand things in a totally different way when you shift your perspective.

My favorite artists play with perspective—Tim Walker's photography that changes the scale of objects in remarkable ways; the subversive, satirical work of Banksy; or examining what happens after "happily ever after" in Stephen Sondheim's *Into the Woods*. I remember the first time I saw Sondheim's *Sunday in the Park with George*, and the second act begins with the song "It's Hot Up Here," taking the audience into the point of view of the subjects in a painting, stuck in one position, forever. I thought this shift in perspective was absolutely brilliant, clever, and comical as well.

Unfortunately, what I had been finding in my early years of moderating is that we all can get locked into our perspectives, myself included—whether it's what we see walking down the street the way Charles and I do, or whether it's on political issues, religious views, social injustice, or something as mundane as what food has to be on the table for Thanksgiving to truly be Thanksgiving. Ask that question of your friends and you'll be surprised at the range of answers you get. What's important to them may not be to you. It doesn't make it wrong; it's just their point of view. Are you able to shift your perspective to see their point of view?

What I've found to be dangerous is when people are so firmly rooted in one perspective that they aren't able to take on the point of view of someone else. After Charles and I talk about what we are seeing on the streets, and he's noticed some incredible style or piece of clothing or makeup that he loves but I've missed, I try to shift my view to see more of what he's seeing. I end up looking at the people more than I normally do. It takes a conscious effort to do that, however.

When I was a kid, I remember my parents would try to help me have perspective on a situation. To see something from the other side. I remember often hearing, "Look at it from their perspective." That helped me as I started to develop the ability to put myself in the shoes of others, to understand where they were coming from. It helped me navigate both school and early work situations. And taking a different perspective also helps lift a worry or concern. When I receive bad news, I feel the weight of the bad news but try to see the other side in order to understand what led to the decision or event. After that, I look to find a bright side, mixing my perspective taking with coping skills, resilience, and a desire for optimism. That perspective shifting has become second nature for me, part of my superpower that helped cover the wounds I endured growing up. Being able to see a classmate's perspective helped me get along with them and hopefully not get beaten up. But how I actually did this and the steps I took were unknown to me at the time.

While I've always been inspired to be open to other perspectives, the person that turned me around and, unknowingly, pointed me on the path to identifying and understanding the 5 Steps to Empathy was a respondent from one of my most favorite projects ever.

The project was code-named "Goldie," named after the actress Goldie Hawn, who, at the time, represented an ideal of aging well to my non-Boomer clients. We were hired to conduct an exploration into the life of aging Baby Boomers. Still fit and youthful in the mid-late aughts, Boomers were rewriting the rules for aging— determined to remain active and vital and to contribute to society.

The fact that Hawn might have had a little work done to help maintain her visual vitality might have been beside the point for the client team. Or perhaps that *was* the point, if you sought to create new food products to help Boomers maintain vitality; it could be the food equivalent of "having a little work done."

We met with Boomers to listen and get a sense of their attitudes toward retirement and the path ahead of them. At that point I hadn't thought much about what retirees go through, as it was still twenty-five years off for me. It was truly eye-opening. I remember people sitting on their sofas or at their kitchen tables, and each one of them expressed how much they wanted to be seen as valued members of society, not shoved off into some corner. All of them were active in the community, as well as helping with elderly parents and their own young adult children. Forget "being put out to pasture"; some of these people had more energy than I did. The clients and I all walked away from the project inspired and carrying with us a new vision of what it might be like to "retire."

It was on Project Goldie that I met Emelia. An everyday American, Emelia was a Black woman in her mid-fifties who'd had an early retirement from corporate America and was moving into the next act in her life.

As we sat in her suburban Philadelphia living room, Emelia told us the story of her life. A marriage that ended but gave her a now grown son. Her daily fears and concerns were for his safety since he had deployed to Iraq several months before we met her. And she had a grandson! The intense love she had for him was expressed in many ways during our conversation, including a high-pitched declaration while showing us a photo of the infant. I can still hear her voice, at an octave reserved for expressions of true love and adulation for people or furry animals. "That face! *Look* at that face!"

I was in rapt attention with Emelia, even more than I normally am while interviewing. There was something special about her, a joie de vivre that I responded to and loved. Her spirit was alive and present. Her eyes, her voice, the way she moved through her home. I felt connected to her. Because of that connection, I was really paying attention and noticed that I was "listening" to Emelia with all of my senses. I was hearing her words, but I was also in sync with her body language and other unspoken cues. I now refer to this form of listening as "active listening," and it's now Step 3 on the path to empathy. Active listening is paying attention with all your senses. It helps fill in the blanks and can reveal unspoken truths as well.

Emelia was saying a lot in both spoken and unspoken language. Paying attention to what I was seeing beyond what Emelia was telling me, I noticed that she kept making a motion with her hands as she'd talk. She'd hold her hands with the palms facing each other, as if she was holding a ball between her hands. And then, she'd rotate her hands around, so her palms were still facing each other but from the opposite position. It was like an imaginary ball she had been holding had been rolled over in her hands. I also noticed that she was making that gesture whenever she was talking about how important it is to learn to look at life from a different perspective. Every time she talked about shifting perspective on a subject, she'd move her hands, rolling that invisible ball over. The hand that was below was now above, until her hands rolled the ball over again. Her hands were demonstrating a physical manifestation of changing perspective!

Emelia told us that, prior to her early retirement, she'd had a corporate job. She traveled a lot, and like all road warriors, she'd relied on a laptop to keep her connected and productive. After years of travel for work, she developed pain in her wrists, diagnosed as carpal tunnel syndrome. In both wrists. And it was severe. Unable to type on her laptop anymore, Emelia was suddenly unable to work. Surgery would be required to correct the condition. With plenty of productive years ahead of her, Emelia wasn't willing to sit on her injured hands and do nothing. She went ahead and had the surgery on both wrists.

While she was recovering, Emelia was unsure if she'd be able to return to her job. It was during that period that her doctor made a suggestion that changed her life and would later influence a change in my own. During one of her follow-up visits, the doctor recommended tai chi as a form of physical therapy. Apparently the gentle, intentional movements of tai chi, which often involves movement of the hands, helps people who are recovering from carpal tunnel surgery.

Initially, Emelia was resistant. The Eastern practice of tai chi wasn't something she was familiar with. The doctor kept encouraging her, and so finally she went to a class to give it a try. And in that class, Emelia said something clicked into place.

If you are unfamiliar with tai chi, it's an ancient Chinese exercise, like yoga, that involves deliberate movement to stimulate the nervous system while also providing mental calm. Prior to this, I had a stereotype of tai chi from seeing groups of Chinese elders standing in a New York City park, early in the morning, making slow-motion martial arts movements. Tai chi didn't hold much appeal to me because it was slow moving. At the time, I preferred a more strenuous exercise like a Vinyasa flow yoga. Tai chi seemed like an activity of "being," incongruous to our Western society, which, prior to the COVID-19 pandemic, has been about going faster, faster, faster, always "doing." The dominant US perspective on exercise, and mine too at the time, was "if you aren't dripping with sweat, you aren't really exercising." Spinning as fast as your legs can cycle and your feet can stay on the pedals. Flowing through Vinyasa with sweat running off you like a raging river. Run, don't walk. And as an "all or nothing" society, it explains why people are either all in for their workouts or rarely get off the couch. If you can't have it all, doing half and at half-speed doesn't seem like it'd be worth the effort.

But what tai chi unlocked for Emelia was a stillness in her mind. The restraint in the practice led to serenity and calm. That helped create the headspace so she could develop her own ability to look at life from another perspective. Tai chi taught her how to take on a different point of view.

"You just have to turn things around. Look at it from a different perspective." She returned to this statement several times while telling us what she'd learned from tai chi and how she thought about the future. And every time, she was making that same movement with her hands, turning the ball over and over.

Then it clicked in my head. My memory of the movements of the Chinese elders in the park was reflected in Emelia's hands. The hand motion that she kept making was actually a tai chi movement. Turning things around. When she was talking about the loss of her career. Looking at life from a different perspective. When she shared her concern for her son's safety on his reserves deployment to Iraq. Her hands repeated the tai chi movement, rotating apace with what she was saying. It was a physical manifestation of this mantra. She kept telling us that she would remind herself to turn things around and look at the situation from a different perspective. The perspective shift it implied kept her in a more grounded place, able to process and handle the stress that came her way.

TAI CHI had changed the way Emelia was experiencing her life. The impact it had on her was so profound that she was inspired to bring tai chi to an inner-city youth program with kids aged four to fourteen. And so she began teaching tai chi herself, to kids who might not have the opportunity to be exposed to this ancient discipline.

There was clear joy for her as she talked about her classes with these young kids. The results, she told us, were also evident. The troubled kids were calmer. They all left class with a state of serenity and focus. Tai chi was helping create opportunities for the kids. It also let Emelia express herself in a new way. She found a way to turn another stressful situation around—to look at her disability of carpal tunnel syndrome as a way to help others.

There's a saying that I subscribe to that the universe delivers what you need when you need it. Sometimes it's hard to recognize that you are being handed that gift, but there it was, sitting on a sofa in front of me in the form of a fifty-something Black woman wearing a baby-blue vest and a turtleneck.

As she was moving her hands, talking about changing perspective, I could envision Emelia teaching a class to the kids, and I imagined their increased calm and focus. In my personal life at that time, after a couple of years of taking in people's stories and nearly nonstop travel for work, I was ready to plug into the universe a bit more directly myself. I needed help to ground and re-center myself. It felt like I was going to have to go beyond my usual self-help fix of an episode of *Oprah*. Could tai chi be that thing? I could see an opportunity presenting itself during this conversation, if Emelia would agree. It might seem self-indulgent, but it might prove insightful, and, at the very least, the clients would enjoy the experience. I snuck a glance at my watch (I certainly didn't want to give off the vibe that I was *bored*). There was plenty of time left in our session; a little detour wouldn't hurt anything. So, I asked Emelia if she could teach us some tai chi. And she said yes!

There were four of us as guests in Emelia's home, me plus two clients and Natalie, the camerawoman. We moved the living room chairs, slid the coffee table back, and lined up as Emelia directed. I gestured to Natalie to keep recording. Emelia took a position facing us. Standing still, she had us close our eyes. That felt awkward, simply because I've never been moderating a session where I completely turned the session over to the respondent. Emelia instructed us to breathe in. As air transited our nostrils and filled our lungs, we fell under Emelia's instruction. She had us raise our hands. "Imagine a ball, like a beach ball, in front of you. Put your arms around it to hold it... face your palms together... move your palms like they are opposing magnets... bending at the knees, shift your body up and down... continue to breathe."

At one point, I peeked to see my two clients following right along to Emelia's instructions. That made me smile. Natalie found some space behind the tripod where she could keep an eye on the camera and also try some of the movements herself. There we were, in a "no-longer-a-stranger's" home in suburban Philadelphia on a sunny midweek afternoon, receiving a tai chi lesson!

I noticed something else. As we gently breathed in and out, the stress left my body. I was relaxing and finding a place of calm and focus. I thought this would just be a nice physical exercise, not realizing that I'd perceive a mental and emotional payoff in minutes. *There's something to this*, I thought to myself. I would never have imagined when I woke up that morning that my eyes would be opened the way that they were. The universe gives you what you need, when you need it. At that point in my life I needed to have my direction shifted to that calmer, reflective place where I could begin to turn things around and see things from a different perspective.

Emelia remains one of my all-time favorite interviews. Ever. Her joie de vivre, her wisdom, and her spirit inspire me to this day. What she initially turned around for me was my own view toward Eastern disciplines like tai chi and yoga. I had dabbled in them prior to meeting Emelia, but hearing her story and experiencing even the briefest tai chi lesson made me reconsider my attitude. I looked at the ancient mind-body exercises with a fresh perspective, willing to explore, experience, and reflect on what came up. That expanded mental space opened up how I thought about empathy. Prior to this turning point with Emelia, empathy was just something I did. I couldn't explain how I did it; it just happened when it happened. This probably would have been just fine had I only needed empathy in my personal life. However, empathy is critical to success in business as well.

At work, I was intuitively empathetic with my colleagues and used it for more positive collaboration, better decision-making, and stronger outcomes. In the actual work that I do as a researcher, clients were participating in the projects in a way that was putting them into a place of discomfort, like at Bailey's house. They were being exposed to people that were unlike them, and in some cases, they were having trouble establishing empathy. I was in the position of being the intermediary between the client and the participant, which meant that I needed to understand and improve my own empathy skills so that I knew how to handle situations like with Rebecca, when she had burst into tears. I should guide my clients to a place of empathy as well. The awakening I had in Emelia's living room fueled the growth in my own self-awareness. As a result, I was able to bring my attention to understanding how I establish empathy across interactions with the thousands of strangers that I meet and interview.

Emelia was yet another example of how being open to learning from others, even the random strangers we might otherwise ignore in our day-to-day existence, can alter your life for the better.

EMPATHETIC REFLECTIONS

• Where does empathy show up in your life today? Where is it absent even though it should be present?

• How easy or difficult is it for you to "turn it around" and look at things from a different perspective?

• Who's inspired you or been a positive turning point in your life the way Emelia was to me?

PART 2

Following the 5 Steps to Empathy

4

Defining the 5 Steps to Empathy

*Effort and courage are not enough
without purpose and direction.*
JOHN F. KENNEDY, campaign speech, September 17, 1960

EMELIA HAD TURNED me around, setting me off down a path of increased self-discovery and awareness, which led me to a deeper understanding of empathy and the steps it takes to achieve seeing a situation from another's point of view. To have cognitive empathy.

My progression in understanding was not linear. I found myself understanding the concepts out of sequence and in varying degrees of depth. For example, I had more intuitive understanding around what it meant to actively listen (Step 3), only to find I needed to go back and practice an earlier step, like dismantling judgment (Step 1). Your own practice may also reflect this imperfect progression. It's okay. This is how we learn. And so it goes, back and forth, two steps forward, one step back, and so on.

THIS NEXT part of *Tell Me More About That* is organized in the order of the 5 Steps, with the intention to help you with an overall understanding of all 5 Steps and how they relate to one another. Please do not burden yourself with the expectation of mastering one step before tackling the next. As I found on my own learning journey and how my empathy practice continues to this day, it's not always sequential. The step you have issues with today may not be the one you have an issue with tomorrow. Success in building empathy also depends on who you are trying to have empathy with. Some people will elicit your judgment, while others may challenge you to be more active in your listening and be present in the conversation. Your stories and experiences with empathy will be different from mine (I'd love to hear from you about them: @empathy_activist on Instagram). What's important as you work through this section of the book are the lessons about building empathy in the moment that you draw from the individual stories and my experiences with them as I grew in my understanding of empathy.

And now, without further ado, here are the 5 Steps to Empathy.

Step 1: Dismantle Judgment. This is the biggest towering obstacle on the journey to empathy. It's imposing, like Mount Everest, and damn it if the hardest mountain to climb doesn't come first. Awareness of when we are being judgmental, what we tend to get judgmental about, and where it comes from is the first step in tearing down the wall that judgment can put up. Be mindful of the source of your judgment. If you notice a repeated pattern, there may be an injury or bias of your own that needs attention.

Step 2: Ask Good Questions. Keep the questions open—don't ask questions that can be answered with a single word. This will frustrate most teenagers, who will still try to give you an "I dunno" or a shoulder shrug, but it helps open people up if they can't cop out with a yes, a no, or a maybe. And eliminate the word *why*—it puts people on the defensive and possibly shuts them down. Use *who*, *what*, *when*, *where*, and *how* instead. Also try starting sentences with, "Tell me more about..." and see where that takes you.

Step 3: Active Listening. Body language speaks volumes, as does looking around at a person's surroundings. Listen to these cues as well as what is being spoken. Be present, and use all of your senses, including your intuition, when you are talking with someone so that you can really tune in and listen.

Step 4: Integrate into Understanding. Take time to make sense of it all. What have you heard? What does it mean? Remember: it's about them, not about you. This step requires you to hold potentially contradictory information side by side. Make room for it because it's just as valuable as the information that you already have. Intellectually you want to be able to say, "Okay, this is what is true for this person. This is how they see the situation, the angle that they are coming from."

Step 5: Use Solution Imagination. This is the moment when, after having taken off your own shoes, you step into the shoes of someone else. What do you imagine their point of view to be? Draw on everything that you've heard and keep your judgment at bay. Look at an issue or situation from their point of view. How would you respond to them? Here you want to consider the *why* and add that to the narrative in your head. Know their story *with* them. That's empathy. Then you formulate a response that demonstrates you get where they are coming from. Use the empathy to forge stronger connection and collaboration, and even to reach compromise that leaves everyone feeling seen and heard.

EMPATHETIC REFLECTIONS

- How do these steps resonate with you? Which step makes you feel uncomfortable? Which one seems like it will be easier for you?

DISMANTLE JUDGMENT

The first step is the hardest. Being judgmental has become second nature in society as we "like" and evaluate everyone's behavior. We have a toxic, codependent relationship with judgment—it's something we need in our life (to protect us), but it's also not good for us because it sabotages us (our ability to form true connection). Judgment forms a brick wall that blocks your ability to listen to and understand another person. Dismantling that brick wall will clear one of the biggest obstacles to attaining empathy.

5

The Moldy Pancake

If you don't like something, change it. If you can't change it, change your attitude. Don't complain.
MAYA ANGELOU

I N MY EXPERIENCE, dismantling judgment is the biggest challenge for anyone trying to achieve cognitive empathy and see the point of view of another person. Dismantling Judgment is Step 1 in the journey and, as you'll read in subsequent chapters, it continues to rear its ugly head all the way through Step 5. We have to constantly be aware of judgment, our relationship with it, and what we need to do to put it aside in order to reach empathy.

Judgment is a "frenemy" in our lives. We need judgment to make decisions—that's the friend part, while *being* judgmental prevents us from getting to empathy—that's the enemy part of the portmanteau. We express so much judgment every day that we don't always realize we are being judgmental, and therefore we have trouble dismantling it or turning it off. Less of a problem is "making a judgment," which includes decisions that you make based on available information. Judgments like this might include which route to take to get to the store, or more complicated decisions involving choices at work or in your personal life.

"Being judgmental" is the enemy. Casting aspersion toward others, putting others down, making sly insults, or withholding approval all get in the way of being able to see someone for who they truly are or hear the story they have to tell. Judgment like this builds up to form the equivalent of a brick wall that needs to be dismantled in order to move past the barrier and continue on the steps to empathy.

Judgment is made up of many different inputs, from our own past experiences to the biases and stereotypes that we carry with us from interaction to interaction. There is a lot of programming in place, which can be difficult to undo or get beyond. In addition, our own personality wiring (such as what's revealed by assessments like Myers-Briggs or the Enneagram) makes a difference in how judgment shows up.

There are many times in my role as a moderator where I need to *make* a judgment while not *being* judgmental. I will make a judgment in deciding the next question or while deciphering the pattern that's emerging from the work. I have to be careful not to *be* judgmental in how I interact with the respondent, how I evaluate their living situation and what they have told me, or even, later on, how I represent them while sharing the findings from the study.

We are often having to make a judgment as we go into a stranger's home in a strange town. You might not think about being offered food as a time when judgment comes up, but it does. Usually, I'm not one to turn down a sample, even on a project. If I am trying to build rapport with someone, keep them comfortable and talking freely, then it feels rude to turn down food. Often, what I'm being offered is something the respondents are proud of, maybe from a cherished family recipe. Taken at face value, that doesn't sound so bad. Who wouldn't want to taste all the different favorite family recipes that are out there? Every family has them. I've often gone into these situations thinking the food must be just as good as my own family's treasures, like my grandma's meatballs, right? Sounds more like a job perk than a hazard? Not exactly. I learned early on while doing a project about baking cookies at the holidays that not every family recipe is as good as your own cherished family recipes, yet you have an expectation based on your own biases, and therefore, you run the risk of being judgmental on the first bite.

Just like cleanliness, "taste" is subjective. While all food needs to be palatable, what actually tastes good is in the eye of the beholder. A dish that tastes perfectly balanced to one person might come across as too salty to someone else. Because I do so many projects about food, and they may include having someone cook or bake something, I end up in the position of getting offered a taste of a favorite food or a family gem of a dish. That puts me in a weird spot, as I don't want to be rude, yet I don't know if I'll like it. Trying other people's food is a way of empathizing with them, in my opinion. You try someone's cherished dish, and you get to experience firsthand what they like and how they taste the world. That's a type of perspective. It adds a richer love to the stories around food, which can reveal a great deal about many facets of someone's life, including expressions of their cultural or ethnic heritage, family interactions, their sense of adventure, and how they manage stress and emotions. I have come to the conclusion that since we're there to learn about someone, the food that they like is part of that understanding. As the moderator leading a conversation, I'm also mindful that I don't want to shut down the respondent and damage the interview by potentially offending or rejecting them. That means if I try food that's offered, I have to keep myself from being judgmental in order to maintain the rapport.

So, not wanting to offend and in pursuit of knowledge, I'll inevitably take a bite. There's a great video clip reel waiting to be made of me biting into everything from cookies to soups, pork chops to brownies. I don't have a terrific poker face, but I think I've learned to hold my face somewhat expressionless, so I don't look like a three-year-old choking down broccoli. And then I have to say something in acknowledgment of this "delicious" bite I've just had.

"Mm, interesting," is my first go-to phrase in these situations. It is the polite Midwestern way of saying, "That's weird; I don't like it," without really offending. It's a "Minnesota nice" way of saying, "This is one of the most disgusting things I've ever tried, but thank you for sharing your prized family recipe with me." Unfortunately, enough people in the Midwest know *interesting* is a word with a double meaning that I can't use it when sampling a Midwestern stranger's cherished chocolate chip cookie recipe. Instead of "interesting," I've developed my own automatic reaction when I try food in other people's homes. I tilt my head to the side while nodding appreciatively, usually with an *mm* sound and maybe a slight furrow of the brow to reflect that I can see how this is far from the worst brownie I've ever tried, and I appreciate the effort they put into it.

I also recognize how it feels to put yourself out there at risk of being judged by others. Seriously. Making food to share is stressful. You are vulnerable to being judged. All eyes are on the person tasting, especially that first bite. As a result, the taster tries not to cast aspersion. (Hopefully.) Instead, you have a sample, chew and swallow a few bites, nod with appreciation, then move on. That's what I do, whether I'm at a potluck or I'm offered food by a respondent during an interview.

I got the chance to refine these nonjudgmental skills during this project exploring baking habits during the holidays. We got to sit in on holiday cookie exchanges among groups of friends. I set out a rule at the start of the project: if you try one person's cookies, you need to try everyone else's, no matter what they look like. It was important to me that we be polite and respect each participant and their contribution. Who wants to be the one at the potluck with the full platter to take home? You want to discover an empty serving tray, the ultimate sign of the popularity of your dish and, therefore, validation of you, your skills, and your choice of recipe (which might also validate your grandma as well).

In my family, cookies at the holidays were always a big deal. Recipes passed down three generations are made faithfully every year.

Some are more common, like peanut butter blossoms; others, like our family butter cookies, are more elaborate. Now I was about to discover what types of cookies other people bake for the holidays. I was disappointed to find it was mostly chocolate chip cookies. Being judgmental, I find chocolate chip cookies are very "Wednesday after school," not a once-a-year holiday special.

At one particular party, set in the inner suburbs of Minneapolis, there were four women gathered together around a table. Each baker introduced her cookie, where the recipe came from, and what was special about it. Remarkably, each chocolate chip cookie did taste different. The balance of chocolate, sugar, and sometimes nuts, as well as the thickness and how well the cookie was baked, made each one different. It was kind of like being a judge on *The Great British Baking Show*, except we could only taste, not provide our opinion. With my Hoosier upbringing, it felt rude not to finish what was offered, so I always ate more than a taste.

And then came one cookie that was different from the others. The woman who had baked them was lovely, with a big personality that added a lot to the conversation. She was in her early fifties, and she had a matter-of-fact "that's the way it is" way of telling her stories and relating to all of us. She also had a lot of love infused into her baking and talked about it that way. I was excited to try her cookies. *These are gonna be good*, I thought.

I took one and passed the container on to the clients who were with me. The cookie looked great. Big chunks of chocolate. Thick. Nicely baked and brown throughout. Not even the slightest hint of charring on the bottom. I bit in. *Texture good.* The first parts of the flavor were coming over my tongue. *Milk chocolate morsels. Hint of brown sugar. Salt.*

Salt?

Yes, that is salt that I am tasting. And it was not the way dark chocolate is made more delicious by sea salt, or the way that the sweetness of caramel is moderated by sea salt. This was like iodized salt. Not so much salt that it was inedible, or a mistake, like the sugar and salt got swapped. But it was definitely a heavy-handed measurement of salt.

In the moment, I was sitting there, eating that salty cookie, trying to maintain my nonjudgmental composure while I figured out what I was tasting. She had said that the cookie was made with Crisco. Would that be the cause? *Keep the slight smile on your face, Rob.* Is Crisco salty? *Rob, visibly engage in the cookie with your eyes and a nod of the head, as though you are enjoying it.* I had never tried Crisco plain, but I didn't think there was any salt in it. *Now just swallow it, Rob, and you'll be done.* No, it's not the Crisco. *Smile in appreciation, Rob; ask a follow-up about the recipe so it appears you're engaged.* There's too much salt in it. *Take a sip of water to cleanse the salt out of your mouth, Rob.* Maybe this works for some people, but it's not to my taste. *There, isn't that better, Rob?* But since taste is subjective, I had to roll with it and dismantle my judgment. *She's revered by her friends as a good baker, so this must be something she does and that her community likes. Plus, I don't want to be rude. It's not going to kill me. Right?*

Food is such a huge part of our experience in America. What we eat and the stories behind each dish are as varied as the people in this country. Food can make the connection between two people even stronger when they've shared something as small as a cookie. All of these reasons make me more open to giving things a try.

In truth, even in a developed country like the United States, the food that we eat can put us in harm's way. We do it every time we lick the beater from the mixer, enjoying the taste of cake batter. It's usually not the raw egg that can get you, it's the flour. (I wouldn't have known that if it weren't for working with the large food companies like General Mills.) We even risk our health when we eat leftovers with a questionable smell or that have a slight fuzz in parts that might go undetected without careful examination. Our kitchens and refrigerators are veritable science labs where we are unwittingly cultivating colonies of microbes that could cause us and our families some serious damage.

YOU MIGHT expect that everyone is doing the same thing for food safety—washing our hands and the cutting board thoroughly after dealing with raw chicken, tossing the milk and other products the day after their expiration date, putting grilled meat on a clean plate instead of the plate that it was carried out on. Not so fast. Just like I warn clients that standards of cleanliness vary from home to home (the lesson I had learned at Bailey's house in Atlanta), the same is true of food safety in the home. Some things might make you blanch if you are a particular neat freak or germophobe. I take an approach to a respondent's life similar to how I want to be treated. It's their life, their rules, and that's what we want to understand.

If I let my judgment get in the way—let's say I had commented on how salty the cookie was and made a face—there's a significant risk that I end up insulting the other person, making her feel as though I am dismissing and invalidating everything that she has to say. That is not good for rapport during an interview with a stranger, as I have mentioned, and it's also not good for people that you know—either at work or in your personal life. If you are looking for collaboration or to get to a decision, you want to minimize being judgmental and instead use your judgment to make good decisions. Less aspersion, more thinking.

Having been on the receiving end of people being judgmental toward me, I know firsthand the power aspersion has to make a person feel bad about themselves. Being judgmental communicates that a person's point of view is unworthy of your time or consideration. That their opinion doesn't matter, or even that their being doesn't really matter. And this is done in the style of "death by a thousand cuts," doled out in micro-doses, or like the slap of a backhanded compliment.

I can say with confidence, as I'm sure you probably can too, that being on the receiving end of unwarranted judgment doesn't feel good. My opinion is as valid as yours as well as the next person's. Dismantling our judgment enables the act of listening to others (Step 3) and then trying to take on their point of view

(Step 4: Integrate into Understanding, and Step 5: Use Solution Imagination). Getting over our barriers caused by being judgmental helps broaden our worldview. I've found that by dismantling my judgment I may even learn a thing or two in the process.

While there are "hazards" if I sample too many cookies, mostly to my waistline, sometimes I run into people putting their own welfare at risk. Two stories from the field come to mind where my clients and I discovered behaviors that didn't jibe with our personal approach to food safety. This created two dilemmas for us: 1) we had to work to keep from being judgmental so we could learn from the respondents and get to a place of empathy, and 2) we also had to make a judgment call on whether or not to intervene for the respondent's safety.

The first story took place in Michigan. I was on a project with an objective to understand how people shop and use products in the dry dinners aisle. "Dry dinners" are products like Kraft Macaroni & Cheese, Hamburger Helper, Rice-A-Roni, and Betty Crocker potatoes, among others. The products come dry in a box, and you have to do some cooking to create the dinner.

Karen, the respondent, was a mid-forties mom with six kids, all college age or younger. The family lived in a good-sized house somewhat removed from the suburbs. Kinda rural but not farm rural. I remember lots of green grass, fields, and trees surrounding their home. Not your typical subdivision for sure.

Given the size of her family, Karen's "voice" was distinct, and she had our complete attention. The clients with me, some of whom were parents themselves, were building some empathy toward Karen's situation, imagining what it's like to have that many kids to feed, drive to practices and events, and still figure out what to make for dinner. Karen was a case study that the clients could sink their teeth into with new products and marketing communications.

And then Karen told us something that was the equivalent of a needle scratching across a record, causing everything to come to a stop. Karen mentioned, in passing, that her family prefers to drink raw milk. Even though it was a quick sentence, I could feel my clients get uncomfortable as their brick wall of judgment started to go up.

I am always curious about behaviors that are less than ordinary, so I asked Karen more about the family's raw milk preference. Apparently, Michigan is one of the few states that allow the sale of raw, unpasteurized milk if you own part of a cow. Karen told us she'd been doing raw milk for five years, and once a week she picked up three gallons that would last the week. "I'm just a big believer, and it has no pasteurization, and it's like my insurance for the kids. I find they have less colds; they're healthier. It's just my own belief," she explained.

For those not familiar with how milk goes from the cow to your glass: the gallon of milk you buy and typically drink is put through a heat pasteurization process in order to kill the bacteria and other pathogens that might be present. Of course, when you heat something, it transforms it. Visibly we would see that with food as melting or browning—for example, the melting of fat off a steak. There is a concern among people such as Karen that pasteurization diminishes or destroys the good nutrients that exist naturally in milk. So that line of thinking implies that the population in general is drinking milk that isn't as nutritious as it could be when it comes straight from the source with less processing.

Now I'll admit, I was kind of intrigued by this. Since I'm not part of Karen's family and was only a visitor for the afternoon, it was easy for me to stay open and keep any judgment dismantled. Thinking about it from her point of view and with the information she gave me, I could see where raw milk would make sense. Taking the other side of this raw milk argument is the other health perspective: if you drink unpasteurized milk, it is generally thought of as unsafe because of potential exposure to pathogens from the farm through the bottling process and into your home. Which side of this debate you land on depends on your point of view—risk drinking something that isn't guaranteed safe but is packed with nutrition? Or sacrifice some nutrition for the safety of drinking copious amounts without risking falling ill?

My clients fell in the camp of pasteurized milk. They were trying their best, listening to Karen explain the health benefits and how she made the trip to the farm to pick up the milk every week. I could see in their eyes and their body language that they were trying to understand her perspective. I didn't care as much as my clients; it was her life and her rules, and she wasn't imposing her beliefs on anyone outside her family.

And then Karen offered us a sample of the raw milk in her fridge. This would be a first for me.

Karen: How do you like the milk? Can you tell the difference or not?

Me: I can. I definitely can. There's like a . . . I don't know how to describe the taste.

Marco (our videographer): Grassy.

Me: Grassy was what—

Karen: You're right. My son, especially the day after I get it, he notices the flavor; you're absolutely right.

Client: That's what I said. It was like, *it's grassy*.

Me: Not in a bad way, either.

Karen: No.

Client: No, it's just a subtleness to it.

Karen: You're right. That's what my son says, too. By the end of the week it'll be okay, but it loses some of that "live" taste.

What does "grassy" taste like, you wonder? If you've ever had a shot of wheatgrass juice, that same taste that is the smell of fresh-cut grass that is in wheatgrass—that was the undernote in the milk. "It's an acquired taste," Karen told us. Indeed, it was. When you first bring the glass up to your face, there is a slight grassy note in the aroma. The initial sip passing your tongue feels just like any other milk. You can also taste that creamy dairy flavor. My reaction started with, *Mm, interesting*, both from my own judgment, weirding out at the thought of drinking raw milk, and from the intellectual curiosity of what I was trying. I'm a pretty evolved eater, but I don't spend that much time thinking about where my food comes from. Raw milk puts the source right there in front of you because you can taste the grass the cows were chewing on before they were milked. It's a little jarring, finding an unexpected taste in something you've been drinking your entire life. You think you know what milk tastes like. So much so that you probably can't describe the taste beyond... milk! *Grassy* would never enter your mind, until the flavor was literally on your tongue.

My second thought while trying it was, *Not as bad as I thought it would be.* Then, as the milk swirled around, coating my mouth as I prepared to swallow, a third and final reaction as I noticed the flavor of... maybe not grass, but hay, rise up. Pungent and sharp, it permeated the roof of my mouth. It was what I imagined the color green must taste like. That fresh-cut green grass with notes of hay bale smell was the taste in the milk. As Karen said, "It's more pronounced when the milk is really fresh." Indeed it was.

So what did I think? I didn't go into judgment and say, "Gross! How can you drink that?" I did my best to hold my facial composure, furrowing my brow in a concentrated look while tilting my head to the side slightly. In other words, I kept my judgment in check. I was polite, interested, and open to what her motivation was for using the raw milk. With my judgment dismantled, I was able to move on to Step 2: Ask Good Questions. As a result, I came away understanding her point of view—raw milk is healthier, packed with protein and other nutrients, and with a large family is a good enhancement to a meal.

Unfortunately, my clients weren't as successful at dismantling their judgment. Forget what we heard about the needs of a large family at dinnertime. Raw milk and the risks associated with drinking unpasteurized dairy dominated the debrief conversation with my clients. It was all they could think of. The conversation went deep into what was harmful with raw milk, the risk the kids might be in, and also where clients had seen raw milk available near their homes and who they personally knew that had dabbled in it.

I tried to refocus them on what else we had heard that was pertinent to the project, which was about dinnertime and meal kits, not raw milk. But their judgment was still up. Judgment had tainted what the clients heard, how they heard it, and what they made of it. Judgment created a barrier to them recalling and internalizing most everything else that Karen had to say. You've probably experienced the same thing with judgment at some point. Judgment got in the way and clouded everything else that you had heard. My clients let their own bias define Karen. She became known as the mom that gave her kids raw milk. Everything else fell by the wayside.

What happened at Karen's is an example of how important it is to remain open to someone's perspective. If you let judgment get in the way, you will just think *ewww* and cast the person as an outsider or a freak rather than asking the questions, listening, and understanding, which can lead to a connection, an insight, or a solution. My clients lost all the other interesting things that we learned from Karen during that interview, all because they couldn't get past the type of milk she drinks.

Like on *Star Trek*, I generally follow the "Prime Directive"—do not interfere with the normal development of life on other planets. I interpret that as "do not interfere with life in other households." We are not there to be judgmental; we are there only to listen to the story, understand, and draw inspiration and insight from it. If I knew for a fact that someone was going to cause themselves bodily harm or injury, then yes, I'd say something, but if it's a behavior they've had for years, I don't feel that I have the authority to tell them not to. I may spend some time talking to them and trying to understand their behavior, but I won't interfere.

AND THEN there are those rare times when someone's food practices just make me go, *Ewww*... Rare situations where I have to consider making a judgment and getting involved while not being (too) judgmental.

Which brings me to the story of the moldy pancake.

I encountered the moldy pancake on a different breakfast project that also had me up before the crack of dawn to go into people's homes to observe them making breakfast. This time, I showed up at their house, along with a cameraperson, filmed them prepping and eating breakfast, and then we left and went on about our day. No questions were asked. In those early morning hours, we got to experience the silence and observe the daybreak rituals. All in silence. We were totally quiet; the people were also pretty quiet, just everyday people going about their morning routine.

One woman, Debra, was particularly notable for the shortcuts she devised to be able to enjoy pancakes on weekday mornings before going to work.

Debra's routine was to make a pancake for herself almost every morning. To expedite her morning pancake (she only made one solitary large pancake each morning), Debra prepared a large batch of batter on Sunday and left it in the refrigerator to use during the week. Pretty ingenious. The messy prep was done in advance, allowing her to draw from a bowl full of batter as needed to make one pancake at a time. And that gave her the freedom to have pancakes whenever she wanted, since she was only dirtying the griddle and spatula, which were easy enough for her to clean.

Debra's kitchen was dark at 6:00 a.m. There wasn't a hint of sun yet. The only light came from beneath a cabinet and over the kitchen sink. I stood silently in the entry to the kitchen while our videographer filmed Debra's routine. She pulled the batter out of the refrigerator. It sat in a big red plastic bowl and already had a whisk in it, I presumed from at least the day before. The batter had separated from sitting for so long in the fridge. A shiny, greenish, watery pool sat atop the heavier layer of thick batter fluid, which I could see just beneath. She grabbed the whisk and gave the batter a good whisking to recombine it, the green water integrating back into the yellow thickness to re-form into batter. Once it was mixed together, she spooned some reborn batter out onto her hot griddle and made her pancake. A few minutes and a flip later, the pancake was done. She transferred it to a plate, sat down at her kitchen table, added a little butter and syrup. Then, using a fork, Debra cut in and removed a wedge of fluffy golden pancake. She grabbed the newspaper and read the news while she ate her pancake. We watched silently and, per our request, she ignored that we were there.

Watching someone eat breakfast without engaging with them is really uncomfortable—for the person eating as well as for those of us watching. Debra sat at her kitchen table, eating her hot pancake and looking through the paper as she usually does. She was silent as she forked off a piece, put it in her mouth, and chewed. Silence as she read a news story, took a sip of coffee, and kept eating. This is morning in America, and probably around the world. Sitting in solitude, slowly waking the brain, gearing up for the day ahead.

We left Debra as the sun was rising. We would revisit with her in the evening. Our plan was to review the breakfast footage with the clients before we came back. Then Debra would watch and provide a "director's commentary" on what she had been doing.

Meeting with the clients later in the day, I was excited because I had witnessed a consumer-generated solution: making a big bowl of batter in advance to address a problem, which provided great inspiration for new products.

After reviewing the footage with the clients, we climbed into the car, and as we started to drive off to Debra's house, one of the clients, a food scientist, turned to me and asked, "Was that mold on top of the batter?"

"What do you mean?"

"Did you notice that green color on top of the raw batter? I think that was mold forming."

My stomach did a little flip when I realized I'd just spent my early morning watching someone whisk mold into their pancake batter, cook it up, and eat it. There was a collective *ewww* from all of us in the car.

In all honesty, yes, when the client mentioned it, I did recall the green shine in the separated liquid. And I remember a thought crossing my mind in the early morning: *It's green; that's weird*, but my brain didn't immediately go to, *That's mold!* I was tired and more focused on observing in silence than asking questions and interfering. Part "Prime Directive," part early morning bleariness. Plus, I hadn't seen overnight pancake batter before, let alone mold growing in pancake batter, so I didn't know what I was looking at.

So, in the quiet of Debra's kitchen in the early morning hours, I had stood silently by, watching Debra stir mold into her pancakes. *Ick!*

So here we are with a kind of ethical dilemma. Our job is to observe and ask questions. Listen and build empathy without judgment. At the same time, help our clients dismantle judgment, build empathy, understand, and be inspired to take action. But when a suburban mom is about to put a pancake fortified with homegrown penicillin in her mouth, do you yank the fork out of her hand or simply watch the story unfold? When would the "Prime Directive," if it were a real thing, apply? Or instead, was I scouting candidates for next year's Darwin Awards? Those people who got themselves killed by sheer stupidity? You can almost hear the headline teasing the local news: "Suburban Mom Dies from Moldy Pancake; Film at Eleven."

You can have empathy for others and also still tactfully share your observations. Armed with information, it is up to them to decide what to do with it. On the one hand, in Karen's case, she had done her research and was making a conscious decision to consume raw milk. I believe that it wasn't our place to try to sway her. Debra, on the other hand, probably wasn't aware of her pancake's fungal fortification. Therefore, she needed to know.

By the end of the evening session, the client who first identified the green mold gave Debra a heads-up that she might be better off with fresher batches of batter.

Judgment comes in many forms. Being judgmental gets in the way of empathy, whether it's personal preference of how salty a cookie should be or a bias against raw milk. Sometimes a person needs help, though, in making a judgment call on whether or not to eat moldy pancakes. That type of judgment making is okay and doesn't interfere with empathy building, as long as you aren't saying *"ewww"* or *"ick,"* casting aspersion in the process. I've found the secret to stopping this type of judgmental feeling is having awareness that I'm doing it. This helps me catch myself in the moment, like I did with the salty cookie and the grassy milk, and approach the conversation differently, without judgment.

EMPATHETIC REFLECTIONS

- How would you rephrase feedback that you've given that might have been judgmental?

- When have you been on the receiving end of someone being judgmental, and how did it feel? What would you have wanted them to say instead?

- What prompts you to be judgmental? What keeps you from just letting people be? What would happen if you weren't being judgmental?

- Can you think of a time when you might have confused making a judgment and being judgmental? What would you have done differently, knowing what you know now?

6

Crawling Away

Sometimes, people can be extraordinarily judgmental and closed-minded to anyone different or special, which is why it's so hard for young people in this day and age to be comfortable enough in their own skin to not listen to the people picking on them.

ARIANA GRANDE

Y GREAT-GRANDFATHER WAS a farmer and a gentleman from South Carolina. Relatives have said that he was always well dressed and wore a hat, even if he was going to work the fields. Beyond that image he was also, I'm told, polite, gentle, and courteous. He would always get the coffee started for my great-grandmother in the morning before he headed out. And he'd make "coffee" of hot milk with a drop of java for his visiting grandchildren, including my mom. I was only a toddler when he passed away. There is photographic evidence that proves we met, but I don't really have crisp memories of him. My memories are framed mostly by the photos I've seen and the stories I've heard.

In one photo, we are outside. I recognize the tall pine trees and dirt roads as the land he owned and worked during his adult life in coastal South Carolina. I'm sitting on his lap. I look like I'm perspiring, which often happens to me in humid climates. It's also evident that I'm slightly pulled away from him. I'm not hugging him or leaning in, like I do in photos with some of my other grandparents. I was keeping my distance. I'm told it was because I was more than a bit freaked out by his voice. By the time I came along, his soft-spoken southern gentleman's lilt had been replaced by a raspy electronic sound, produced by a voice-generating device placed over the hole in his throat where his voice box used to be.

A life of smoking brought cancer to my great-grandfather and ultimately claimed his larynx and vocal cords in 1963. He passed away in 1972. I was almost four. The few years that our lives overlapped, he had to use an artificial voice box in order to communicate.

If I think hard enough, I remember seeing the hole in his throat. Where there should have been the solid skin and substance of his neck, maybe an Adam's apple, there was a hole that pierced into darkness inside him. A hole that wasn't supposed to be there. If anything gave me the willies when I was a toddler, that was it. I can remember seeing him bring the device to his throat in order to speak; it was beige-white in my mind. Then, instead of a human voice with the rounded edges and intonation you'd expect, a raspy sound emitted. I don't remember much else from that scene, but I do have a memory of that electronic voice. I'm told I would crawl away when he entered the room. It makes me sad to think that I was afraid of this man who was known to always have a twinkle in his eye and to be very loving.

My great-grandfather's stoma generated an early-age "trauma" that has lived on deep in my subconscious. As long as I can remember, I've been uncomfortable seeing people with physical disabilities. I try hard not to have a visceral reaction, and my inclination is to want to look away, just like I'd turn my head away from the hole in my great-grandfather's throat. As a toddler, I was afraid. It wasn't what was "normal" to my two-year-old understanding. This past experience has rooted to create a reflexive judgment within me that I have to dismantle when I meet someone who is disabled.

It's not easy to admit that I do this. I'm not proud of it, and I continue to make progress on overcoming my judgment. In other situations, I find the judgment acts as a brick wall preventing me from reaching another person. To use another analogy, judgment can be like noise-canceling headphones that prevent you from actively listening, which I'll discuss in Step 3.

In my situation, if I let my aversion get the best of me, then I don't even show up at the conversation. Judgment is preventing the start of connection, which means there's no hope to get to empathy.

I share this about my own behavior because each one of us is formed by our own past experiences. They can be significant and difficult—not technically "traumatic" but still unsettling, disturbing, or concerning, and they can form these negative opinions and drive behaviors.

The past experience that has created a dismissive or aversive reaction in you is probably not the same as mine. There are so many events, big and small, that can take root and cause this that I don't have enough pages available to list them all. If you pause for a moment and reflect on your own lived experience and resulting behaviors, you can probably identify what it is for you.

For me, I needed to work to overcome this. First and foremost, I don't like this response within me; it goes against my values of compassion and accepting humanity in all its many sizes, shapes, colors, and figures. Second, in my line of work, it is only going to get in the way, just like the other types of being judgmental.

It's taken a lot of work over a long time, but now, when I find myself in those situations where I'm uneasy, I remind myself to simply make eye contact. Easy enough if I'm not directly engaged with the person, like if we were to pass on the street or be in the same store together. I can prepare myself for what I'm seeing and then make eye contact in my own time. In situations where I'm suddenly placed face to face with someone, like in an interview or alone in a narrow aisle of a grocery store, I've found it harder to regroup than when I'm on the street. What I've found I do is make eye contact, say hello, then look down at papers or the shopping cart in front of me to quickly process and get beyond my judgment. Then I look up, begin the conversation, and work hard to maintain eye contact. There is a saying that the eyes are "the windows to the soul," and I believe that. Focusing on someone's eyes lets you connect on a deeper level than if you are fixated on another part of their body or their room that may or may not be what you are used to seeing. This helps me keep the conversation going, and we can focus on the matter at hand. I used this approach during a project where we were testing a new type of yogurt packaging.

In marketing research, we are often looking to see how many people like, or validate, a new product idea. Through various methods, we expose a concept to potential consumers and then they give us the thumbs-up or thumbs-down reaction. I like to include a thumbs-sideways option as well. The "murky middle" can often be just as insightful as to why someone does or doesn't like a product. It creates a chance for someone to express an ultimatum on what they feel could be stronger about the idea to get the thumb turned up, or what would ruin it for them and give it the thumbs-down.

Thumbs have become integral in expressing our feelings to others. We "thumb our nose" at something we don't like, while we give something we like a thumbs-up—which, thanks to Facebook, is now a universal icon. The thumb has become increasingly powerful beyond its original, opposable, purpose. It delivers validation, both in research projects as well as to our own self-esteem and sense of self-worth.

Among validation projects, there are some where you want to see how people react to a concept described on a piece of paper, and others where you want to see how people handle a mock-up of your potential product. It's a type of usability test. As the creator, manufacturer, or publisher, you want your product to be as easy and intuitive as possible for people to use. The physical interaction and engagement can enhance liking (thumbs-up) or be a barrier or a turnoff (thumbs-down). This type of work, observing how people interact with a product, can lead to great innovations and improvements. Researchers for OXO noticed that people bent over to look at the level in a measuring glass, which creates strain on the back, unnecessary movements, and imprecise measurements. To solve for that, they created a system where you can see from above how much you've filled the measuring cup—an ingenious design built upon empathy and inspired by watching people interact with a product.

For this particular project, we were looking to understand how people interacted with the packaging for a new type of Greek yogurt. Earlier, Pepsi had decided to enter the yogurt category through a partnership with Müller, a German yogurt brand. In Europe, Müller already had a distinctive package that you might now recognize as the Chobani Flip package found on shelves in the United States. It's a flatter, square container with a diagonal divider that creates a larger "cup" for the yogurt and a second smaller "cup" next to it for a "mix-in" like granola or chocolate or nuts. The part of the plastic that connects the two cups is scored, so you can fold the cup with the mix-ins over the yogurt base, thereby adding flavor and different textures to your yogurt. This package structure is known to me as a "sidecar," and it has the benefit of giving the consumer control over how much mix-in to add while also preventing the mix-in from absorbing the moisture from the yogurt and getting soggy.

This project predated Chobani Flip, and, from my understanding, the announcement that Pepsi was bringing Müller and its crunchy mix-in sidecars to the United States sent the other yogurt manufacturers scrambling to beat this potential juggernaut to market.

My company, Ignite 360, was brought in by one of the manufacturers to test reaction to their own version of this new sidecar idea. We had versions of the concept on paper, which would be read and evaluated while samples of packaging that resembled what the final offering might look like were mocked up with product so we could see how consumers handled the package. Would they dump all the crunchy bits in? Would they spoon in a few bits at a time? Was the score in the plastic deep enough to make it easy to fold over? Did the consumers even like the idea? Would they give it a thumbs-up?

In the middle of one of the focus groups, I noticed one of the respondents was having difficulty with the packaging. A middle-aged woman was handling the package in a way that wasn't so much clumsy as it was deliberate, yet with a lot of awkwardness. In particular she was having trouble getting the package to fold over.

When people are trying out a product, my role is just to observe what is going on and make mental notes on what to explore with some good questions later on. I'm in observation mode—"listening" to the actual interaction, including any body language that might indicate a pain point or difficulty or other reaction. I also pay attention to facial reactions and expressions. Are they happy or looking frustrated? I stay silent, withholding any questions until they have finished testing the sample out. Then I ask for their reaction—Who gave a thumbs-up? Thumbs-down? Thumbs-sideways?—and the conversation goes from there.

In this one group, the respondent (I'm going to call her Helen) was really nice and had some thoughtful comments in the first part of the session when we discussed everyone's usual habits of eating yogurt. Later on, as she was trying out the package, she started having some difficulty. On the second and third samples that we put in front of her, I noticed that Helen held the package closer to her body than the other people. And where some were using a single hand, Helen used both hands to manipulate the package and hold on to it. My eye caught that because her movements were different from all the other respondents. The package wasn't that large. Once you had flipped it over and were eating, other people easily held it in one hand. But she wasn't. That wasn't obvious to me at first, but those differences start to be noticed when one person out of eight is doing something slightly different. It was like lining up a group of people and asking them to demonstrate the same task, say hammer in a nail. There might be some minor differences—right- versus left-handed, number of fingers to hold the nail to start, placement of the hand on the hammer handle—but the primary action of swinging the hammer should look very similar person to person. Not true with Helen and these sidecar cups. No one else was manipulating it the way she did. She would pull the package close to her body and use her chest to help keep the package in place while she flipped the sidecar over. She fumbled with it as though she was "all thumbs" when it came to dealing with this package.

Observing Helen compared to the rest of the room, my eyes were registering that something was different, but I couldn't quite decipher it. It was starting to feel like those tests where you look at pictures and try to identify the thing that's subtly off or missing.

I didn't want to stare at Helen, but I couldn't help continuing to look in her direction as I was trying to figure out this mystery. As part of the study, everyone was directed to tip in the mix-in and then try the yogurt with it. Then I had them write down their thoughts.

Again, something with Helen caught my eye. Was it the way she held the spoon? I paid closer attention. She grasped the spoon with all four fingers wrapped around the handle. It was a palmar supinate grasp, like a child might do before learning the correct way to use utensils, balancing them on your finger and side of your hand. I've seen plenty of grown-ups with similar less-than-pristine table manners, so it stood out but didn't strike me as unusual.

As people started writing down their comments, I noticed the way Helen held the pencil. She was holding it between her index and middle fingers and moving it around with just those two digits. Again, my brain was registering that this wasn't what I usually see with people. I started walking around the room. As I neared Helen, I looked at the pencil in her fingers. Then I looked at how the woman next to her was writing, with the pencil between the thumb, forefinger, and middle finger. And then, I broadened my vision to see Helen's entire hand and the pencil. And that's when it finally registered with a jolt of revelation. There *was* something missing. It turns out Helen wasn't "all thumbs" with the package because Helen was clumsy or there was a problem with the package design. Helen was "all thumbs" because Helen didn't have thumbs.

No thumbs. At all.

Of course, in the moment, just like at my great-grandfather's house in South Carolina, I wanted to crawl away. Inside I squirmed, uncomfortable with what I was seeing. I knew I couldn't look away, but I knew I couldn't stare either. I also couldn't believe my eyes at what I was seeing. I had never seen a person without thumbs. I started thinking about what the cause of this could possibly be. I took another peek as I walked around the room, looking at her hands. The sides of Helen's hands where her thumbs should extend looked just like the skin you find on the side of your hands. No scars, blemishes, or underdeveloped digits. Just no thumbs.

In this moment I was trying to wrap my head around what had happened to Helen's thumbs while I also wrangled my mental focus to elicit feedback from the rest of the group about the packaging and product concept. Had I stepped on another land mine? I needed to get the group's reaction. The clients were all behind the glass mirror, unaware of what I'd seen, unaware that I was having a little mental freak-out, just waiting for the answers that would inform a fifty-million-dollar capital investment decision. I had planned to ask the group for a thumbs-up, thumbs-down, or thumbs-sideways. That would have been horrible—unkind and insensitive to Helen's situation. I wouldn't want someone to do that if I were her.

I needed to find another method to get feedback. I'd never been in this situation before. I wanted to crawl away, like I had from my great-grandfather, but I couldn't. I had to face it and find my way through. My mind was filled with all sorts of distracting thoughts— from curiosity to discomfort. Oh wait, there were still seven other people in the room, waiting for me to lead them in conversation. My brain was buzzing. *How should I handle this?*

I noticed, once pencils went down on completion of the exercise, that Helen tended to keep her hands in her lap and out of sight. I realized she had done that earlier in the session as well. I just hadn't registered it as important. I thought she was being polite, but I started connecting the dots and realized she must have had a natural inclination to keep her hands somewhat concealed. I took that as my cue. Since Helen was not showing her hands off or using them to accentuate her conversation, I wouldn't draw attention to them either. Your goal, whether as a moderator or in everyday life, should always be to respect the person you are speaking with and treat them as you treat others and want to be treated yourself. It's the Golden Rule. I think this applies to everyone and all conversations.

In the end, I did not ask for the "thumbs-up/-down/-sideways" indication of how everyone felt about the product. I just asked them what the positives, negatives, and things they'd want to change were. Helen joined in the conversation just as she had earlier. She offered her thoughts based on her experience using the package. Ultimately, her feedback wasn't all that different from everyone else's. She didn't call out her condition, nor did she take a stance that the package failed to be friendly to those without thumbs, although she certainly struggled more than the others and had a right to remind us of the need to be sensitive to the needs of the differently abled in all of our product and service designs. I've learned on subsequent projects addressing accessibility needs that more than one billion people have some type of disability. That's 15 percent of the Earth's population. It's time to move beyond prejudice to create solutions with empathy.

What appeared at first to be someone being "all thumbs" was in fact someone who was in complete control over their situation and just had a different way of getting tasks accomplished, like so many people do, regardless of whether they have a disability or not.

Later that night, back in my hotel room, I kept thinking about Helen and wanted to find out more about what was going on with her hands. I entered a Google search for "genetically missing thumbs" and discovered a condition called thumb hypoplasia—a range of congenital abnormalities of the thumb. I'm not a doctor, nor did I discuss it with her, but it appeared that Helen had Type V, which is missing thumbs altogether. There is a surgery that can create a pseudo-thumb from the index finger, but it appears that it isn't as strong as a naturally occurring thumb. Helen didn't appear to have had any sort of surgery; there were no visible scars. Clearly, she had learned to adapt.

MEETING HELEN in a work setting pushed me to get more comfortable meeting people with accessibility needs. In the months and years after having Helen in my focus group, I've begun making conscious attempts to be open and more warmly engaged with people who are visibly different from me.

And then I had my moment where I became the one with the disability.

I spent much of the summer of 2016 with my foot in a boot, healing from a fracture in my heel, right where the Achilles tendon connects to the foot. I had to rely on the wheelchair service at airports that summer in order to get to the gate and down the jet bridge to the plane. I remember the first time I was wheeled through the airport in a wheelchair. It was in Minneapolis.

The first thing I noticed was how my perspective shifted when I was seated in the chair. Suddenly I wasn't at eye level; I was gazing at people's stomachs. And as I was wheeled down the hallways, I saw more than one fellow passenger look away rather than meet my gaze. That felt awkward. "Hello, I'm right here; just look down a little bit." They were choosing instead to "crawl away," just as I used to do.

I remember that one woman, probably in her mid-fifties, casually dressed, saw me, tilted her head, and gave me a look that said, "Oh, poor thing." I was dumbstruck at that. I just had a boot on my foot. I didn't need her sympathy. I wanted empathy. I was starting to see how people with disabilities might feel: ignored or met with pity. Neither of those felt good, particularly when I was making do with my limitation. I decided I was going to help people understand how I wanted to be treated by treating them that way first. I started to make sure I had a smile ready and that I was waiting to respond to them when we made eye contact. It was a choice to connect with people from a positive place rather than let them take me to a place of pity. I didn't want to be a pity magnet. A broken foot was nothing, really. *Look at me as a person who just happens to be in a wheelchair. Smile and say hello or nod in acknowledgment, but please hold the droopy-eyed sad face. I'm still me.* And that is the lesson I keep reminding myself of when I see others that might be disabled in some way. Treat them as regularly as possible rather than as objects of pity or something to crawl away from.

A couple of years after my experience in a wheelchair, I spent time at the Beth Israel Deaconess Medical Center in Boston, visiting my sister-in-law, Becky, who was a patient in the oncology ward. It had been years since I'd been in a hospital. In this particular ward, people were in all stages of getting better, getting worse, and approaching death. I was overhearing very emotional conversations addressing end-of-life realities. I remember being really nervous in the cab on the way to the hospital the first time. I wasn't sure how I was going to react to seeing people wasting away, the vibrancy drained from their persons, including someone I knew and cared about. Would I crawl away?

I took a deep breath as the doors to the elevator opened on the floor. I went through the double door airlock, sanitizing my hands on the way. I could see into rooms as I walked by. Some patients were asleep or in a daze, unable to make eye contact. Patients that were alert were able to look out from their beds toward the hallway as I walked by. I thought about what I might want if I were in their shoes. A warm, caring smile seemed like something that would be welcomed. And if I made eye contact, to give them a nod of acknowledgment so they knew that I saw them as fellow humans.

When I entered the room and saw Becky for the first time, she was much thinner and smaller than I recalled due to the invasive surgery and the complications that had put her back in the hospital. Various tubes delivered oxygen to her nostrils and fluids to her veins, while wires measured her vitals. I lit up my face with a big smile and a twinkle in my eye and said, "There she is!" I gave her as big a hug as I could, considering her situation.

No matter how bad Becky or any other patient might have looked, the staff always looked the patients in the eyes, saw them as fellow human beings, and engaged with them on a human level. They expressed empathy with what the patient was going through, which nurtured compassion in their care. As they got to know their patients, the staff would reveal little things about themselves too. Stories about kids and pets were common, and occasionally photos would come up on phones to be shared. Care isn't just clinical or purely emotional; it's a blend of both. Just like when you scraped your knee as a child, you wouldn't want your mom to have made a fuss but *not* put a Band-Aid on it. You need both the actual care and the compassion from empathy in order to get better.

Becky lost her battle with kidney cancer, yet through that experience I've grown in my own understanding of how important it is to respond to people with a recognition of their humanity and with compassion, no matter their differences—visible or otherwise. We are all human and looking to be seen and acknowledged, which should be a fundamental right that we all grant each other out of decency.

I can't fault my two-year-old self for being freaked out by an old man with a hole in his throat and a box that helped him artificially speak. I wish I hadn't crawled away. I'm sure that didn't make my great-grandfather feel very good. Now, in those moments when I feel that "crawl away" reflex, my inner voice reminds me to imagine what it might be like for the other person. To move through the world with something noticeably different, a visible minority. As a gay man, I wasn't a visible minority, so people wouldn't look away the first time they saw me. Even so, I have felt persecution and aversion from others in my life. I know what that feels like, and it isn't a good feeling. It hurts. Even if you tell yourself you don't care, deep down there's a nick of pain etched into your heart each time it happens. I draw on how that feels for me in order to help me overcome my own judgment and imagine the feelings of the other person so that I don't crawl away and inflict pain on them. I certainly wouldn't want them to crawl away if the shoe were on the other foot.

EMPATHETIC REFLECTIONS

- When have you been judgmental because you were uncomfortable about someone's appearance? How did that feel? If you were in that situation again, what would you do differently?

- Think about a time when someone looked at you with pity. How did it make you feel? Was that what you wanted in that situation? What *did* you want?

- Where does your judgment come from? What prompts you to be judgmental?

7

Mother Would Never Do That

You know how bitchy fags can be.
JENNIFER NORTH IN *VALLEY OF THE DOLLS*, by Jacqueline Susann

WHEN YOU SLIP into a state of "being judgmental," you are basing your thoughts on your own values and opinions and negatively applying them to someone else. Even when the action or person you are being judgmental about is not harming you, and you still insist on being judgmental, you can cause injury and harm to the other person. It's what I suffered through while growing up in the smaller small town in Indiana, and it's what all of us suffer through at the hands of our tormentors and bullies. Being judgmental creates a power dynamic and is unempathetic. It's childish behavior that follows us straight into adulthood.

In the end, when you are being judgmental, it diminishes the way the other person feels and is never a good look for the person doing the judging. Yet it's a default that we go to in order to protect ourselves and our worldview, just like we have since we were kids. In the moment, it makes us feel bigger—that we are "better" than the other person. That makes us momentarily feel good about ourselves, which is why being judgmental repeatedly gets in the way, and why it's so hard to overcome.

When someone doesn't fit with our expectations, we judge in that "being judgmental" way. We call attention to any characteristic, feature, or attitude that is divergent from our own. It's an awful inclination and one I try so hard to keep under control. But even for someone who's an "empathy activist," coaching and training people on how to be more empathetic, I am guilty of slipping into being judgmental myself. One work situation when judgment comes out for me is when I've been with a respondent who I feel isn't totally forthcoming or willing to go deep on topics. I get frustrated with what I perceive (judge) to be discomfort, a lack of self-awareness, or even secretiveness. It's frustrating for me because it's my job to get them to open up. When they don't, I feel responsible for that "failure." And in that moment, I'll cast some type of judgment against them to deflect from anything that I might have done wrong. The truth is that I may not have been at the top of my moderating game that day. Or the person may have their real feelings so locked away that they will never share them, particularly in front of a group of strangers with a camera recording them. That's happened to me on more than one occasion, including one memorably hot, semi-sticky August afternoon in Pennsylvania.

I had pulled up in front of the respondent's home in my rented Ford Expedition SUV packed with clients and equipment. The single-family home we were about to visit was two stories, all brick, with a porch on the first floor that was elevated five to six feet above the street level. The house felt about eighty years old. It was like a detached row house. I was reminded of one of the homes FBI agent Clarice Starling visits in *The Silence of the Lambs*. Hopefully this wasn't the house where the killer lurked amid moths and what I imagined were putrid smells. This was just another house we were about to enter, instead of a chamber of horrors. But it somehow felt oppressive.

Yes, I pulled up in front of this house and immediately went to a place of judgment. Squeezed in between the clients and the videographer were a lot of my own biases and prejudices—against summer heat and humidity, against old houses, and even against Pennsylvania (while I had no valid reason to dislike Pennsylvania, it was there, irrationally gnawing at me).

We unloaded the oversized SUV and started up the creaky steps to the porch. Frank, a jovial man who appeared to be in his mid- to late forties, with graying hair and a good, hearty body size, greeted us and invited us in. *Okay, he seems like a really nice guy*, I said to myself to quell the overwrought judgment-based fears brewing inside me.

Whenever I enter a respondent's home, I am bombarded with stimuli and sensorial input. The eyes, ears, and nose come alive, taking in and processing the sights, sounds, and smells. What pictures are on display? What is the state of harmony or disharmony in the home? How quiet is the house? Are there dogs barking? Can I smell the pets? Can I smell something else? Do I want to smell that? And I am taking all of that in, making little mental notes, while also talking to the respondent, sizing them up, trying to make them feel comfortable. I come back to all those details later when I am trying to piece together the puzzle of who this person is, what makes them tick. Hopefully by then, the clients and I are closer to understanding.

Entering Frank's house, what first struck me were all the exposed two-by-four beams and drywall. Several walls were that way. Clearly there was some renovation going on. However, there were no tools or tarps or evidence that the work was ongoing. That meant that Frank had either seriously cleaned up for us or this was a side project happening over many months or even years. What's more, there were objects placed on display on some of the crossbeams. He had made use of the new "shelving" created by the exposed two-by-fours to hold small, framed pictures and some souvenirs from his travels. Frank had moved into his state of repair. He had adapted to it as his new, normal living situation.

When I am first taking everything in, I try not to be too obvious that I am scanning every inch I can see to take in my new surroundings. I really can't help it. It tells me a lot about a person or a place. Frank must have picked up what we were seeing and how out of the ordinary it was. He quickly apologized and explained that he was renovating his home and it was a long, ongoing process. I found I was being judgmental about why someone would want to live with so many walls half completed and not finish the job. His "work in progress" explanation helped me dismantle my judgment somewhat, although I remained a little wary of the half-finished setting.

We sat down and started the conversation. In every interview, I try to get a little personal or biographical information to help me have context for who this person is. Those questions include what they do for fun, or how a close friend might describe them. Then, if it's a food-related project, like this one, I might ask them how they'd describe their philosophy toward food. This led me to then ask Frank how he approached cooking, and where he got recipes and learned about new things. He was also going to be preparing dinner while we watched, so this initial conversation established what we would see later on. I also pay attention to the word choices people make. I will adapt to their selection of words and pronunciations to make them feel more comfortable. See if anything stands out to you in this excerpt from the transcript.

Frank: My mother taught me how to make a really good meat loaf.

Me: What do you like about cooking?

Frank: I think probably it mostly reminds me of growing up, because my dad, he had a regimented schedule where at five o'clock every day on a weekday, we had dinner, so I'd come home from school at three-thirty—I went to the local Catholic school up near my house—and I'd meet my dad, and at five o'clock every day we had dinner, and my mother was always cooking it. So I'd help her in the kitchen with stuff, and that's why I learned probably even more than my sister. I don't know how she did not learn how to cook, but I learned a lot. Even from my dad I learned how to wire a house and all that stuff, so I learned a lot from both of them.

Me: Where do you start in terms of planning the meal out?

Frank: [My ideas] come back to my mother. Pretty much the way I make the food is the way she did. I don't think I've ever prepared chicken other than Shake 'n Bake. That's what I do. I've never fried it. I just don't do that. I just do the Shake 'n Bake and the pork chop—every once in a while I'll try, like, a stuffed pork chop, and I'll put Stove Top stuffing in between stuff, just to try something a little bit different, because Mother would never do that. She would never do Stove Top stuffing, either. Just trying different things, but pretty much staying with the basic preparation that I grew up with.

Me: And so did your mother use Shake 'n Bake?

Frank: Yeah. That's where I learned it.

Me: Has Shake 'n Bake changed at all?

Frank: To me the box did, because I couldn't find it, actually, but no, just exactly what it was as a kid. She wouldn't cook hers as much. Dad didn't like dried-out meat, but I liked the well-done stuff. So I will cook it longer than she ever did. I put it in milk to keep it moist, and dip the pork chops in milk first, then put it in the Shake 'n Bake. I don't know if that's the instruction or not, but that's how I was raised.

Me: And so Mother did that?

Frank: Mother did.

Me: So, like, you're doing pork chops, then you're doing some rice—and salad?

Frank: Today? Salad with cherry tomatoes and, like I said, fresh bread I just picked up.

Me: So is that pretty much what Mother would have made?

Frank: Absolutely. Like, she would have a dessert with Dad, but I don't do that, just because, for some reason, I don't have a sweet tooth anymore. That's exactly the meal she would have.

Me: And when you do your mashed potatoes, you said you do them from scratch?

Frank: From scratch, but extremely simple; just boil the potatoes. Mother taught me how you cut the potatoes up instead of putting the whole potato in. Otherwise it takes ten times longer to cook. I found out how you chop those up, just mash them with butter and whole milk, salt, that's it.

Me: And how would Mother—

Frank: Just like that. We were always in charge of the potatoes, so she taught us how to do that, but, of course, it was an army kettle of potatoes, so we'd sit there: "It's time to peel the potatoes."

Me: And how do you prepare the green beans?

Frank: Just in a bowl. I microwave the green beans in a normal bowl, and it has its own water, of course, and I put salt and pepper in that. I didn't this time, but I'll throw the chili oil in it just for a little spice. Again, Mother would never do that.

One way to go "inside" a conversation is to listen for key words that people use and try to use that same language with them. It helps build a connection and make the other person feel more comfortable. This works in everyday conversation as well, especially if you are talking to someone you don't know very well. You just have to be careful not to come across like you are making fun of them or mocking them. If they mispronounce something, I'll mispronounce it the same way. Perrier and Fage are two brand names that get mispronounced often. Sometimes I'll acknowledge that I'm not sure if it's pronounced "Perry-er" or "Peh-ree-ay," which gives me permission to use both. Even though I know it's "Peh-ree-ay," in an interview I don't want someone to feel "less than" for not knowing how to properly say a word. That creates a power dynamic that isn't conducive to honest conversation since the respondent will be wondering if they got it right. While it might offend the client's ears, I don't care how they say it.

Similarly, with a person's lexicon I've really got to pay attention and incorporate the language. Did you pick up what I did with Frank? It's subtle, especially in written form. You may have noticed that in my questions to him, I referred to his mom as "Mother." Personally, I've never referred to my mom as Mother, and I find the word comes across very stiff and detached. But it wasn't about me; this conversation was about Frank and building a connection with him. If I had referred to her as Mom, I would have been referring to someone else. This was "Mother," and for Frank only one person fit that word, and that's who I wanted to hear about. So I, too, was referring to his mom as Mother.

What I was struggling with was that the word *Mother* has such a formality to it. Yes, I know it is used more often in some parts of the country, like the South, and that's fine, except we weren't in the South. To me, *Mother* doesn't feel as loving or nurturing as saying *Mom* or *Ma* or any other number of nicknames. Despite the formality, I didn't get the sense that Frank was detached from her. Quite the contrary. He seemed overly attached. His father, he always referred to as Dad. But his mom was always Mother, and she clearly had played a really big role in his life. Maybe that outsized importance was because we were talking about cooking, and she had taught him the skills and passed on the family recipes. Or maybe he was just really close to her. Either way, it struck me as unusually prominent.

What also struck me as unusual was what I found when I excused myself to go to the bathroom mid-interview. I transitioned the moderating to one of my colleagues who was there in a training capacity, left the room, and started climbing the creaky old wooden staircase toward the only working bathroom in the house.

As I got toward the top of the stairs, I saw through the banister that there were two bedrooms to my left. The doors to each bedroom were wide open. The bathroom was straight ahead of me. Once I got high enough up the stairs that I could see into the two bedrooms, out of the corner of my eye I caught the shape of a person. I inhaled sharply. Frank hadn't mentioned anything about a roommate, a significant other, a child, or another person living in the house. I tensed up as I continued creakily up the stairs. We hadn't heard a sound from upstairs this whole time, and we'd been there for almost an hour. Who was up there? Even though climbing the stairs caused creaks and squeaks to come from the floorboards, I couldn't detect any movement in the room. Surely the noise would prompt someone to look up, but the head of blond hair that I could see remained still. As I advanced up the stairs, my line of sight shifted so the figure slipped out of view, but what I gained in vision was more of the room itself. There was weight equipment taking up a lot of the space. Mostly free weights and a barbell perched above a lifting bench. I'm positive no one was working out while we were there. I'd have surely heard the clanking of weights during the interview. Who was sitting so quietly in that room?

I reached the top of the stairs. Instead of moving straight ahead into the bathroom, my curiosity got the best of me. I quietly inhaled and held my breath. Mentally, I thought through what I might say to this mystery roommate that Frank had never mentioned. The bathroom door, now behind me, was open and visible, so any "where's the bathroom?" pretense wouldn't work. As I gingerly stepped down the hallway toward the open door, I decided to go with an almost-as-lame, "Oh, hi! I didn't know anyone else was home." I was nearing the doorway when I again saw the blond-haired figure. I was still not sensing any movement. No riffling of pages of a magazine or book, as if that was a distraction from hearing a stranger come up the stairs. No sound at all except the conversation coming from the interview continuing without me downstairs.

I peered around the edge of the open door. More weight equipment came into view. Finally, I saw a chair. Sitting on the chair facing the doorway was the blond-haired figure I had seen. Instantly I saw that the hair wasn't groomed particularly well; it was sticking out like a head filled with cowlicks. The straw-like quality of the "hair" made me realize that this wasn't a person at all; it was a full-size human mannequin! It looked like one of those Resusci Annie or Andy mannequins that you use when learning how to perform CPR. My mind continued to spin. *Why does he have this here? Who is this guy?* And with all this talk of Mother, I was beginning to creep myself out. My mind went from how I felt seeing the exposed studs downstairs, to how I was reminded of *The Silence of the Lambs* when we had first arrived, and to all the references to Mother. I was starting to wonder if I might find "Mother" preserved in the basement, like in Alfred Hitchcock's classic horror film *Psycho*. It was all of these improbable thoughts that led me to start questioning our safety in Frank's house.

I calculated that, since there were four of us and only one of him, we would probably be able to take him if he tried anything. Unless he spiked our drinks, of course. But we'd brought in our own water, hadn't we? And since one of my colleagues had talked to Frank a few times in the recruiting process, someone on the outside knew where we were. That might not increase our odds of survival, but at least our bodies would be found. Or whatever was left of us would be found, and the police would have Frank as a really strong suspect. So ultimately, he would see justice for his crimes. Considering the situation, and since Frank hadn't put on a Hannibal Lecter voice or said anything about making fava beans for dinner, I calmed down and assumed we'd get out of this situation in one piece. That said, I still didn't want to end up chained in his cellar.

Yes. All these thoughts were going through my head and stayed in my mental mix. As I finished my business in the bathroom and returned to the group, I was pretty certain I was being irrational and that we were safe. That was me *making* a judgment about a situation with a person I was *being* judgmental toward. But then Frank would bring Mother back into the conversation, and my mind would replace his kind, smiling face with images from *Psycho*. And just like that, I started *being* judgmental again. I was disparaging this man, likening him to fictitious serial killers for no reason other than the fact that I was uncomfortable with how he referred to the woman who'd given birth to him, loved him, and raised him. I didn't like that this ugly side of myself was coming forward. In the moment, I couldn't stop it.

EVEN THOUGH I'm aware and mindful of empathy and the steps to get there, I still succumb to these base tribal actions of being judgmental, and it results in me not always being as accepting of my fellow humans as I'd like to be. I try to be an accepting individual; I really do. Particularly when it comes to our differences as human beings. I enjoy finding those differences and understanding how they impact our actions and inform our beliefs. It's what my career is based on. I feel enriched when I hear from people about their lives. But I can be judgmental. And I know I'm not alone. For me, judgment creeps out of the dark recesses of my mind, wraps its tentacles around my brain, and squeezes the breath out of my ability to reach empathy and compassion. Replacing the empathetic oxygen are the noxious fumes of negative thoughts. That aspersion, being judgmental, can be expressed by a put-down, either direct or subtle. It can be in thought form or let loose verbally. It can show up as thoughts on why someone is wrong or what they don't understand about something, all without my own understanding of where they are coming from. Or I can be judgmental about what they should be doing differently to make their life better, regardless of how attainable or realistic that might be.

These moments of being judgmental slip out from all of us, and we need to move past them in order to get to empathy. I try to catch myself as the tentacles begin to reach out, telling myself that I'm being judgmental, and I try to see it from the other person's perspective. Or I ask myself why I feel the need to criticize them. Is it based in something real, or is it my own issue? Sometimes that's enough to put the monster back in the box. Other times not so much.

As you can see, my abilities at being judgmental are well honed. Yours might be as well. Judgment is something that has existed in my family for generations, like a dominant gene. Brown-eyed and judgy. That's us. The judgmental commentary I've heard offered up from others in my family often comes from a place of caring, but it can also be pointed and sharp. Regardless of how "good" a place it's coming from, for me, I feel the hurt and sting it must inflict upon others. It takes me back to the judgment being cast on me when I was ten years old and a stranger in a new school. And that pain, etched so deeply in my brain, makes me uncomfortable when I hear others in my family being judgmental. Fortunately this "know it all" attitude comes out mostly in private. Proclamations on what people "need" to do and "should" do to make their life better. Or why someone isn't living up to their potential, or to the standard set by someone other than them. As if they even need fixing or improving. And as if we are the ones wise enough to offer advice. We aren't. I've come to understand I'm not.

And yet we keep doing it. All of us. I bet you have family members who do it too, and that you sometimes take part. Like a disease that's spreading out of control.

Except I've been searching for a cure, which has led me to this understanding of the 5 Steps. The problem is, can I follow them myself? I've got to try.

A few years ago, in conversation with my therapist, Greg, he pointed out my "shoulds" and "needs" language and how that sounds.

It was like a lightbulb came on. I'd spent my life wanting to help people by sharing advice, but I was using a "being judgmental" voice.

The irony in that behavior is that I'm also a coach. And I believe in the power of coaching. Coaches help inspire and guide people—not tell them what they should do but help them see the path forward and how they can make modifications to improve. "Shoulds" and "needs" language feels more like a pious know-it-all casting "wisdom" on others. And then the other irony is that—hello!—I'm in the business of trying to get people to understand one another, and to see them for who they are, not how they should be or need to be to fit the worldview of someone else.

There's one other factor that has contributed to my judgmental self: I'm a gay man. And sometimes it feels like the gay tribe has written the book on being judgmental. At the very least, we took good notes on how to do it best-in-class.

Yes, gays can be overly judgmental—of ourselves and those around us, strangers and friends alike—and it seems at times like we take no prisoners. The moniker "bitchy queen" didn't come from nowhere. Some call it "shade," and there is a side of shade or "reading" that can be good-natured—like how you tease a good friend and "give them shit" for something they said or a habit or mannerism that they have. That can be the fun side when all parties are willing participants. And then there's the other side, that ugly side that can have us turning our noses up at our own kind.

The range of insults that we sometimes fling so callously at one another (and our own reflections in the mirror, most tragically) are far and wide. I've heard gay men criticize others for being too thin, too fat, not ripped enough, too tall, not tall enough, too hairy, not hairy enough, too smart, too boring, too into partying. If we can criticize others so easily, what must we be saying to ourselves in the mirror? Years ago, I had one friend consider rejecting a potential suitor because he didn't like the shape of the other guy's fingers. Seriously! And there was nothing unusual about the guy's fingers. With all this judgment, it's amazing gay men are willing to get undressed in front of one another, let alone have sex. Bitchy queens can turn on our own kind instead of truly bonding together, being victors of our personal struggles to come out, supporting one another, and loving ourselves (which might be part of the problem).

Racism and disdain over income and status are also prevalent. There is an LGBTQ+ caste system that sadly mirrors society's larger pecking order. Outside of the Pride festivals once a year, how integrated do you see the entire LGBTQ+ community? We are filled with subcultures, one for each letter in that acronym and other groupings, for people of color, for fetishes and fantasies, and more. Aside from Pride, I've not seen much reaching out from one subculture to another. That means we don't listen to the needs of the other parts of our own community. For all the unity we present at Pride and related to civil rights, the LGBTQ+ community is just as segregated as mainstream America. Perhaps you see something similar play out in the tribes and communities you belong to as well?

What's the effect of all this judgment? Shame. We gays can end up loathing ourselves. Wanting our waist to be tinier, our abs to emerge in a six-pack worthy of a god, or our face to be symmetrical like a Hollywood star. God forbid we ever have a sagging belly or a droopy jowl or floppy triceps. Get thee to a gym! And thus we lash out and start the cycle anew.

It's tragic since many of us, myself included, spent our younger years being judged by our tormentors, which instilled in us a deep well of shame and hurt that many still carry today. You'd think after being so suppressed and punished for being who we are, we'd emerge from the other side of that horrible, dark voyage filled with love, compassion, and empathy for others. But no, that's not always the case. Sometimes, our unresolved traumas can leave us quick to judge and even quicker to tear someone down with a cutting remark. We can be so cruel to each other, sometimes I wonder if we're even aware of what we're doing. For some of us, our tongues are sharpened from coping with years of pain at the hands of others. Instead of providing comfort and support, we strike out with what seems like a witty comment but is actually a put-down as hurtful as the suffering we felt as children. We are reliving our childhood traumas, but with the roles reversed. We are now the persecutors. We relieve the pain from our own psychic scars by inflicting more pain on others. It's as though we learned nothing from our suffering except how to be bitchy and dish it out after suffering through years of taking it.

And yet, all we really want is to be loved and accepted, just like every other human being—whether it's on a dating app or in a bar or at a friend's party. We crave to be seen as worthy and enough. We desire to be accepted just as we are, flaws and all. What we want is what had been denied us in our youth: To be absolved of the shame of being different, of never quite being sure if we are going to measure up, to be enough. To be treated with empathy.

AND SO there I was. Standing in Frank's house, wondering what was up with this guy, my own judgment rising. The tentacles were starting to reach out to suppress my empathy and compassion. My judgment was taking over, readying to flip me from the persecuted to the persecutor.

My judgmental self, aided by my intuition, had me convinced there was more to Frank's story than met the eye. I wasn't able to just accept him at face value. There was something about him that wasn't adding up. And just like the kids in that smaller small town in Indiana, who couldn't let me be and pounced on me if I said something the wrong way or my body language wasn't "manly" enough, I couldn't let go of it. I was being controlled by my judgment.

I let my colleague continue on with the "make-along" portion of the interview, where Frank was to make dinner and we would watch and ask questions. That gave me the freedom to sort out what was going on with his story.

Every in-home related to a food topic includes a tour of the kitchen. As we took in the sights in his pantry and he showed us his refrigerator, the story Frank had told us about his food values totally held up to what we were seeing. There was the Shake 'n Bake and Hungry Jack he said he bought. Even the items he bought to add spice, like chili oil, were there. Mother hadn't used chili oil, as her cooking was to please her husband's tastes. Chili oil was Frank's break with tradition.

Frank was showing us how he defrosted pork chops in the sink when I noticed what was staring at me from the edge of the sink. Propped against the hand soap bottle on the sink ledge was an action figure I immediately recognized from my 1970s childhood. The red jumpsuit and molded plastic hair were instantly recognizable.

It was Steve Austin. Astronaut. A man barely alive. Yes, the action figure Frank had was the Six Million Dollar Man. Steve was slightly used (the "action eye" that you could look through for magnification, simulating the character's bionic-powered eyesight, was missing), but overall the doll was in pretty good condition. (If you don't know of *The Six Million Dollar Man*, please Google it now.)

I also had the Steve Austin action figure when I was younger. I loved that show as a kid. I loved the spin-off, *The Bionic Woman*, even more. What was even more curious to me than the action figure itself was the strand of green Mardi Gras beads wrapped around Steve Austin's neck. Clearly Frank had been to New Orleans at some point for the annual celebration.

On their own, those beads wouldn't provide too much insight. But the fact that there were Mardi Gras beads on a Steve Austin action figure: that started to give me a clue about Frank. Right there in the kitchen, Frank had this one-eyed action figure for a little wink of personality as he did the dishes.

Intrigued by this small but potentially significant piece of "evidence," I let my colleague continue on with the interview. I stepped out of the small kitchen, turned to the main client, Ken, who was observing the action, and said I wanted to have a better look around the house.

In that moment, I was still acting in judgment. Frank had me confused. Yes, I had my weird, creepy serial killer bias still in my head, but another picture was starting to come together, thanks to the Steve Austin doll, a few other observations I noted, and a tingle of intuition.

A couple of steps removed from the kitchen, in the entryway by the base of the stairs, I started to look around. On some of the exposed studs and on a few tables around the house, Frank had placed photos. I started looking at them for any further information they might reveal. As a rule, I don't open closed doors or drawers; I only examine what is on display or what a respondent has opened for me to see. The people in the photos must have been Frank's family—perhaps his sister and her kids. There were some vacation photos, but they were just snaps of Frank alone at the sunset or on the beach. Who was he with on this vacation? Who was on the other side of the camera? Who else was in Frank's life? It was a secret the photos weren't going to reveal.

Nestled behind the front door on a small table, I found a photo of Mother and another photo of both of Frank's parents together. The pictures were carefully framed and displayed, with a rose in a vase and a Catholic prayer card on the table. He'd created a shrine in honor of Mother. My judgmental side thought about how that wasn't how I would pay my respects to my loved ones. I pushed that bitchy thought aside, dismantling my judgment for a moment, and allowed myself to be touched by the meaning of his gesture. Frank really missed his mother, and he'd found a way to honor her. I asked myself: *Why can't I just let him be a guy who misses his mother?*

Dismantling judgment goes beyond "really hard." It's asking you to change an instinctive response. When we are working with clients and coaching empathy, this first step to empathy is *the* step that keeps coming back up again and again as a challenge. You will see judgment return in later steps in this book as well. Turning your ego off from defending deep-seated beliefs, and being open to new ways of thinking or behaving? That's hard stuff. Even after all the writing and speaking and coaching I've done on the topic, I find I *still* have to be mindful, checking in to see if I'm being judgmental, asking myself where that thought is coming from, and putting it aside so that I can connect with the individual or group I'm trying to understand. It's a never-ending journey, but I can report that with practice it does get easier, and you can get better at getting to empathy. And the end result is worth the hard work.

But while I should have been putting my judgmental inclinations toward Frank aside, my intuition was telling me that there was more to the story than he was letting on. Yes, he missed his mother, but that wasn't the end. There was something more. What was it? Where was the next clue?

I moved over toward some of the "renovation" work. Drywall was up on one side, but exposed two-by-fours were on the other. Placed on the horizontal supports were various objects. I spotted a purse, most likely Mother's—a sensible-looking handbag from the early '70s. Small, with a snap closure and a short strap. And then, there it was. Sitting on another one of the "shelves" formed by a two-by-four, I spotted it. The clue that brought Frank's story into focus for me. Frank had nestled, on one of those shelves, a small coin purse—tiny, but loud and proud. On that coin purse was beading that formed the rainbow flag, a symbol of the LGBTQ+ community. Combine that with Steve Austin sporting Mardi Gras beads, the fact that he was in his mid-forties and single, with no mention of a spouse, partner, or kids of his own, and a question that popped in my head when we first met and I thought *he seems like a really nice guy*—eureka! My earlier hunch might be correct: Frank must be gay just like me!

Now, I just typed that and thought to myself: *Shame on me for thinking that.* Why was I jumping to conclusions about this man? Because I was being judgmental. I was so focused on figuring out his story and wanting to have a connection with someone from the gay community, that I ignored everything else he was telling us about his cooking and eating habits. I had even handed off the moderating to someone else! I was distracted from the things that really mattered to the project because of my own judgment.

In the moment, I grew confident I'd finally solved the puzzle of Frank's story. The evidence was scant and circumstantial, but I convinced myself only a gay man would have this combination of items on display. He was a semi-closeted (or at least very private) gay man who was really close to his mother, now deceased. I had a feeling early on that he might be gay, but he wasn't responding to me with any acknowledgment of our shared homosexuality. I couldn't understand why he wouldn't open up to me. Even just a little bit. But that was my issue and what I wanted. Frank wanted to remain private about his personal life. I became judgmental about Frank when he didn't give me what I wanted: connection to my community through the commonality that we shared. Being a minority living and working in the majority's world can feel isolating. When I got an unexpected moment to "be gay" with another member of the LGBTQ+ community, I wanted to take it. I wanted the easier, comfortable path of having empathy with someone similar to me rather than having to reach deeper once again to get to empathy with someone who was different. Even though I promote having empathy with everyone, sometimes I just want the easy route, to be with my tribe. Being denied that hurt.

I became fixated on discovering Frank's truth, whether he wanted to reveal it or not. I disguised my judgmental bitchiness as a quest for his "truth." As though my knowing his truth would have made any difference in how I interpreted Frank's feelings about Shake 'n Bake. Once I thought I had put it all together, I didn't dismantle my judgment and hold Frank in a positive regard. I had to trumpet my findings to Ken and the other clients afterward. Sharing what I was up to while they watched Frank with his Shake 'n Bake. Proud of myself for solving the puzzle, like a gay Nancy Drew.

After the project was over, I brought my understanding of Frank's story into a session with Greg, my therapist. I find hearing a psychologist's perspective on what I am observing and experiencing helps me better understand human behavior and how to interpret my observations. Frank and his relationship to Mother was definitely one I wanted to better understand.

Greg and I conjectured, based on the information I had, that someone like Frank might have had a highly codependent relationship with Mother, and when she died, he was left alone, lost. So much of his identity was connected to Mother that he wasn't a full, true expression of himself. And his homosexuality might not have been something that he'd shared with her. If he kept it suppressed, it might end up peeking out in the subtlest of ways that only another gay man or a really astute observer would pick up. Like the coin purse tucked away on a shelf, or the Mardi Gras beads on a Steve Austin doll—subtle clues that let Frank express himself, but not so much that he was exposed and put in a place of discomfort.

At Frank's house, I'd let my judgment get in the way. It wasn't my proudest moment as a moderator or empathy activist, but now I recognize a valuable lesson from my experience with Frank, a lesson that I myself desperately wished the kids who'd teased me when I was growing up had understood. Let people be. Who cares if he was gay? It wasn't germane to the parts of Frank's life we wanted to understand. It was only important to me personally in that moment. However, Frank wasn't willing or able to go where I wanted him to. Instead of accepting that, I let my judgment flare up and get in the way.

Even now, when I retell Frank's story, I can't recall most of the insights that came from him related to making dinner, only the story I've relayed here. In the end, Frank was just a guy, living out his life. He'd been missing his mother for a long time, and one of the ways he felt close to her was when he cooked dinner, trying to re-create some of the foods she used to make.

Frank: I don't know if anybody's a psychologist here, but it's like, I don't know if it comes from when I was a kid, where we had basic meat-and-potatoes food. My oldest brothers, after

Mother passed away, were like, "Oh, her cooking was horrible." Never once in my life did I think she made bad food, but they didn't think she could cook. I don't know if the stuff I cook has much more flavor than what I had as a kid. My mother, she passed away, but my favorite meal she would make me was spaghetti and meatballs, and I can't make them as good as her. My sister finally figured out how to make them as good as she did. Finally. Mother's been gone twelve years, and my sister finally figured it out!

Judgment can create so much trouble. It took me off course and got me fixated on the wrong things with Frank. Frank loved his mother very dearly, and he still missed her. That has to be enough. It didn't matter if he was gay, straight, bi, or asexual. Forget the rest of it. Frank, I see you now, and I'm sorry I judged you.

EMPATHETIC REFLECTIONS

- Have you had your own experiences like I did with Frank? Were you able to let go of your judgment and see the person for who they were or the situation they were in? Or did your judgment get in the way? What might you tell yourself to defuse your judgment in the moment of being judgmental?

- What have you noticed about how easy it is to see the point of view of people like you compared to people who are different? What do you need to let go of in order to see the perspective of people who are different?

8

Fear

The only thing we have to fear is . . . fear itself—
nameless, unreasoning, unjustified terror which paralyzes
needed efforts to convert retreat into advance.
FRANKLIN D. ROOSEVELT

A GAY, A BLONDE, and a South Asian man walked into the
2012 National Rifle Association (NRA) gun show in St.
Louis. Outside the convention center, the largest American flag I've ever seen stretched from the ground to the top of the
building. Inside, every surface was festooned with red, white, and
blue. Symbols of patriotism abounded like it was the last Fourth of
July we'd ever have. Right along with the flag, there were guns on
display everywhere. The latest in handguns, shotguns, semiautomatics, and more. Cautiously in awe, we made our way through the
booths on the exhibit floor. Two of the three of us were feeling very
out of place. The blonde wasn't one of them.

I've never handled a gun in my life. Haven't had much interest in
it, either. I'll admit it: I've got a healthy fear of them. Or at least of
the violent outcome of their use. As a result, I'm fully loaded with
both types of judgment on the topic of guns. I am able to make a

judgment about whether a gun is right for me (it's not), and I'm also likely to be judgmental about other people having guns. I get the use of rifles for hunting, but I also wonder... if hunting is meant to be a sport, why not use a bow and arrow to make it a little fairer?

No one I knew as a kid talked to me about hunting, even though I lived in Indiana. As an adult, I've met plenty of people who get excited for deer season to kick off, and I've come to respect that. I just don't want to handle a gun. My father-in-law has several hand-guns and rifles. Sometimes they are visible in the house when we arrive (never when children have been present). Just seeing his guns gives me a queasy feeling. Rationally, I know they are not loaded and aren't going to harm me or anyone else in that moment. Yet they could if they got into the wrong hands. That's a line of thought that gets very disturbing for me very quickly. There have been far too many mass shootings in the United States, and I don't accept the NRA's defense of why anyone needs to have a semiautomatic rifle. The political stifling the gun lobby has wrought seems to have erased any sort of sane collaboration between both sides of the aisle to prevent the slaughter of innocent people. You don't hear about mass shootings in many other countries. It seems to me that we'd be better off without guns around. Hence, my position on gun control. I was filled with judgment against gun owners, even though I'd never really talked about the issue with a gun owner before, only with friends in my own bubble who served to reassure me of my views. And here I was walking into a gun show.

We got to go to the NRA show thanks to a new client who came to us looking to understand the practicalities of how people use their "concealed carry" permits. When do people carry, how do they conceal, and so on. The project had two parts. One was focus groups with a mix of inner-city and suburban residents in a major metropolitan city, and the other was doing intercepts with people at the NRA show. After years of doing intercepts in grocery stores, cafes, and clothing retailers, who could say no to exploring another side of day-to-day life in such a "new to me" setting? I was totally a fish out of water, and I loved the opportunity as much as I was scared of who I thought I would meet and what I might hear.

Since I was not immediately empathetic with gun owners and I've already revealed some preconceived notions and stereotypes I held about guns that may show up as judgment, I was going to have to work hard to make sure I maintained an open mind, or a "beginner's mind." This meant dismantling my judgment completely, letting go of those pre-existing attitudes and stereotypes I might have, if I truly wanted to understand the world of gun ownership through a gun owner's point of view. Thoughts about how guns shouldn't be allowed in people's homes? I had to let those go. Only then would I be able to see the perspective of a gun owner. As Scott Cook, cofounder of Intuit (makers of TurboTax, QuickBooks, and Mint) once said, and I paraphrase, "If having empathy is being able to walk a mile in someone else's shoes, you have to take your own shoes off first." Those shoes that we so comfortably wear is our being judgmental.

For the three of us who were going to the show, each had our own individual baggage that we needed to let go of. Each of us had our own shoes to take off. The blonde in our group, from Texas, had the smallest adjustment to make. She owned a small pistol that easily fit into her purse. She showed it to me once. It had mother-of-pearl on the handle. That meant the shoes she had to take off were mostly about letting go of her perception of herself so she could see the point of view of a man or a woman, younger or older. The South Asian man in our group had his own shoes to remove, quite different from hers. Of Indian descent, he was 100 percent American and was raised in an upper-middle-class neighborhood in a Texas suburb. Like me, he had not had a lot of exposure to guns, so there was his own discomfort to overcome. Added to that, he was well aware of the stereotypes and judgment he might receive from people based solely on his skin color.

In any interaction, we have to be mindful of a conversation as being a two-way interaction. A dialogue risks being derailed by the judgments of either party. That judgment can show up as bias or stereotypes simply because of the color of our skin or our appearance. The other person is being judgmental about us as soon as they see us, just as we are being judgmental about them based solely on their appearance and the stereotypes or biases we hold in our minds. As a gay white man, especially in a situation with people that might be "hostile" to the LGBTQ+ community, like those at an NRA show, I had my guard up and would take care not to say anything that might be interpreted as "gay," and I'd monitor my movements so that I didn't come across as gay. This monitoring of behavior occurs much more constantly, I'm told, if you are a person of color engaging with people outside your own race or ethnicity who don't know you and accept you. I've had several Black friends describe it as "exhausting," and I'm able to relate to it because of my own experiences having to conform. It's like hiding part of yourself.

This is one part of what privilege is: not having to worry about how others might judge you based on your skin color, ethnicity, gender identity, and/or sexual orientation. Many people are not aware of their privilege but reap the benefits and advantages simply for being born one way and not another. And so if you are not born into one of those groups, you then have to deal with how that plays out.

So my South Asian colleague was mindful of how he would present himself and start the conversation with people in order to get them beyond any judgment they might have and open up to talk with him. That's a tall order at a gun show in St. Louis, where there were plenty of people that were "other" from him and who may have had stereotypes of their own about people with brown skin. At the same time, he recognized he had to open his mind and overcome his own stereotypes of the gun show attendees in order to really listen to them and see them for who they truly were. As did I.

Achieving an open, beginner's mind is critical in order to build empathy. It's part of dismantling judgment. If biases and attitudes can't be dropped, then it won't matter what someone else is trying to tell you—you will only hear what you want to hear and continue to see them through your biased lens. It's easier said than done. I'm all ears if you want to talk about computer operating systems or new TV technology. Dinner, breakfast, yogurt? Easy. I can hang with that. No judgment from me. Hot-topic issues where I might already have a strong opinion, like guns? Now that's something altogether different. If I let my own attitudes get in the way, I was going to have a problem doing my job building empathy and understanding others. So, for the sake of the job, I put my feelings aside. To help me dismantle my judgment, I let my intellectual curiosity take over. I pretended that I didn't know anything on the topic, meaning I adapted a beginner's mind. If you are at the beginning, you can't have judgment. I walked past yet another giant American flag, arrived at our client's booth, and readied myself to hear the stories of gun owners.

All in all, the three of us talked to more than sixty people over the course of two days. The questions we asked in those ten-minute conversations included the when and how of their carrying. We also showed the respondents photos of people appearing to be in dangerous or threatening situations and handling or about to handle a weapon. We wanted to get their reaction as to which photo best represented how they thought about concealed carry. Aside from that, we were open to wherever people took us as they told their story.

Personally, one of my biggest curiosities was, *Why do people own a gun and carry it with them in the first place?*

The answers to this question all had a theme to them. Here are some excerpts from the several different conversations that we had over the course of those two days:

Chris: Being more confident about being able to go to wherever I so choose, well, you know, within reason.

———————

Bob: Because I live in the city. I mean, it just seems safer.

Me: Okay. Are there particular situations where you're, like, oh, yeah, I need to bring my gun with me?

Bob: I wouldn't say there was, like, specific situations. I would just say it's just, I don't know, common sense, like, obvious. If you're just going out, you know, in the city, you probably want to bring it. I mean, there's a lot of guns in this city to begin with. There's a lot of crime, so you [ought] to have one.

Tim: You know, I'll be carrying, and I'll know that should something happen, I will be able to protect myself accordingly. You know, it's just looking out for myself, is what it is.

Kent: I just thought it was the right thing to do for self-defense, and things are getting worse out there. I don't know of anybody that's had issues, but I know it's probably going to come.

Me: So is there, like, a particular scenario that you're worried about when you think about it?

Kent: No, not really, because there's a lot of them.

I was struck by how many answers I was getting that didn't cite a specific incident but were about generally maintaining personal safety (a basic, primary need according to Maslow's Hierarchy). I paraphrase it as, "It's a big bad scary world out there, so I need to have a gun to keep me feeling safe." It seemed to me that people were afraid of a "boogeyman," of what *might* happen, rather than what had happened or would happen. The NRA show attendees I met were unable to articulate an exact situation they were concerned about but wanted to be prepared just in case *something* happened. Since that *something* they were concerned with was so nebulous yet omnipresent, it had a powerful, gripping effect, motivating them to have a gun. Just in case. Something bad *could* happen. To my rational mind, this all just seemed preposterous. Afraid of the boogeyman, so carry a gun, even though you may never need it. I heard "may" and "maybe" many times in the rationalizations I was being told, although what I was hearing was being warped because of my judgment.

The NRA show was one of the hardest projects for me to maintain my neutrality and keep my judgment dismantled. As I've said, I'm not a fan of guns. I'm sickened by mass shootings and the innocent deaths that happen when kids handle guns that haven't been properly locked away. And while those are my feelings, I still believe people have the right to choose to own a weapon. I believe even more strongly in people's right to calmly share and discuss their beliefs on this or any other topic. The onus was on me to stay open rather than closed in judgment. If I could manage to keep my judgment dismantled, I'd be able to hear the underlying message of why carrying a gun was so important to them.

An older gentleman, Steve, soon approached the booth. He had a look about him that said he was both well lived and not shy to voice his opinion. He told me he was an ex-Marine who had served the country for thirty years. I could still see the strength and stature of a Marine within a now-weakened body frame. And something about his swagger seemed decidedly pro-gun. Of course, just by being at the NRA show you'd qualify as pro-gun, but he seemed like he held it as a deep conviction. So I was curious, why did he want to carry?

Steve: Because I want to defend myself.

Me: Okay, and in what sorts of situations are you most interested in defending yourself?

Steve: Hopefully none.

Me: But what are you concerned about; what's happening?

Steve: Well, I'm getting old. I will be seventy next month, had a major heart attack. I went to that class the guy was talking about on how to keep lean and stuff like that. And he said do karate and kung fu and things like that; he didn't know I was in the Marine Corps for about thirty years. So, if I got to punch my way out of [a situation], forget it; it's not going to happen. Because [after] a few seconds of punching, I am going to run out of breath. So if I want to defend myself immediately, that's the only way I know to defend myself. That and get the hell out of there. I try not to put myself in certain situations where it would be an issue.

Me: What situations do you try not to get into?

Steve: Well, it can happen anytime. When you go out to a restaurant in the evening—my wife and I travel a lot—and you're going into a restaurant or you're coming out, the sun's gone down and it's dark, and someone wants to hit you up for money for drugs. It happens often enough. When you got a gun, what are you going to do with it? I don't want to get shot.

Steve's story, like so many others, was still banging up against my own judgment and stereotypes, which I had to deal with. My first judgmental thought was, *Just where are a seventy-year-old white guy and his wife going to dinner where they are getting hit up for money for drugs?* Of course, this was me being judgmental because a) I was not Steve, b) I had not been to the places he and his wife went to for dinner, and c) I hadn't established empathy with him. So, if I didn't want to be judgmental, I had to take his word for it and accept it for what it was. I wasn't at the NRA show to question Steve's restaurant decisions, nor did I want to debate the crime rates outside of an Olive Garden. I was there to listen to people's stories and make sense of them. In order to do that, I had to keep my judgment dismantled so that I was open to what they were telling me. What I'd heard was that Steve's diminished physical condition had left him feeling vulnerable and less able to defend himself and his wife when they were out. Getting past my judgment, I was able to follow the remaining steps to get to empathy with Steve, imagining what it might feel like not to be physically as strong as you once were or to be unable to fully defend a loved one. And there was probably an element of frustration for Steve because he used to be able to do that better than most, given his Marine history. The restaurant scenario he laid out was less important than the bigger issue I needed to have empathy with—Steve's fear of not being able to protect his wife.

Taking my own judgment out of the equation helped me open up to hear what Steve was saying. Often a person's true motivation for behavior lies just beyond what they are saying. You can catch it in the inflection in their voice or in select words they are saying, or by reading between the lines. Judgment cancels out your ability to hear any of those subtle signals that speaks volumes. That's the real "boogeyman."

What I was hearing and picking up on was that there was a very real fear that people had that led them to gun ownership. Whether or not it was founded in reality, well, yes, you can debate that point, but I couldn't argue that people were exhibiting a fear of the world and the bad things that might happen. That made it real for them. If put in a position to fear for their safety, of course a person is going to want to protect themselves. When that safety is threatened by a perceived violence, then you would want whatever it takes to protect yourself and make yourself feel better. That takes you to a gun, which then makes you feel safer in your ability to protect yourself and your family.

The gun owners I met, like Steve, wanted to feel safe and have more confidence when they were out and about. They used the weapon as a sort of security blanket to give them more confidence. Having lived in big cities my entire adult life, I was aware of the bad things that can happen, but since I knew that Steve and some of the other people I interviewed at the NRA show were living in the suburbs and rural areas, I couldn't easily understand or relate to the concerns that they had. I had to dismantle my judgment to shift my point of view and think about what it must feel like to live in a relatively safe suburban or rural area and venture into "the city," where violent crime is a much more frequent event. By adopting their perspective, I could see where they might be fearful.

TO BALANCE out our learning at the NRA show, we also did some focus groups in Philadelphia. We had a mix of individuals recruited to make sure we were hearing a broad range of voices. Sure enough, the same themes of fear of what might happen out in the world came up in these groups, just like it did at the NRA show.

One focus group was a mix of men from the inner city and the suburbs. I didn't realize how profoundly different this dichotomy of lived experiences would be until I was in the session with these men. From the very start, the guys that commuted in from the suburbs, several of whom were named Dave, coincidentally, were commenting that they wanted to feel safer in Philadelphia's Center City because of the number of homeless and mentally ill people on the streets. It was one example of why they carried a gun. While the Daves from the suburbs carried, they never had to use their gun. They talked about staying vigilant and alert, looking a block ahead to be on the lookout for any trouble. The role of the gun was to enhance their sense of personal safety, security, and protection in case something did happen. And then Deshaun, one of the city dwellers, shared what his life was like living in the inner city.

Deshaun: I've never been bothered by homeless people. They're the least of my worries. Where I live at, it's usually crime. You might walk into something that's about to happen, like somebody is shooting at each other, or I got robbed a couple times. I actually got robbed *and* shot one time.

With that admission, the suburban guys' jaws all dropped. Mine did too. The suburban Daves had just had their worst fears confirmed by Deshaun. The city is scary. Bad things do happen. And this was Deshaun's lived existence, not just his fear of something that *might* happen, but something real that had already happened to him and could happen again.

Deshaun: I kept getting robbed. I was like, *that's it, man.* I was scared. I couldn't keep going on like that, getting robbed all the time.

Me: Have you been able to use your gun to foil a robbery?

Deshaun: Actually, yes. I still remember the first time. I never had to fire it or anything like that, but I remember one time I went to see this girl real late at night.

Dave #2: There's your first problem right there. *[He said this in a joking tone to alleviate the tension.]*

Deshaun: I was leaving her house, and I had to catch the number 33 bus, and it was real late, nobody outside. There was a Chinese store across the street, and that was open. Nobody's outside, so I'm standing waiting for the bus, and I see this car coming. And it slows down, and the guys are looking at me. They're kind of moving in slow motion; they're looking at me as they ride by. So, then the car turns all of a sudden and goes down a street, and there's a little block there. He stopped, let the guy out, the one guy gets out, the other guy circles around, he's walking down. So, I said, "Oh man, I know what they trying to do." So, I took my gun, I untucked it, put it in my coat pocket. And so, I'm standing there because I'm already expecting this guy to come walking up. He went through the back alley or whatever, and the car drove around. So, then he pops back out the alley and comes walking toward me. And so, I wait till he gets right up to me, and I pulled it out. I don't think he saw me pull it out, but then I let him see that I had it. So, he stopped in his tracks. He just stopped and stood there. And I was like,

"Man, you better go back the other way, man. You trying to rob me?" He was looking; he tried to ignore me, and then he walked across the street to the Chinese store and tried to play it off like he was trying to get something from the store. So, I see the car come, and the car comes; he's riding up and he's just starting to pull over, and I turn around and I'm like this with the gun *[makes a gesture indicating that he revealed he had the gun in his coat pocket]*. And so then he just kept driving. I'm just standing there the whole time, the other guy's standing at the store, and then I put my hand in my pocket, and I'm holding it in my coat. [And I just waited like that] all the way until the number 33 bus came, then I got on. I was glad I didn't have to shoot at him or anything like that.

Another man, Camron, who worked in a North Philly barbershop, echoed the same reality as Deshaun. This was life. The threat of crime was real, and he had to deal with it.

Camron: Well, at the barbershop, you get unfamiliar faces. Down there, I know basically everybody. But there are shady people with hoods on and hands in pockets, especially in the wintertime. So, usually at work I have at least two guns on me.

Me: On you, at work.

Camron: Well, one be up on the counter. Yeah, at least. I usually close before nighttime, but sometimes I run over, and there are shady people. So, I just make it known that if I'm looking at them, I have it right here. Just let them know. Nine times out of ten, the robbers, bad guys, they have a gun. If I see a gun—I've never had to use it, but if I see a gun, I'm shooting. Nine times out of ten, they've already got records and they'll leave. My gun is registered. And make sure you don't overkill. That's the whole thing. After dark, men would come in off the street. It wasn't always the barbershop usuals. These guys had their hands in pockets, hoodies up over their heads. Our barber says he can tell these guys are looking for trouble. So he keeps two guns. One on the counter and one on his person. He makes it known he's got a gun, and that has kept trouble away.

Once the men from the city started telling the truth of their experience, the men from the suburbs went quiet. I could only wonder what they were thinking as they were hearing real everyday stories about the *need* for guns, versus their want for guns out of a concern that something *might* happen someday. My judgmental self was tempting me to turn on the suburban guys and say something snarky about feeling silly with their worries compared to these men who have legitimate concerns. But that, of course, would not have helped the situation. I would have been minimizing the very real concern of the suburban men. Just because I might think someone else's fear is imagined doesn't make it any less real or motivating to action for them. Had I asked something like that, it would have further split the group into two and kept it at a more juvenile level: people who were afraid of the dark because there *might be* monsters under the bed versus people who have actually run into *real* monsters in their daily lives.

Having an unplanned schism like this in a focus group, where one side is shutting down like the suburban guys were, is not good. Ideally, a moderator strives to have a cohesive group conversation with equal participation reflecting different viewpoints. The same is true of any group conversation. In this case, the guys from the city were beginning to dominate because they were speaking from a position of reality compared to the guys from the suburbs who were speaking from a place of perception. Since they couldn't contribute to the same degree, the guys from the suburbs were clamming up. It's possible they didn't want to risk being judged by the guys from the city. To get beyond the rift that I sensed was forming, I decided to continue to "unpack" the motivations of both sides around what had prompted them to get a concealed carry permit in hopes of finding some common ground.

> **Dave #1:** I'm in the restaurant and bar business, and I felt like I had a target on my back. Too many times I've gotten in my car late at night and felt cornered in the parking lot. Just closing up, I've felt cornered. Needed a backup plan.
>
> **Ted:** For me it was just, I had meant to do it for ten years before that, but just never got around to it. When you get older, you just realize it makes more sense to be legal than deal with the hassle of if you get in a situation and then you have to explain it away somehow; how expensive that would be. So it just made sense.
>
> **Me:** So you were carrying before, just not—
>
> **Ted:** Oh yeah.
>
> **Me:** So what got you started carrying?
>
> **Ted:** My grandfather came from Ireland, and he was part of the Easter Rising in Ireland in 1916. So guns were a big part of his life. He was in the IRA [Irish Republican Army] and all that. And that's just the way the world was back then. So I kind of came up with, it was just always part of life.
>
> **Me:** What keeps you carrying it now, though?
>
> **Ted:** The world we live in.
>
> **Bill:** Yes, society.
>
> **Lavar:** It's not like it used to be. It's really, really bad out there.
>
> **Bill:** I think it was probably my old neighborhood where I lived. Next door to me, one night I found out the husband—older people, they were—he went upstate to his house, and she was home.

Come to find out somebody was in there robbing the house. And then around the corner, the same thing happened. They were older people. I was young. We're talking twenty, thirty years ago. And then I said, "Wow, what's going on around here? They're robbing houses and [cars and] stuff like this." So, that's about when I decided to get it.

Me: Who else?

Howard: I just wanted the license. I had purchased firearms before I got the permit, but I was just going to the range; I wasn't carrying. But I wanted to get the permit so I could carry. I've had instances where I wish I would have had one but didn't have it. And then just experiences of other people in neighborhoods and things happening to them and just wanting to be prepared. So, I got one. My attitude is not the greatest, so I try to limit my carrying. My personality, I've got to curb it, so I try to make sure I'm adhering to that when I'm carrying.

Shifting the question from the present "what has you carrying now?" to the past "what prompted you to want to carry?" brought out more specific, original fears, based on real-life events. Being a witness to a robbery or knowing a victim of a crime aligned more closely to the lived experiences of the city guys. And the city guys were able to participate. Then, when I asked, "What keeps you carrying now?" as a follow-up question, I got more about the fears of the uncertain world we live in. Listening to more of their stories helped keep the group together as they found shared history as their common ground. It also helped me further dismantle my judgment.

I shifted gears to the next area of inquiry. We were evaluating reactions to stock photos that represent situations where people might have a concealed weapon.

"Stock photos" are pictures that represent a scene, a situation, or an emotion. They are not always the best representation, but when you are trying to get a general reaction and draw out conversation, it's more affordable than doing a custom photo shoot. The selection of photos we put together mostly involved scenes of men or women attempting to draw a firearm. When I put them in front of the group, these gun owners were all over it.

> **Adam:** I can tell you I don't like this one because this one looks very submissive, like she's not, she has no idea what's happening to her, and she's not being very alert. So that's a bad example of what you should do. This one, her finger is on the trigger a bit too early. She shouldn't be doing that, so that's also a bad technique. I mean, what's she going to do, shoot her purse?

> **Dave #2:** You have to understand the laws. It's like, if I'm in a situation where my wife is threatened and I have to use a gun, and let's say I do something very stupid, like, maybe have a caliber that's too high or use a full metal jacket [a type of bullet] where it could potentially go through somebody and shoot an innocent bystander, you know, that's a manslaughter charge against me, and it should be because I'm not using the gun properly. So that's a very, very, very serious thing, and that's something that should be taught as good technique.

This conversation about the photos was eye-opening for me. I was impressed. These gun owners really knew their stuff! Perhaps this is a broad statement, but everyone I met was very well versed in gun safety and usage. Just a quick glance at the photos and they were calling out improper technique and handling that would not end in a "positive outcome" for anyone. From panicking to having a slow response, and from breaking the law to shooting a hole in your purse, this was a knowledgeable and capable group of citizens. They had been to the safety classes, done regular training, and recognized the importance of training and the responsibility that goes along with gun ownership. Because I had been dismantling my judgment throughout the course of the conversation, hearing the gun owners talk this way, with such knowledge and confidence, made me feel better about them as gun owners. I was able to really understand their perspective and reach empathy about why they wanted to own a gun. And I could respect their opinions as a result.

Now that I had empathy with them, did that mean I changed my personal feelings about gun ownership and gun safety? Not at all. Just because I understand someone's point of view doesn't mean I have to agree with them (see Step 4: Integrate into Understanding).

The 5 Steps to Empathy let me see another person's perspective. Hopefully I can then relate to them better. By expressing empathy, I demonstrate that I respect the other person even though I may not agree. Empathy and respect lead to more productive conversations and interpersonal relationships. In this situation, I came to understand that gun owners, at a base level, are afraid for their own safety. I am too, just from a different vantage point. I can work with that in order to work with them on solutions.

A WEEK after the focus groups, back home in San Francisco, I was having brunch with friends. Of course, they were curious about my experience at the gun show and the focus groups. Both of the friends joining my husband and me lean liberal to progressive, and both are vocal proponents of gun control. Their words on the topic went something like this: "People don't need to have guns. If there was better gun control, we wouldn't have as many random shootings. Why should everyone have a gun? They [gun owners] don't know what they're doing, and yet they are free to run around carrying a weapon to fire it whenever they feel threatened!"

And there it was. I could hear that the tone beneath their argument was that same powerful emotion: fear. Just like the gun owners at the NRA show, my friends were afraid of the possibility of something happening in this unpredictable world. It was a similar line of thought as the suburban guys in Philadelphia—it's a big world, and anything can happen. Except my friends, city dwellers themselves, weren't worried about being attacked by a homeless person or the random person outside a restaurant; they knew how to avoid those situations. Their fear was of the people who have guns. So both sides are afraid of strangers. And both sides let their judgment block their willingness to engage in conversation with the other side of the gun safety argument.

Having this aha moment, I told my friends about the training and awareness the gun owners I'd met had, and how impressed I was with their level of knowledge and how much more comfortable this made me. Because I had firsthand knowledge and spoke to the issue understanding their perspective, my friends were able to dismantle their judgment and hear what I had to say.

Both sides in the gun safety argument are driven by fear. At its core, people are afraid of what might be. Constant examples in the media of gun violence reinforce the fear non-owners have of what someone who has a gun might do, and they also create fear among gun owners about what might happen (or, for some, did happen) to them out in the world. Each side has the same fear, and the stories and lived experiences merely reinforce people's positions on the topic—which leads to reactionary solutions to assuage that very fear, which further fuels the fear of the other side.

Fear is one of our most base, primal emotions. It informs fight or flight. In response to fear, people take positions and make decisions to help calm their fear. Some choose to buy a gun, and hopefully get trained on it and be prepared to protect themselves, because who knows what some random person with a gun might do. Others choose to support the restriction on gun sales, arguing that guns don't need to be widely available and they need proper regulations, because who knows what harm some random person with a gun might do.

Imagine what could be achieved if the opposing sides in the gun debate came to the table and began from a place of cognitive empathy with each other. Knowing that fear drives both sides of the debate, each side could then more calmly and respectfully address the concerns of the other. Gun owners are concerned about their safety and the right to protect themselves, their property, and their loved ones. Non-owners are also concerned about their safety and the threat presented to themselves, their property, and their loved ones by who has access to buy a gun and the types of guns available for purchase. With the mass shootings that have become so common in the United States, from Sandy Hook to Orlando, Las Vegas to Atlanta, Columbine to Boulder, plus all the smaller but no less frightening acts of terror in the workplace, there is tangible evidence almost every day on the evening news that justifies the fears of the gun safety advocate. How do you change the conversation on gun safety? Can we find a way to rationally and respectfully work together to find a path toward preventing a gun capable of overkilling from getting into the hands of someone who is mentally unstable? And at the same time, can we find a way to make those who don't own guns more comfortable with the safety training and knowledge that responsible gun owners have or are required to go through?

If there was ever a topic in our society that could benefit from cognitive empathy, it's this one. Fear is often irrational, and even if it is based in reality, our minds can get the best of us. Fear has the infectious ability to grow, twisting and turning in our minds until it's much greater than reality. And once we live in that heightened state of fear, it drives our thoughts and actions. Cognitive empathy can help us get to a rational state that overcomes the fear. If you take the time to unpack what people are worried about, then see their perspective alongside your viewpoint, and think through how you might talk with them in a manner that addresses their fear and helps them also see your perspective, you'll be on your way toward understanding and developing solutions.

Empathy has the power to be transformative. We just need to have the courage to overcome our own judgment and open ourselves up to experience empathy and put it to good use.

EMPATHETIC REFLECTIONS

- What stereotypes came to mind for you at the beginning of the chapter, with the descriptions of "a gay man, a blonde, and a South Asian man"? How did that judgment influence your perception of each of them as individuals and in relationship to guns?

- What's a topic that you have a lot of pre-existing judgment on? What would it take to get to a beginner's mind?

- Think about a time when empathy helped resolve a disagreement for you. What lessons from that experience would you apply in the future? How about a time when empathy wasn't present? What would you do differently next time?

STEP
2

ASK GOOD QUESTIONS

Achieving cognitive empathy requires that "good questions" be asked in order to gain the context behind a person's thinking or behavior. A good question is one that is open-ended and exploratory, often stated from the attitude of a beginner's mind. It has no judgment in it. Ask a good question and you will get a great answer.

9

Peeling
the Onion

---

*The irony is that we attempt to disown our difficult
stories to appear more whole or more acceptable, but our
wholeness—even our wholeheartedness—actually depends on
the integration of all of our experiences, including the falls.*

BRENÉ BROWN

I
T'S LATE APRIL. I'm driving an SUV on a two-lane country
road forty-five minutes outside of Birmingham, Alabama.
Spring is in full swing, with warm temperatures and threatening storms. This project is exploring working-class America—who
are these people, what are their lives like, their day to day, their
hopes and dreams, their values? The cell reception was getting spottier the farther we drove. GPS was going in and out. We rounded
another bend in the road and finally arrived at our destination: a
trailer at the end of an inclined gravel drive with a green yard. This
was Emmajean's home.

As we pulled in, we found Emmajean in the yard, tending to her
dog and a litter of puppies. She greeted us from a distance with a
warm smile and a hearty wave. Solidly built, she was an attractive

woman with soft brown hair and a warm demeanor. While she was not physically imposing, Emmajean's energy displayed a quiet strength.

In those moments, as we arrive on any in-home, it feels like "showtime." We're all getting out of the car, pulling out our gear, making introductions; the respondent is a bit nervous, and we're still cautiously evaluating the setting, looking for indications of the type of interview this might be. Maybe it's having camera equipment with us, or maybe it's my performer's nature, but it feels like an interview for a TV show is about to start.

In my mind, qualitative interviews are similar to putting on a "show." Whether I'm moderating a focus group with my "audience" facing my back or it's an audience of one or two sitting next to me on an in-home, live qualitative research is like a form of "infotainment." I, as the moderator, feel a responsibility to make sure the clients, my "audience," are engaged and getting something out of the content they are viewing live. That might create a slippery slope for some moderators to try to elicit the salacious or not respect the participants, but I search for truth rather than dig for titillation. If the session elicits something more exciting on a personal level, that's great—and it makes for a great story afterward, as long as we've asked the questions we need to ask and get the information we're hired to uncover.

Emmajean finished up with the pups and headed over toward us. We had only said hello and asked, "How are you?" when she started sharing her stories with us. The puppies belonged to her dog, and it was a surprise litter, so she planned to adopt them out. She lived on property that once had belonged to her mom. Apparently, her mom had lived all around the country because her husband, Emmajean's stepdad, had worked construction. Then the couple moved south and settled in the area. The property used to have an old homestead, "a big old two-story house," on it, which was now long gone.

Emmajean shared quite a bit of information right there in her front yard! Usually the team and I are settled inside the house on a sofa when this type of info starts to come out. Instead, we were standing in the yard, torn between cooing over the puppies and focusing on Emmajean. Once she started to open up, however, I had to start focusing. The paperwork, the releases, and the explanation of what we were doing—we'd do that during a subsequent part of the conversation.

I made mental notes on what she'd told us in case I needed to circle back to something later. The property had been in the family for generations. She'd lost her mom a while back. She had a son who was fifteen.

Me: I'm sorry, how many kids do you have? I was looking at the puppies.

Emmajean: Four.

Client: Oh my gosh! Really?

Emmajean: Yeah, I have two sons and two daughters. A twenty-seven-year-old daughter, a twenty-two-year-old daughter. Then I started over and I had the two boys; one will be fifteen in May, and my baby boy will be thirteen in October, two days before my birthday.

Client: Wow!

Me: And what do you mean, you started over?

Emmajean: I got with their dad and had them. I done had my girls raised, you know, they were big girls in school, you know, and had them took care of, had a career, and then I met him and—

Me: So you've got two teen boys now.

Emmajean: Mm-hm.

Client: Wow!

Emmajean's life, like everyone's, is like an onion. You peel back one layer and then the next layer reveals itself; peel that back and there's another, and so on. Usually you have to ask a good question to get to the next layer of the onion.

"How are you?" is a great question to start with. It's what we asked Emmajean when we pulled up. It allows the person you are talking to the opportunity to steer the conversation to whatever is on their mind. Next, ask another good question when trying to get to the next layer of the onion. For this follow-up question, the goal is still to get someone to open up and go deeper. That means the question will need to be broad and allow for any type of answer. "Tell me about…" is one example. Another would be to ask *how* that topic made them feel, such as, "What were you feeling in that moment?" Good questions get the respondent to reflect and are so open that it makes room for any answer. And then, based on what the answer was, you pick up and follow that thread.

Some people are open books, and it doesn't take much to get them to share. Emmajean was one of those people. Right away, after my client asked how she was, she revealed a lot about herself and what she had gone through in her life. Those comments elicited a *wow* reaction from my clients (and a silent *wow* from me).

"Wow" comes across as an immediate reaction of surprise, but depending on the tone and accompanying facial expression, it can also express judgment. Don't believe me? Go to a mirror and say "wow" three times. The first with a smile, the second with a look of disbelief, and the third with a tone and look of hurt or anger. The first was surprise; the second and third could have elements of judgment in them.

The word *wow* is also used in acknowledgment of, and reaction to, the "mind-blowing" degree of what is being shared. It's not an "I can't comprehend this" mind-blowing expression so much as an empathetic recognition that you are comprehending what is being told to you, taking it in, and quickly imagining yourself in the other person's shoes.

So there we were, standing in the front yard, and not five minutes in, my client was having an empathetic connection with Emmajean and what we were understanding of her life story. And, it turned out, there was much more to come.

Emmajean told us more about her boys. Her youngest, twelve, had size twelve feet already and was playing football locally. She said football was possible because they were more financially secure now that she had met a guy three years prior. In fact, they'd gotten married at the courthouse on a beautiful fall day the previous year. While we offered our congratulations, I made an assumption, thinking about Emmajean's relationships that we knew of; two relationships had produced children, and now there was a third.

Me: So, your third marriage?

Emmajean: No, my second marriage, but my fourth serious relationship, you know, for years. Yeah. And I hope he's the last.

My assumption on the number of marriages was a guess, and the question I asked wasn't good. Had I listened more carefully, I would have noted that she had only mentioned two husbands. At other times she mentioned the dad of her kids. Those are not necessarily one and the same, and that's what I missed—subtle lingual cues that would have told me a great deal, if only I had heard them. Instead I was left making assumptions. I had no idea if her relationship history was a sore spot for Emmajean or if she might have felt some amount of shame if she'd perceived judgment in my question and the way I'd asked it. In this case, judgment wasn't getting in the way of my question, but there are other ways I could have asked it. One that comes to mind: "Congratulations! Have either of you been married before?"

Not bad, as it doesn't make assumptions; however, the way it is phrased is what is known as a closed question (as opposed to open). The risk is that she could say "yes" and not elaborate. Then, I'd have to ask a follow-up question to "peel the onion."

It would also be okay to ask: "How many times have you been married?" although that's also a closed question. She could just give me a number and no other information. If I were to do it all again, I'd try something like: "I just want to make sure I'm following what you've told me; tell me more about your relationships and marriages." This phrasing keeps the possibilities open for however she might answer. It also puts her in the position of helping me make sure I'm tracking what she's telling me. Since people like to help other people, it's a good tip to use "help me understand" as part of asking good questions.

Emmajean continued on:

> **Emmajean:** Yeah. I haven't had good luck, especially with their dad. He just went to work one day and never came home.

According to the time stamp on the transcript, this detail was coming out only seven minutes after we'd arrived, still in the yard, looking at the puppies. Her forthrightness and honesty moved our conversation right along. I'm a believer in speaking your truth, and Emmajean seemed to be doing just that—an open book and open to sharing.

During the few minutes it took us to head inside her home and get "officially" set up and settled, I realized that I had to be careful about the assumptions I was making about people on this project, which was focused on working-class America. What made me assume that she was married when she had her kids? That was my bias. I was ascribing a "traditional" view of life: be married when you have your kids. That might be true for some people, but certainly not for all people, and not for her. I needed to approach my conversations with more of a beginner's mind. That means asking questions that don't rely on assumptions. Let the person being asked fill in the blanks.

We continued our conversation with Emmajean. She gave us some of her work history. She had worked for a retailer, getting merchandise boxes ready to go from the warehouse to the store locations. She had been doing that when her youngest son was born.

He had some medical complications, though, and needed to have surgery at two months old. Emmajean requested medical leave, but she was told that she was still on her maternity leave, so she had to use that leave plus her accrued vacation days. Near the end of the extended leave period, she was told by the retailer that since she hadn't come back to work at the end of her maternity leave, she was going to be terminated and replaced.

To make matters worse, when she went to apply for unemployment insurance, she was told she wasn't eligible because the retailer had said she voluntarily left her job. Our first thought, right there in her living room, like yours might be reading this, was that Emmajean had a good case and should have gotten a lawyer. Unfortunately, she didn't have the resources to hire a lawyer, and the unemployment board wasn't receptive to her complaint. That left her with a toddler but lacking a job.

At the time that we met her, Emmajean stayed busy raising her boys, and she made money by doing some sitting with an elderly woman that lived nearby. Years earlier, before working at the retailer, around the time of the birth of her first daughter, she had attended and completed nursing school. She was motivated to learn nursing because, at the time, she and her boyfriend and their infant daughter lived out in the country. "If I'm out in the middle of the woods somewhere and something happens to my daughter, I want to know what to do," she explained.

However, an aspect of nursing that didn't appeal to her was the fact that it was an indoor job, and "I can't stand to be inside all the time." And while she liked nursing itself, for the clinical portion of school, she would go into the nursing homes and found it depressing. "Oh God, I'd cry every day, you know," she said, because she'd get close to her elderly patients. Seeing what a big, open heart she had, it wasn't difficult to imagine how hard it would be for her to be a nurse and manage to keep compassionate distance from her patients.

I was learning a lot about Emmajean's life, and we seemed to be going back in time from one job to the previous one. I was curious to go back further to an earlier life-stage transition, like when she would have graduated high school and what she'd imagined her adult life would be.

> **Me:** So, let's go back to, I don't know, when you were eighteen years old, maybe.
>
> **Emmajean:** I'm eighteen?
>
> **Me:** Back when you were eighteen years old.
>
> **Emmajean:** Oh, Lordy!
>
> **Me:** What dreams did you have for yourself?
>
> **Emmajean:** At eighteen?
>
> **Me:** At eighteen.

Usually when I ask this question, I go with age twenty-two or twenty-three, right when someone might be out of college. That's often an age when people are still finding their way and having dreams for themselves that may be far-reaching. They also generally haven't experienced too many of the curveballs of life that might alter or crush their dreams. As I was quickly formulating this line of questioning in my head, I made an assumption that, beyond the nursing program, Emmajean hadn't gone to college. This means she'd have been in the midst of work and life stuff in her early twenties, so in my question I rolled her age back to eighteen. If you aren't continuing on to college, when you finish high school, you are filled with that shining hope of dreams for the future and notions of "freedom."

The problem with my question was that I was still making assumptions about the course of Emmajean's life, and I should have phrased the question differently, so that it was less tied to a specific age. Not everyone is in the same place in life at eighteen, as she was about to teach me.

> **Emmajean:** Oh my goodness! Well, I hadn't started nursing school then. At eighteen. I had just divorced for the first time at eighteen. I got married when I was young.

Another "wow" from us. Divorced for the first time at eighteen? In hindsight, I should have asked her, "What dreams did you have for yourself when you were a young girl?" That would have been more open and exploratory rather than locking the conversation to a specific time. As a result, she shared what was a jaw-dropper to me and my clients. She was getting divorced at eighteen.

> **Me:** Emmajean, tell me more about that.

> **Emmajean:** My dad, when we moved down here, he got with a very much younger woman, and me and her did not get along. You know, it was like the evil stepmom and the wicked stepsister or whatever you want to call it, because she was so much younger; she was more my age, like an older sister, and she was trying to be a mother and telling me what to do, you know. And me and my dad had been alone for like a year and a half when we moved south. And then when he met her, she was like real young, like twelve years his junior. And so, it was like a competition, you know, with me and her about his attention, I guess.

Emmajean told us about how her stepmother liked to go to the bingo hall with her own mother and didn't do much around the house, which was then left to Emmajean. "I had to clean the bathroom, I had to wash the dishes, and I was still in school," she recalled. "And so, I left. I left home at an early age. I left when I just turned fourteen."

To earn money, Emmajean got a job at a nursery at the age of fourteen, her love for being outdoors showing up in her first job.

Emmajean: And the guy I married, he was older than me by about ten years. But I was going to run away from home; we were going to run away and get married, blah blah. And my dad found the letter, and so he signed for me to get married. And I asked him years later why, and he said, "Because I always figured you might run away, and I didn't know where you would run to, and then I didn't know if I'd ever get to see you again. So, this way I knew I would still have you."

When I hear stories like Emmajean's, I wonder what would have happened and how her life would be different today if one of those variables had been altered. What would have happened had the stepmom not entered the picture, or if the stepmom was an older woman rather than someone close in age? And what if the father hadn't signed the permission to marry? Where would Emmajean have ended up then, had she gone through with her plan to run away? Each and every action causes a subsequent reaction, sometimes pushing you in the opposite direction. Dad marries younger woman, which creates tension with daughter, driving her away. She meets an older man and wants to run away. In order to keep his daughter in his life, the father signs permission for the daughter to marry at a young age. Life is a series of sometimes unintended consequences, resulting from the decisions we make and the way they ripple out, impacting us and the people around us.

So, fourteen-year-old Emmajean got married.

Emmajean: I married the guy, and thank you, Lord Jesus, I never had no children by him. But he was very abusive. Very abusive. Mentally and physically. And I left him, just, I worked at the nursery for the whole time we were married. He never worked. You know, he was more like a house husband. He would have supper cooked when I got in, and he'd clean house and stuff, but he did not do the work, like, you know. So, I seen, within four years, you know, he just, he was so abusive and mean to me that I just couldn't. I had a dream, actually, and it was like, I believe in Jesus, you know, believe in God, and it was like the Lord come to me just in a dream and said, "If you don't get away from him, he's going to kill you." So, and he *had* done shot at me a couple of times.

Emmajean proceeded to tell us how, after having "got into it" with her husband, she was walking with her sister-in-law down a long country road, on the way to a relative's house. "It was what I call 'country country.'" Suddenly, shots rang out and the dirt kicked up just ahead of their feet. Someone was shooting at them! "Yeah, he was mental, I'm talking about. I never knew how mental," she told us. By the time they got to the relative's house and called the police, the shooter had gone. Not long after that, she decided to leave him.

Emmajean: So, I had been packing my stuff little by little because I was scared of him. You know, he had always told me, "If you ever leave me, I'll kill you and won't nobody find you," you know how they do. But anyway, so I was young, I had packed my stuff little by little, and one day my cousin's wife, her car had broke down, and she had asked him to take her to Birmingham to the doctor. Well, he had told her he would, but she got her car fixed in the meantime, but I told my aunt, "You better tell her; don't tell him you got that car fixed because I want him out of the house that day." You know, I had done planned this, you know. So the whole time I had been packing my stuff in a big old toilet paper box, I will never forget, and I was packing everything, my hot rollers, you know, that was about the only thing he ever gave me of value was a set of hot rollers.

Packed all my clothes, all my stuff. Well, I had borrowed a friend's car and it was a two-door, you know, it had the seats that you lift up. Well I had packed, I had, like, four boxes and that big old Northern tissue toilet paper box. I had a bunch. It was heavy; I couldn't tote that thing through that house. Just waiting on him to pull up, I was terrified. So I had done packed everything else [in the car] but that one big box. Well, I go to put the seat up and the box was too big. I couldn't get it in; it was wedged. Oh, I just knew he was going to pull up and catch me, you know, leaving. I was terrified. So I just took my foot and I just hauled off and kicked that box, jumped into that car, and I was gone.

Emmajean fled to the grandparents of the coworker who had loaned her the two-door car. While there, she called her mom to check in.

Emmajean: I called my mother, she said, "Yeah,"—his name was Danny, the one I had left—She said, "Yeah, Danny's been calling here telling me, or asking if you're down here and wanted to know if I've heard from you. And I told him, 'No, actually, I haven't heard from her.'" I said, "Well, you tell him now you've heard from me." I said, "Tell him I was in a white Trans Am heading to California with a good-looking man."

We were all sitting in Emmajean's living room, transfixed, listening to her. Emmajean knew how to tell the stories of her life. It was masterful. The oral storytelling traditions were alive within her. She set the mood, provided enough backstory to let us fully imagine the setting and the personalities of the players involved. The tension was palpable as we thought of her wrestling with that giant toilet paper box, stuck in between the car door frame and the back seat of the car—all the while worried that her abusive husband may come home at any minute. Then the surge of relief she must have felt when, after a hard kick or two, the cardboard succumbed and squeezed its way through and into the back seat. Then, the unfamiliar feelings and isolation of her rural hideout with the grandparents of a colleague. And finally, the image of her driving off into the sunset toward California in a Trans Am. I could visualize a younger Emmajean, in early-'80s aviator sunglasses, her long brown hair catching the wind from the open car window. Like in a movie, her foot, clad in an espadrille, pressing down on the accelerator as the view pulled back to take in the entire scene. I saw the car race ahead, dust kicking up behind her, the Trans Am heading directly into the orange blaze of the large setting sun, where the road meets the horizon. A life filled with possibility lay directly ahead of her. And then the credits to this movie began to roll.

I couldn't help but think of myself at eighteen, graduating from high school, leaving Indiana, about to go on to college, dreaming about my future. And Emmajean, at the same age, had already been in one abusive marriage, been shot at, and had to make a stealthy escape from her first husband. It would have been hard to imagine, but because of how vividly she told her stories, it made it easier for me to step into her world. I could picture the small house way out in the countryside, what it must have felt like to see the dirt kicking up as it was being shot by a "stranger" in the woods, the stress mounting as the oversized toilet paper box wouldn't fit into the back seat. The relief as a sharp kick forced it into place, enabling her escape. We were all right there with her.

My colleague who had done the prescreen interview with Emmajean told me afterward, "I knew Emmajean would be an interesting interview; she's had a lot of adversity in her life." I found that fascinating because she attached the word *adversity* to Emmajean, while the word that comes to my mind when I think of her is *resilience*. Yes, there was a lot of adversity that she faced, but she had the inner strength and self-reliance to get through it. That's resilience. Adversity wasn't part of her character; resilience was. Adversity was part of Emmajean's circumstance, but she had the resilience to deal with it. I related to her more easily because of the adversity I'd faced in my own life growing up. I had the inner resources to make my way through and figure out how to survive what I was going through. I connected with Emmajean, and even

Emelia before her, because of that shared resilience. By drawing a connection between my own experience and theirs, I was able to imagine what it might have been like to be them. Stepping into their shoes, as it were.

Building that connection is so much easier when you identify with someone's trials and tribulations. You relate to it and therefore you can more readily draw inspiration from it. That's part of the reason why some gay men attach to and adore iconic women, from Marlene Dietrich to Barbra Streisand to Madonna, Cher to Britney to Beyoncé and Lady Gaga. We see their resilience in ourselves. They've fought their way through a straight white man's world and succeeded in spades, doing it their way and not conforming. That is the ultimate hope of many young gay men (and pretty much anyone that's been marginalized by society in some way)—to be accepted and successful for being who they are, rather than conforming to an image of what they interpret society wants them to be.

I learned many lessons from Emmajean that day. I learned not to make assumptions about people based on the little scraps of information I had, like her ratio of husbands to relationships. I also learned not to apply my judgment on when things should have been occurring in her life, like her first marriage. I also realized that, in order to minimize the effect of those assumptions and judgments, I needed to keep my questions open and broad.

After dismantling judgment, asking good questions is the second step toward building empathy. I never know the answer someone's going to give, so I want my questions to be as open as possible when I'm getting to know someone or exploring a topic. That means not leading them toward an answer. It's like in the courtroom dramas, when a lawyer is leading the witness toward a specific answer. Had I asked Emmajean, "Why do you prefer hot rollers over curlers or getting a permanent?" then I would have been leading her. That question has a subtle inference that I'm looking for her to tell me that she likes hot rollers instead of other options of keeping the curl in her hair. It's subtle, but people are good at picking up those types of leads and will gladly follow along. The more open question would be: "What are your thoughts on the different ways to keep your hair curled?" With that rephrased question, she would be free to answer in any number of ways depending on her own beliefs, rather than trying to please us with what she thought we might want to hear. And people instinctively want to please on a certain level. Keep the question open, and they can still please while giving the answer that's most true to them.

That's not to say adding specificity to a question won't help focus it. I made the decision to ask about Emmajean's dreams at a certain age. Had I not done that, had I just asked what dreams she had for herself, we might have heard about her current dreams, or what she wanted after she had her girls in her twenties. By asking about her dreams at eighteen, I was looking for that point when she might have been transitioning into adulthood. As it turns out, at eighteen, Emmajean was also dreaming of escaping, but she had already transitioned into adulthood. I should have asked that differently to be open to where she was in her life.

This whole conversation had begun with one question to Emmajean when we first arrived: "How are you?" We got a lot from asking just one good query.

Asking a good question is the start of "holding space" for someone. Put the question out there, keep it broad enough and open enough, and see where they go with it. Let them fill in the space. Notice how little I talk in these conversations. I mostly listen to answers. By listening to what they say in reply and keeping your judgment dismantled, you can pick up and guide the conversation to go deeper, learn more, or focus on another area of personal truth you want to understand. This leads to connections forming. A deeper understanding of a neighbor, a colleague, or a client comes from forging a deeper bond and creating a new level of personal respect.

Emmajean had openly shared her truth with us. It just took one good open question to get her sharing her personal history with a group of complete strangers.

"HOW ARE YOU?" is such a beautiful, simple, broad, and open question. It's also a powerful question because it can be answered in any number of ways. How we choose to answer is up to us. From time to time, I find myself answering that question with a perfunctory "I'm good" when I know, particularly during times of stress, like the pandemic, that there's really so much more going on. I have to make the decision whether to open up about a specific subject or stay at the surface. That decision can be based on my comfort level with the person asking, the mood I happen to be in at that moment, and if there really is something deeper that I'm ready to explore. I certainly don't want to overshare with the wrong person or at the wrong time, but we have to be willing to open up if we want people to understand us in return.

One of the greatest ironies is that we have more ways than ever to open up and share our thoughts due to social media—yet our shift to social media as a primary mode of "communication" has created a scenario where we are seeking validation instead of sharing with any depth, let alone building empathy. The lifetime of resilience that Emmajean had displayed required us to listen to the whole story. That might not have come through in individual tweets, posts, or stories designed for immediate affirmation.

Every "like" that I get on my Instagram or Facebook or LinkedIn posts (or any other social media that I don't use but that has this validation function) releases a hit of dopamine into my brain, which makes it feel good. Therefore, I, like everyone else, want more, so I've learned to repeat the function that successfully releases the dopamine. In other words, one like creates a craving for a second like, and we start chasing that sensation of being liked.

Yet where on social media do we ask, "How are you?"—that beautiful, broad, open-ended question that lets you explore how someone is really doing. Fortunately, we have chat and text-based communication where someone can privately open up, but it can never replace the depth of a live conversation where you can hear the other person's voice.

Even in a text format, a reply to, "How are you?" might be, "Fine." That's not revealing very much. Even less when it's just four letters on a screen. Hearing someone's voice provides cues as to where to take your next question. It allows you to pick up on someone dodging the question, being distracted, or being sarcastic or insincere. That helps you understand where to go with your next good question. In text format, you are left guessing what to ask next.

"How are you?" isn't about collecting likes or sympathy. It curates a more enriching collection: connections. Asking good questions allows you to form these connections with others. That leads to understanding and, ultimately, empathy. Making the connection in person or by voice helps build stronger conversations, which contributes to better understanding and even conflict resolution.

The next time you are tempted to just click "like" on a post, take a moment to send a message instead, or better yet, pick up the phone and call. Start the conversation with one of the best questions of all: "How are you?"

EMPATHETIC REFLECTIONS

- Thinking about a recent conversation, take a piece of paper and write down the questions that were asked. Now evaluate if they were open or closed questions. How broad were they? Any that were leading? Next to each question, rephrase it as a "good question."

- The word *why* puts us on the defensive. Challenge yourself for one full day to replace "why" with other words while still getting at why. Notice how often you use that word. *Pro tip:* Use who, what, where, when, and how as replacements when rephrasing your why questions.

10

Let's Talk About Sex

I have no objection to anyone's sex life as long as they don't practice it in the street and frighten the horses.
OSCAR WILDE

W HEN WE ARE younger, it's not unusual for friends to chat about their dating trials and tribulations as well as the intimacy of their sex life (or absence of one). *Sex and the City* brought pretty frank conversation among friends about sex into the mainstream. It also popularized the "girls brunch," where friends gather and share feelings and behaviors on dating and sex. It empowered women to be okay with their sexuality and not be ashamed or embarrassed about wanting and pursuing it. I was living in New York City in the late '90s, and I could see the transformation of the city's residents happen before my eyes. And I'll be honest: gay men, myself included, did the "girls brunch" too. Freewheeling, leisurely, sometimes boozy brunches, where pretty much any topic was open for honest discussion. From blow jobs to leather fetishes, dating hang-ups to the latest hangouts, my friends and I talked about it all.

At that age, it seemed like our happiness was measured, in part, by the frequency and quality of our sex life. We were around thirty, settling into our careers and enjoying the liberation of being openly gay, young, and in good-paying jobs relative to our age. And by sharing, we were also helping each other learn about dating and sex and how to do both better. It felt incredibly freeing to be able to share with friends, since that wasn't available to most of us growing up in the closet. And having characters in a TV show as role models demonstrating how to have sex-positive conversations took down some of the remaining barriers we were facing. Pushing beyond the walls of our "closet," we were liberated by *Sex and the City*. Beyond brunch, you could readily find groups of young women going out on the town, decked out in heels and their LBDs (Little Black Dresses), each one perhaps adopting the "role" of one of the four main characters—although most fancied themselves the Carrie of the group, when they might have really been the Charlotte, the Samantha, or the Miranda. Sex was coming forward in our society in a way that it hadn't since the '70s, before AIDS and the conservative eighties made sex a taboo topic.

And so that's sex. In your youth, it's topic number one, particularly when you are single. Then, as we age, perhaps we get into a long-term relationship, and happiness starts to get measured not by the quality and caliber of the sex but by the quality and caliber of our bowel movements. Yes, poop conversations. Don't believe me? Ask someone over fifty. They'll either confirm it or they might blush or even yammer a bit, which is another nonverbal way of confirming something they are slightly uncomfortable with. While bowel conversations haven't become a regular brunch topic in my social circles, I have been known to espouse the wonders of the Squatty Potty, proper bowel position, and the feeling of bliss after a good evacuation. Welcome to middle age!

While talking about sex and bodily functions with people you are intimate with or really close friends with may have become more acceptable, both are still awkward topics with strangers or casual acquaintances. These are subject matters too personal for idle chatter with a stranger on the subway. But just because it's not as comfortable and open a conversation topic doesn't mean that people working at the companies supporting the sex and pleasure industry, as well as companies involved in bodily waste elimination, are incurious and don't have any questions for their consumers. They have lots of questions. And someone has to put those questions to consumers. Guess who!

While a good qualitative researcher should be willing and comfortable talking about *any* topic, that's not the case for people that aren't in the business of asking questions. But if you are a truly good friend who wants to use cognitive empathy to show support and compassion, then you too will benefit from being willing and comfortable to talk about any topic. Regardless of the subject matter, asking good questions is fundamental to navigating your way through uncomfortable conversations.

A few years ago, we were approached to assist another firm in conducting some frank conversations about sex and the use of personal lubricant during sex. I was going to talk to the men, while a female colleague handled the conversations with the women.

As it turns out, some of the men I was going to talk to, and that the clients were interested in hearing from, were gay men. As a gay man myself, that wasn't a problem. I understand gay sex, the mechanics, most of the gadgets, and any enhancers that might be involved. I thought of it like a throwback to my *Sex and the City* brunches in the late '90s in New York. Easy enough to do. However, heterosexual sex and talking to the straight guys about sex with women, now that's virgin territory for me.

As the schedule of interviews developed, it worked out that I got to talk to the gay men first. That was helpful because I got to "warm up" to the questions in the discussion guide and how the respondents might react to this topic. It gave me what marketers might call "fingertips," initial familiarity with the topic—a term that could sound inappropriate in a frank conversation about sex, but that really was allowing me to get more comfortable helping people open up.

One of the gay men I talked to was very "sex positive"; he had no evident shame or shyness about sex. It was something he enjoyed, and he didn't feel the need to apologize or cover it up. As a result, he was very open and comfortable sharing details about his sexual activities, the toys he used, and the different types of lube he had tried. Another guy, also gay, was a bit more reserved and hesitant in our conversation. It wasn't that he was less comfortable with sex or his sexuality, but he was less adventurous sexually, so he didn't feel like he had as much to offer on the topic. He used lube for self-stimulation and anal penetration. Toys and fetishes weren't part of his repertoire. These two men shared many traits in common but were still different in subtle and sometimes not so subtle ways.

While any topic can be discussed provided you treat it and the person sharing with respect, every topic is easier if you have some ability to relate to it. Gay sex, I got. Even if it involves a fetish or role-play or toys that are outside of my comfort zone, I at least understand what man-on-man sex is like. Some of the sex acts were out of my league, but I still had a base of understanding of what goes on. A conversation on a sensitive topic like this is one of those times when you cannot be judgmental in thought or in word if you're there to keep the conversation going and gather more information. What someone else chooses to do is their own business; it's not our place to judge, only to hear what they have to say and consider their perspective. It's the same as talking with a friend on a sensitive topic.

Does this make it any less awkward? No! Any conversation, including interviewing, like good sex, has a warm-up period where you get your conversation partner comfortable and ready to share more. Then, as you enter into the main part of the conversation, you have to maintain composure—no smirking or judgment allowed. An understanding nod of the head can go a long way to getting someone to let you in and share a part of themselves.

Finally, it came time that I got to talk with a heterosexual man about having sex with a woman.

Like when I was at the NRA show, a beginner's mind is a great way to approach a conversation where you may have judgment or know little about a topic and need an open mind. This mindset will enable you to ask good questions. Then, as you develop a point of reference, you are able to connect and build empathy. I may never have handled a gun before, but I went to the NRA show with a beginner's mind, which helped me develop empathy with the need of gun owners to stay safe. For this project, as a gay man who has never gone further with a woman than a single kiss, and a tame one at that, my mind was so rudimentary in comprehension that it wasn't a beginner's mind; it was a blank slate!

Since the project wasn't about the emotions in sex—it was strictly focused on the functional role of lube—I didn't have to ask questions from the perspective of pleasure and desire. This took the titillation out of the conversation but raised the stakes in other ways, as I needed to understand anatomical parts I hadn't looked at since eighth-grade health class.

To make the interview situation even more unusual, we were on the phone, a tactic used to give a sense of anonymity to the respondents so that they'd feel more comfortable opening up to share their thoughts. During this interview, Adam, the subject, was driving home from work somewhere in the Midwest. The phone call in the car during a commute gave him privacy, but it's hardly my preferred setting for intimate conversations—although when my dad and I had "the talk" to discuss the birds and the bees, we had been in the car, so this didn't feel totally unfamiliar.

I was about thirteen. I still remember that it was a cloudy day, and we had barely merged onto the interstate when Dad started explaining how two adults merge. There we were, on our way to the mall on a Saturday afternoon, like we did every weekend, except my mom and sister mysteriously had taken a separate car. Later I learned it was all planned by my parents to give my dad and me some privacy. My dad's hands were perched at the top of the steering wheel. While driving, he extended and spread his index and middle finger on his left hand and said they represented a woman's legs. His right hand was closed except for an extended index finger that he said represented a (hopefully not to scale) man's penis. I remember he told me that the man's penis would get hard. "How?" I asked, with a combination of innocence and closeted dismay. "Don't worry about that; it'll happen," he replied. "Or you'll play with it a little," he added. On the outside, my beginner's mind nodded in interest while inside, my adolescent brain was spinning. *Oh God, does he know I'm gay? Is that what this means, that I'll always have to play with it first in order to have sex? With a* woman*?!* I'm sure Dad offered an explanation of what was between the index and middle fingers of his left hand, our imaginary woman, but I've blocked that out of my memory. Then, at sixty miles per hour on the interstate, driving toward the mall, he brought the "male" index finger in between the "female" fingers to illustrate the act of sex. I wasn't sure if I was going to die of embarrassment or of a high-speed car crash. I struggled not to show my discomfort, while on the inside I was totally discombobulated. Then I started to hear my dad, the college chemistry major, provide the clinical explanation of what was transpiring inside the woman's body. With two parents that have science degrees, there is never a shortage in my family of clinical explanations of how things work. And that's how I learned how babies were made. A brief discourse on intercourse in a 1980 Honda Accord hatchback on the way to the mall.

And now, on this project, with this interview, I feared I was going to relive that experience all over again.

Even though we wanted to know about purchase decisions and perceived differences between two brands of lube, the main thrust (pun intended) was about how the product was being used. I get how lube is used on a male penis, and it plays an important role in gay sex, but again, the female anatomy is foreign territory, and my passport doesn't have a single stamp. Much in the way that many Americans can't identify foreign countries on a map, that's the female anatomy for me. Ask me to identify a clitoris or a labia and I'll point in the direction of Southeast Asia. It's somewhere there, next to the other thing and the inner thighs, which resemble the V-shaped space between my dad's fingers. I truly have a beginner's mind in this situation.

Of course, while I was dying inside from the sheer awkwardness of the conversation with Adam, I couldn't let him pick up on that. Admitting that I'm a forty-five-year-old "virgin" to vaginal intercourse—that would raise questions. And if I revealed to Adam that I'm gay, that might have risked making him feel uncomfortable enough to change his answers and the level of depth at which he was willing to share. And most importantly, I had to treat the respondent and the topic with respect. Otherwise, the whole thing would go off the rails.

Here's a bit of the conversation.

Me: Are there certain sexual acts or positions when you use lube more frequently? *[A closed question I should have phrased to be open.]*

Adam: I would say more when she's on top; it seems like she enjoys it more.

Me: *[Trying to understand how this helps her out]* It's enhancing her pleasure or reducing friction, or what's happening?

Adam: I want to make sure it's worthwhile for both of us.

Me: When you say worthwhile, can you elaborate on that?

Adam: Sometimes, you know *[no, Adam, I don't]*, there's certain positions I get more enjoyment out of, and certain ones it's more work for her. And I think that's where lube comes into play, where we can, so she can last longer and actually enjoy it more rather than worry about being tired.

At this point we'd been talking for about thirty minutes. Adam had arrived home and transitioned to taking the dog for a walk so he could continue to have some privacy. I could hear in the background the noises of his suburban neighborhood somewhere in the Midwest. As he neared other people, he went quiet and waited till he got farther past them. I'm sure it would have been the talk of the town if someone had heard him explicitly, yet functionally, talking on the phone about sex. But the presence of neighbors passing made our interview even more awkward, as we'd stop and start several times as he kept on his walk, and I kept asking questions. I tried to keep them open and exploratory in order for him to take the conversation in whatever direction suited his truth.

> **Me:** When you talk about prolonging it, is that a measure of time, or how are you thinking about that?

> **Adam:** It's more in the space of time that she can have multiple orgasms, and I kinda think that's a big thing that helps, so I think that's kinda the main reason for that and so forth. So that way, uh, she's not taking it . . . basically, I think it's more fun for her because if it's just up to me, it'd just take a few minutes; that's just me being a guy and everything like that. And not trying to be rude and everything.

I get the concern about reaching orgasm too quickly; that happens to most guys at some point in their lives. But I really just needed to make sure I had it all straight.

> **Me:** So, just to kind of lay it all out, you guys might have intercourse, and you might achieve an orgasm, and then you use the lube to continue to stimulate her? [*On the audio, you can hear*

my voice going way up with the words "stimulate her."] Or how does that work? *[Never has there been a more honest, open question because I honestly have no idea how that all works.]*

Adam: Um, it's usually starting with her and easier for me to have one, and there may be one more go-around where we may or may not use it at the end.

Me: Where there's still penetration involved?

Adam: Correct.

And then, just like during sex, we were done. Phew. Exhale. The awkwardness for me was over.

As I later reflected on it, this conversation with Adam wasn't all that different from my discussions with the gay men that I talked with on this project. It also aligned with what my colleague heard from the lesbians and hetero women too. What I was realizing in all of these conversations was that people use lube for largely the same reasons; what makes the difference is the anatomical equipment that's in use at the time: penis only, penis plus vagina, vagina only, with toys or without toys. It was an important reminder that we are all similar, regardless of gender, sexual orientation, or ethnicity—we are all sexual beings, looking for contact, connection, pleasure, and love from each other. Because I kept a beginner's mind and asked open questions, I was able to open the door for these stories from people of different backgrounds to emerge. Then, laying it all out, I could connect the dots, find the insight for our clients, and, also, importantly, develop cognitive empathy with Adam, the straight guy.

MORE OFTEN than not, the other person is introducing a topic and you are following on with a good open question. If you are in a position to introduce a topic, start broadly with, "Tell me more about…"

or, "How are you doing with..." Both are comfortable, nonintrusive ways to start exploring a topic, whether at work or in your personal life. (And I feel obligated to remind you to be mindful of topics that are not appropriate at work or could be construed as harassment.)

Sometimes I use a little humor to help break the ice, or I give permission for someone to take on a different role in the conversation. I've had a couple of situations with middle-aged women in a small group setting that we call friendship circles because the respondents all know each other, and we are in someone's home. The topic of menopause starts to come up, but the women aren't sure if they should go down that path or talk around it. Typically, I will disarm their discomfort by saying, "You may have noticed that I'm a man, and so I don't know anything about menopause." That use of humor, stating the obvious, usually garners a laugh and puts them at ease. It also reveals my beginner's mind, which shifts the dynamic to where they are given the power in the conversation to instruct and teach me, rather than remain respondents answering my questions. I'm still guiding the broader conversation, but I've given them the reins for this portion of the discussion.

Unlike straight sex, I have some knowledge of menopause: I've observed women, including my mom, steam up their glasses while having a hot flash. I remember one woman having hot flashes during a session. Her glasses would steam up, yet she kept on talking right through it. She likened it to stepping in and out of a hot steam sauna. Having been in and out of a steamy bathroom before, I can imagine how uncomfortable that would feel. (This is an example of me having cognitive empathy.) Having the sauna analogy made it easier to imagine what hot flashes would feel like. And with that empathy, I admire women everywhere who put up with hot flashes on a daily basis.

The first time I had the menopause talk was still relatively early in my moderating career. It was on that project talking with Boomers, the one where I met Emelia, and I happened to have an in-home friendship circle of five women. They were our evening session, and they all knew each other. They had already had a light dinner and cocktails by the time we got there. Appropriately enough, alcohol is a wonderful conversation lubricant, provided you don't let people get past a second drink. I've found that more than two drinks and they start to become impaired, which is a danger to both the interview as well as to the respondents themselves.

In this case, they were lubricated just enough and ready to share. Mention of menopause would enter the conversation but euphemistically rather than directly. They were dancing around the topic, as people will do when it's something they may have shame or stigma about. For this interview, I was the only man in the room, so I presumed the shyness was because I was there, and I was a man. That's when I pulled out my line showcasing my beginner's mind: "So, you've probably noticed I'm a guy..." which got a laugh and got them talking openly about menopause.

They covered off on hot flashes, then went on to discuss vaginal dryness as well as the irritability and "itchiness" they feel as their hormones are shifting all over the place. Once I got them feeling comfortable sharing with me, they included me in the group like I was one of them. The clients loved the candid, honest conversation, and it became one of the project's stand-out sessions due to the answers to my beginner's-mind questions. I was able to draw them out by how I treated them and the topic with respect, which led to such great honesty in their answers.

Even important yet difficult topics like sexual harassment, racism, social injustice, and politics can be brought up in a conversation as long as people treat each other with respect, hear each other out, and try to speak with recognition of the perspective of the other person.

In my personal time, I was at a dinner party in rural South Carolina with my maternal grandmother, who lived there. The party was filled with septuagenarians from the Deep South. It was just days after Matt Lauer was fired from the *Today* show for allegedly harassing female staffers. The light being shone on sexual harassment and assault kept growing brighter and brighter, and it was entering conversation for everyday Americans. As the couples were arriving, the men were being cagey and a little jokey about the whole thing, holding their hands up and saying to the women, "Oh, I'd give you a hug, but you know, sexual harassment!" indicating that they wouldn't be touching anyone.

I was saddened at their reaction, as I felt like it was belittling the cultural moment and was insensitive to what these women had experienced in their lives. So while we were standing around the kitchen counter, nibbling on appetizers, I brought the topic up for real. "So, ladies, let's talk about sexual harassment, because I'm sure you've experienced a thing or two in your life." I used an exploratory question that gave them an opportunity to agree or not, without resorting directly to a closed "yes" or "no" binary. And that question got the women sharing about what it was like working in the '60s and '70s, a time when there was no apparent recourse to harassment. One woman was a nurse, and she talked about how she'd get pinched or propositioned every time she'd bend over for something. And that was by the doctors!

As the conversation continued, we talked about the differences between harassment and assault. One by one, the men scooted off to take a look at the game on TV. I was disappointed and was hoping they would share observations, but that might have been challenging for them without accidentally incriminating themselves. Instead, they chose to "plead the Fifth" and seek safety in front of the TV. But at least the topic was out there. And their wives might have circled back to the discussion later on in a private moment when the husbands might not have felt so uncomfortable. I was really proud of this group of women for being willing to speak up, at least with each other. It didn't take much to get the conversation going; they were that ready for it.

ANOTHER WAY to ask a good question is to share a story about something that happened to someone else and get reactions to that.

A week after the septuagenarian dinner party, I was on Long Island visiting my paternal grandma (I've been incredibly fortunate to have had both of my grandmothers alive and with me well into my fifties). I shared with my then ninety-nine-year-old grandma what had happened in South Carolina. And that sharing of the stories I'd heard from the women in the South prompted my New York grandma to share her own #MeToo story.

During World War II, in 1943, she was working in an office and one of the men in the office would get too close when they were reviewing paperwork together. Suddenly, she'd find his elbow pressing into her breast. She said she would move away slightly, and he'd move over and do it again. Finally, she stepped far enough away that he couldn't continue to touch her. She said she couldn't say anything to her managers because she would have been accused of being a tramp or a floozy, doing something to invite it. The shame of being thought of as the guilty party when you are the victim has silenced too many women for too long, including my grandma.

By sharing the stories I'd heard in the South, I gave my grandma permission to share her own experience. You can use stories of others in order to get people to share their own. It's about time that we have these conversations about harassment and the way we treat each other. Whatever your gender, you can ask others about their experiences as long as they and the topic are treated with respect and you're in an appropriate forum or setting. Just like any conversation where you are building empathy, start by dismantling your judgment. You want to hear what the other person has to say. Ask good questions—in this case, it's opening the door for the topic to come out, not chasing it down.

THERE'S ONE more sexcapade that I walked into because I asked a good question while moderating that I should share. We were on a project talking to people about dinner, how they plan for it and what they turn to for solutions. One of the selected respondents was a young Millennial couple from outside of Sacramento. The wife, Karen, had an office job, while her husband, Ryan, worked from home.

When it came time to introduce himself, Ryan was cryptic about what he did. "I'm thirty-three, and I install floors and also do online sales," he told us. Typically, I spend time probing to find out more about people. Sure, you say you are in sales, but what do you sell? It really didn't seem like he would be selling the flooring online. I'm also curious to hear how people got into their jobs. Do they like what they are doing? What's a typical day like? What would they really like to do? Hearing that additional information is so critical to getting a full 360-degree view of the person. Having that fuller perspective makes it much harder to put a one-dimensional label on someone you understand in 3D.

I remember reading in the advance bio we got that he was involved in online sales, which he confirmed. But I couldn't remember what he was selling. In person, he was still not admitting what he was selling. And there was also something to do with floor installations, which could be a full-time job. I wasn't sure how those fit together, so I asked.

Me: And you said you do online sales. Of what?

Note the open, exploratory question. Ready for wherever Ryan might lead the conversation.

Ryan: Of the adult entertainment variety.

Except there.

Me: Oh, okay.

I gave an understanding nod of the head, trying to keep my lower jaw next to my upper jaw instead of letting it drop to the floor. Another "wow" moment like we had from Emmajean, except this time I had asked a well-phrased, open question; I just wasn't anticipating this answer from a suburban thirtysomething man.

I couldn't see my clients directly, but I could sense their body language behind me tighten up and constrict. (This is an example of that feeling of "putting on a show" during interviews. As a moderator I'm acutely aware of how my "audience" is responding in real time.) Only one client that was in the room stayed pretty chill. Ryan was a gem that you don't uncover too often, plus I knew the clients would be judgmental if I didn't draw out more from him, so I decided it was worth taking the time to explore. I wasn't sure where "adult entertainment variety" sales was going to go, but it was definitely going to be interesting.

> **Ryan:** I work as an agent and model in online adult entertainment. I find other "talent," if you will, and then basically [make] commission off of that and then work modestly at my own pace as well. It's good money, yeah, if you know what you're doing.

Ryan went on to tell us how he had worked in the corporate world, in hospitality, for eight years after putting himself through college as a bellman using the GI Bill after his military service. He realized working fifty to sixty hours a week on a fixed salary wasn't for him. "All my days blended together, one to the next, and then the next thing I knew it was, like, three years later," he said. After he and Karen met, he got into the adult entertainment business. "It worked, slowly but surely," he admitted. "It's fun. We have an interesting lifestyle, and we have a house, so we're doing okay, right? That's me in a nutshell. Do you have any questions I could answer for you or specifics?"

Questions?! Of course I had questions! I had lots of questions that could fill the whole two-hour session. This revelation felt like finding a hidden room filled with treasure. Tell me more! Tell me about the experience. How many of your friends know? What do they think? How long do you plan to continue doing this? The questions racing through my mind were countless. But I also knew that my clients might need help dismantling their judgment. It's not every day you meet someone who works in porn. This might very well have been outside their comfort zone. I needed the clients to stay connected to Ryan and Karen so they would accept the insights that would ultimately be shared about dinnertime, which was the actual reason why we were there. I had to first ask a few good questions that would help them get beyond judgment and continue with the 5 Steps to Empathy.

Me: How did you get into the adult entertainment industry?

Ryan: Because of her [Karen]. No, that sounds crazy. I was breathing a little bit harder when you were asking her about her. I was like, *Man, I didn't tell them specifically what my online job was; is this going to sound weird? [Yes, Ryan, it wasn't what we were expecting, but it makes for a helluva story! Thank you!]* But hey, we're good. [Karen] told me that I'm attractive, I'm in great shape; I am endowed well enough to make it happen, just to be honest with you. And I said, "Really?" She basically was like my manager. She's getting red now, but she's a business-woman at heart; I can tell you that right now.

Me: I can see who's wearing the heels. Those are some serious shoes. *[Karen was wearing some serious four-inch stilettos for our sit-down conversation.]*

Ryan: I know. I have to take those down to my little shoe shop downtown to get those things replaced often. She wears those out.

Karen: I said, "Look, if you're going to be doing stuff anyway, you might as well get paid for it."

Ryan: So, I gave it a shot. I'm clearly a yappy, Chatty Cathy kind of guy, and it just kind of worked out. It doesn't work out for everybody. As they say, of a hundred people that think about it, ten may actually sign up, and then one may actually, out of those hundred, go through with it and actually make some money. And then as far as the fact that I worked in sales for hospitality before, I've always kind of been a salesy guy. It doesn't matter if I'm actually selling a product. If I believe in something, it sounds like I'm selling because I love things that much, you know what I mean? And so, who do I love more than myself? I don't know. So that's an easy sale, right? I'm just being facetious, but it just worked out. People like the chatting aspect, as well as the physical aspects, but that's a whole different story to begin with.

Me: It has nothing to do with dinner.

Ryan: It doesn't, although that interrupts dinner sometimes.

By having Ryan tell us more about his sales focus and how he got into the field, it made him seem like any other salesperson (more or less). We took the sizzle out of the sex and revealed that a job is a job. Isn't it? That made him relatable again to my audience, the clients. Had I ignored the uncomfortable part and just focused on how Ryan cooked and ate dinner, there would have been an elephant in the room. Once that cat was out of the bag, I had to ask good questions, to dive into it, give it more context. That helped my clients dismantle their judgment and listen to Ryan. Otherwise, it would have been the equivalent of them listening to the Charlie Brown teacher for two hours. *Wah, wah wah wahhh.* Sounds with no meaning.

As we synthesized learnings a few weeks later, the session with Ryan came up several times. Not for his work in adult entertainment, but for what he *did* tell us about dinner. He and Karen ended up contributing some breakthrough insights for us that live on to this day. Had I not asked the questions that helped the team learn more and dismantle their judgment, he would have been a lurid footnote to the entire project.

When you treat a topic with respect, and you respect the opinions of the person you are talking to, you can talk with nearly anyone about nearly anything. Respect removes barriers of class, gender, ethnicity, sexual orientation, political leanings, religion, and values. Then we see each other simply as people, with stories to tell. Listen with respect; ask good questions that are open, respectful, and with a beginner's mind, and you will understand more than you imagined possible. Even about sex.

EMPATHETIC REFLECTIONS

- In my conversation with Adam about sex, I asked a closed question (Are there certain sexual acts or positions when you use lube more frequently?). If you were the researcher in this situation, how would you rephrase that question to be more open and exploratory?

- Think of a topic that you are uncomfortable with. Write down three to five questions you might ask someone about that topic. Keep the questions open, broad, and nonjudgmental.

- Now that you are learning more about good questions, take note of people around you and interviewers on TV. Who is asking a good question? How can you tell? Who is asking a not-so-good question? How would you rephrase it to make it better?

STEP 3

ACTIVE LISTENING

Without listening, it is impossible to achieve any type of empathy.
Listening is about more than the sounds that enter your ears.
Everything that we hear, see, touch, smell, taste, sense, and intuit
becomes data points and stimuli to be processed and synthesized into meaning in the moment. We must be present and
paying attention in order to pick up the signals being transmit-
ted. That is active listening.

11

Mirror, Mirror...

You use a glass mirror to see your face;
you use works of art to see your soul.
GEORGE BERNARD SHAW

I F IT WEREN'T for active listening, I would have missed some of the greatest moments of empathy, fascinating discoveries, and inspirations in my career. Listening, as you know, is synonymous with hearing. But listening goes beyond hearing. Listening is a form of "sensing"—taking in what you are detecting with all of your senses, not just your ears. Similar to hearing—where you pick up auditory signals—sensing is where you pick up the other signals coming at you. Visual, textural, olfactory, flavors, and that energetic "sixth sense." Combined, those signals take listening way beyond merely "hearing." For people who are focused on the tangible five senses, it can be challenging to tune into this sixth sense.

Like radio waves and cell phone signals that surround us at all times, these sensory signals are also ever present. We only pick up on them when we choose to tune in. It's like "selective listening"—you are choosing when and what to listen to. Like a radio, you pick up one station or "signal" at a time.

"Active listening" takes tuning in a step further. To be actively listening, I have to expand my awareness and take multiple signals in as they come to me. We hear words and sounds while active listening fills in the blanks and provides inspiration. It can turn noise into a form of music. It confirms what I heard, or it points out the contradictions that I need to ask about for clarity of understanding. Active listening also gives me a sense of the boundaries of another individual. I may hear their words, but I can also see discomfort in their eyes. The fidgeting body movements tell me when I am near a breakthrough or when I am pushing them too close to the point of shutting down. Active listening is about really noticing and paying attention to what is being communicated. It's being truly present in the moment. Otherwise, I'm not sensing or listening; I'm just hearing, and that's just noise.

I've learned to never stop my active listening, particularly when I'm meeting someone new or when I want to be truly present in a moment. This includes business meetings, research projects, and conversations with my own friends and family, whether in person or on Zoom. Active listening helps me see things I might otherwise miss. And it's usually those things that we miss that are what we should really see. Like in a stranger's bathroom.

I advise my clients joining me on an in-home to use the bathroom in the respondent's home at their own risk. I've learned that standards of cleanliness are subjective, as I discovered early in my moderating career at Bailey's home in Atlanta. In the same breath that I warn them, I also tell them that they should make a point of visiting the bathroom.

That's because the bathroom is one of the places where you get to see who a person really is.

The bathroom is where you can find the contradictions as well as the fascinating glimpses into a person's true personality. Take an affluent home as an example. What type of shampoo brand might you expect to find? I've been surprised by the number of times I'll spot a "value" brand shampoo in a home that I would expect is using premium products, based on the rest of the home furnishings. The reasons why someone has that shampoo while spending more on other things is what I want to understand and build cognitive empathy with. Either they are saving money and view it as an economical choice, or they don't value the benefits of a premium shampoo. Or maybe I'm in the guest bathroom, which says something else altogether.

The bathroom can also be its own version of an entertainment center. There's often amusing artwork and reading material stacked next to the porcelain "throne." What strikes me is that we, as humans, don't spend a significant amount of time in the bathroom compared to other rooms in the house. However, the bathroom is where we put things that might be too "silly" for other rooms. Why not put something that will make you laugh in the living room right next to the TV? Or by your bed so you can have a chuckle to foster sweet dreams? No, it's the bathroom that is the place where artwork affirmations get posted, humor is prevalent, and personality is on display. These are our moments of relief in our palace of relieve.

That is, unless it's the "guest" bathroom, in which case you'll find nothing but a sterile picture from Pottery Barn or Anthropologie, some potpourri covered in dust, and hand towels from Macy's. Maybe, if you peek in the shower, you might find that "value" shampoo. The good news is, many homes don't have the luxury of a bathroom just for guests, so when I ask to go to the bathroom, I get to use the one that the family uses. And that means I get to see the good stuff!

What's more, people often don't "tidy up" their bathroom prior to our arrival. They will clean up other parts of their house, just like you would if you were having friends over. When we arrive at someone's house, they usually have in their minds the place where the interview will take place. More than one respondent has carefully guided us through to that room that they've curated for us, all tidy and neat, pillows karate chopped to a crisp crease. It's part of the "story" that they want us to know about them. It's not really their true story, however; it's only a story they've been conditioned to believe is what they should present—the stereotype of the "perfect" American home. Like we find on TV or movies, where people lip-sync together into kitchen utensils substituting for microphones in order to solve their problems and reach a happy ending. People also compete with the façade given off by the neighbors. Everything is perfectly happy and okay with "the Joneses" next door, and so it is the same with us. And thus, the respondent attempts to shunt the real truth to the side, leaving us nothing but platitudes and niceties. The truth is that the Joneses have just as many problems as you do, maybe more. And they don't karate chop their pillows on a regular basis. That happens only if they are having company over. How do I know what's going on with the Joneses? Because I've been in their house. And since I used active listening—paying attention to the details in front of me, like the appearance of the pillows in other rooms in the house—I've been able to deduce their truth as a result.

The rooms people tend to tidy up are the kitchen, the living room if that's where they think we are going to do the interview, and usually one of the bathrooms. Since I haven't come across that many people who really like cleaning the bathroom, I suspect it just gets the once-over. Toilet is flushed, lid down (sometimes), no toothpaste caked to the side of the sink, no obvious stray hairs anywhere; we're good to go! And as I've learned, since everyone's standards are different, people typically only get it to the point where it looks good to them, which sometimes isn't much nicer than a public toilet in a city park on a hot summer day. But I do appreciate the effort.

I will say that while I'm infinitely curious, I also do respect people's privacy. That means that I don't open up anything closed, like medicine cabinets or drawers. If we're touring through a space together, I may ask the respondent to open whatever is closed in order for us to look inside. But if I'm in someone's bathroom by myself, I observe what I can take in based on what's in my line of sight, and then return to the session. Even then, you can discover some incredible finds, provided you are paying attention by actively listening.

On one in-home project, we were having a fantastic interview and conversation. We heard the respondent's life story and took a detailed tour of the entire house, which included a look into the bathroom. I had two clients with me, both women, and Natalie, the videographer. As we went room by room through the house, we'd look or step into the bedroom, bathroom, workroom in the basement, kitchen, and backyard; take a look around; ask some questions; and then move on. We then returned to the living room to continue the rest of the interview. Prior to getting started again, we decided it was a good time to have a "bio break."

I let all the women use the bathroom first while I sat in the living room, waiting my turn. I continued to make small talk with the respondent, careful not to go too deep into any topic that should be captured on camera and heard live by my clients. After a few minutes, it was my turn.

It's important to the story that I be really honest here and "overshare" just a bit because it helps explain what happened in the bathroom and why what happened was more likely to happen to me and not the women, although had they been actively listening, it would have happened to them too. You see, I had to pee. And since I'm a guy, I, like many men, pee standing up. Which is what I intended to do in this bathroom. The toilet was at the far end of this long, narrow, pink bathroom, at the end of a large tub and shower, which had a plastic curtain wrapping around it. From the door, which is where we had gathered during the house tour, the curtain obscured the view of anything but the front edge of the toilet seat. Directly across from the toilet was the sink and a cabinet.

I closed the door behind me, walked over to the toilet, unzipped my jeans, got into position, and looked down to make sure my aim was correct. (It is the worst feeling of panic when you miss in a respondent's home!) Then, I began to urinate. I tend to drink a lot of water and therefore often have a full bladder, which isn't conducive to long sit-down interviews like this one. A big mental sigh of relief crossed my mind and my bladder as I started to relieve myself.

While I wasn't experiencing an "Austin Powers just out of cryo-sleep pee of a lifetime," it lasted long enough for me to adjust my gaze up and away from where I was aiming. I looked up and saw my reflection in the mirror hanging above the toilet. The first thing I noticed was that the image of me was split in two by a somewhat diagonal, not completely straight line. So, I shifted my head a little to the left so I could see my full face in the mirror.

While I try to pay attention and use active listening at all times, you'd think I could take a break in the bathroom. But active listening is about taking in everything that's around me, including not being myopic or too narrowly focused in my vision. Otherwise, I risk missing the bigger picture. Fortunately for me in this case, that diagonal bisection of my initial view of myself cued me that there was something more to this. That I should widen my field of vision to take in the rest of the mirror. I adjusted my gaze and noticed there was stained glass around all four sides and that just the center portion was the actual mirror. But I was still looking too narrowly. I wasn't taking in the entire piece hanging on the wall above the toilet in front of me. What kind of shape in a mirror would have a diagonal line? It wasn't something I'd seen in a store anywhere.

I broadened my view even more, moved my head back, and glanced up and down to take in the full shape of the mirror.

That's when my eyes widened slightly, and my jaw dropped. I wish I had a picture of my reaction. I'm not sure which expression of "wow" I registered. And it is ironic because I was looking in a mirror at the time. I didn't see my reaction, though, because I wasn't looking at my reflection in the mirror; I was looking at the mirror itself.

The mirror was actually a piece of art. A larger frame of stained glass held inside it the exclamation-mark shape of a well-endowed, erect penis and testicles made of mirror glass.

Like I said, you don't have to violate someone's privacy to learn more about them. Personality and truth are on display right there out in the open. You just have to actively listen by keeping your eyes open and being aware of your surroundings. And there I was, eyes wide open, staring at a penis mirror! This respondent had a penis mirror hanging in the primary bathroom in her house! Forget potpourri and dainty hand towels from Macy's; this bathroom contained a significant, epic declaration of self. We had heard some great stories from this respondent earlier in the session, but nothing that would have led me to believe she'd have a penis mirror in her bathroom. I finished my business, washed my hands, and left the bathroom, dying to find out the story behind the mirror.

THE DISCOVERY of the mirror is a perfect illustration of active listening. I saw it because I was open and paying attention to my surroundings, not just the task at hand. As I returned to the living room where we were having the interview, I recalled that my female clients had all been in the bathroom before me. None of them had said anything about it. Not a single one. Surely, had the rest of my group seen this, it would have elicited some sort of reaction from them. It's not every day you find a penis mirror in the bathroom of a respondent's home. In fact, this moment ranks for me as one of the greatest finds in my professional career. I know, I know. It's a penis mirror. But as I was about to find out, it had meaning far deeper than a mere *objet d'humour*.

I sat back down in the living room, directly in front of the respondent. I composed myself and said, with a slightly puzzled look on my face, "Emelia, I was just in your bathroom, and I couldn't help but notice—" I couldn't get the full question out before she roared with laughter, which made my female clients wonder what was going on. Yes, it was Emelia's home, and it was that same wonderful laugh that she had seduced us with in the first part of our session, when she was telling us how to "turn it around" and inspired my journey toward tai chi, greater self-awareness, and empathy.

I was eager to hear Emelia's perspective on men, penises, and the story behind that mirror. Amid her laughter, I suggested that my clients go into the bathroom and take a look over the toilet.

One by one they proceeded down the hall to Emelia's bathroom. From the living room we could hear their own burst of laughter. Then they came back in, still smiling, and sent the next person in. This repeated until everyone had taken a look, even Natalie the videographer. And then we sat down to hear Emelia's story behind the penis mirror.

Emelia, as I've mentioned, was a middle-aged African American woman living in the near suburbs of Philadelphia. She had divorced her husband years ago and had dated a string of gentlemen, but none of them had won her over. She was also spending a lot of time with her girlfriends and observed how they made themselves crazy and changed themselves for the sake of having a man.

One day, Emelia told us, she was at an art fair, and at one of the booths was an artist who worked with stained glass, and one of her girlfriends knew him personally. Emelia asked him if he did commissions. He said he did. She took a piece of paper and sketched out what she wanted, an erect penis and balls with a ropey vein running down the shaft.

A few weeks later, it arrived. Emelia chose the bathroom as the place to display it. She told us, "Every morning I come into the bathroom, see it, and remind myself that I have *that*. And I don't need to do anything to have *that*. I can enjoy *that* as much as I want. I've seen too many women change themselves and go crazy for *that*, and I won't do it anymore."

That fierce piece of female empowerment art and the declaration of independence was worth ten thousand words. She was like every empowerment anthem and Terry McMillan character all rolled into one wonderful human being.

While I'm sure Emelia has her own support networks and close relationships, she was clearly standing on her own, a survivor who knew how to keep life in perspective and, in turn, reminded me to do the same. Active listening, paying attention, and being present enabled me to move toward a stronger empathetic understanding of Emelia. What was surprising was that we had already toured the house, including the bathroom. And no one had noticed the mirror! Not during the house tour, not even the second visit when all the female clients went to the bathroom! Was that because the toilet was at the very back of the bathroom, which was narrow to begin with, so we didn't step all the way in? Did they miss it, but I saw it because I was facing a different direction when I used the toilet? Or were we so focused on the conversation in the living room and getting back to it that we simply missed the bigger picture every time? Were we not really present? Had I not employed active listening when I was using the toilet, I would not have widened my field of view. Without active listening I could not have been able to notice what was right in front of my face the entire time.

EMPATHETIC REFLECTIONS

- Next time you are at a friend or family member's home, use active listening and make note of the items and nonverbal cues you notice. How does it align with what you know about this person? What else does it tell you? How does it help you understand who they are as a person?

- On a scale of 1 to 5 (with 5 being highest), how present are you in a typical conversation? With a loved one? An acquaintance? A boss/client? A friend? A neighbor? A clerk at the store? What's the difference in each scenario? What could you do to improve by 1 point on the scale?

12

The Birth
of Venus

---

*You may encounter many defeats, but you must
not be defeated. In fact, it may be necessary to encounter
the defeats, so you can know who you are, what you
can rise from, and how you can still come out of it.*

MAYA ANGELOU

JUDGMENT IS THE noise-canceling headphones of active listening. It blocks out everything, so you only hear what you want
to hear, not what you need to hear. In other words, it stops you
from being present.

Here's an example you might relate to. You made plans to go to
the movies with a close friend or romantic interest. You showed up
on time and waited. And waited. You began to get annoyed. Finally,
you got a text or a phone call. The other person was flaking; they
had to cancel. At that point you had a choice. You could either let
your emotions out, lay into them, and "tell them what you think,"
letting your judgment spew, or you could put your judgment (those
noise-canceling headphones) aside and listen to their explanation.

It may require taking a deep inhale and exhale breath to return to an emotional calm where you can focus, not just listening to the words themselves but also to the intonation, the emotion behind the words. You might even have been sensing something that wasn't said. If you could see them, there are nonverbal cues you may have picked up on: Were they making eye contact or looking away? Was their body language defensive or open? What do you feel they might have wanted to say but weren't saying? Could you keep your judgment at bay throughout the conversation or did it want to keep poking its head out? Once you have actively listened, then you can Integrate into Understanding (Step 4), then Use Solution Imagination (Step 5), and then, at that point, respond.

If we can't get beyond our judgment, it gets in the way of how we actively listen. It's why we have to use Step 1, Dismantle Judgment, repeatedly before we can achieve Step 3, Active Listening. It can feel like one step forward, two steps back. Getting to a place of empathy is anything but linear. Remember to take off your noise-canceling headphones.

ONE INTERVIEW in particular presented a lot of work for me to actively listen in order to get to a place of empathy. It was meant to be a sit-down in-home, but the respondent had seemingly "flaked" on the interview and left us hanging. The clients were beginning to brim with judgment. It was like they had those noise-canceling headphones on. Once an interview gets going, I can't turn and tell them to dismantle their judgment. Instead, I have to guide by actively listening and asking good questions, in the hopes that the clients will take their noise-canceling headphones off, dismantle their judgment, and also actively listen to the point of understanding and reaching empathy.

It was a slightly humid Texas morning when we rolled up to the house, an unremarkable deep-olive-green ranch situated on a corner, with a large fenced-in backyard in an older neighborhood. The clients, the videographer, and I gathered our bags and gear and climbed out of the car. A moist, sunny warmth greeted us on the driveway. Together, we walked up to the front door and rang the buzzer.

A dog was barking in the distance. Was the barking coming from inside the house? A neighbor's? Hard to tell. There was a lengthy wait. No one answered.

One of the clients walked around the side of the house and noticed another door by the carport with the letter B on it. Maybe Iris, the respondent we were scheduled to meet, lived in the "in-law unit." We all trudged around the house under the weight of our backpacks, camera equipment, and moist Texas sun to door number two.

I rang the buzzer. It was now 9:06 a.m. No answer on this "B" side either, although the dog's barking did appear to be coming from behind door B. If Iris was home, surely she'd hear her dog and get the door. No answer.

I texted my colleague, Jen, who had set up the interview. Had she heard from the respondent? Last-minute cancellations are rare, but they do happen. Jen texted back that she'd heard nothing but that she had called Iris and only got voicemail. It was now 9:13 a.m.

The time was coming for me to make a decision on whether or not to cut bait and move on to an alternate's house. I was feeling some stress. The show must go on! Even though we take extra care to talk to people ahead of time, building rapport and trying to determine if a person will flake on us or not, it can still happen. Sometimes life comes up, like a child gets sick, or the respondent can't get out of work at the last minute. Sometimes they just bail. All of these scenarios were running through my mind. I was half expecting Iris to drive up in a car at this point, late getting home from working an overnight shift or running an errand or some other random life-gets-in-the-way excuse. She must have been out. I didn't see how anyone could be inside the house after all of our buzzing, the dog barking, and repeated phone calls and texts. Except there was a car parked in the carport. Hers?

I made small talk with the clients while practically leaning on the doorbell. The mood was starting to get tense. *Where is Iris?* we were all wondering. *This is bizarre*, I thought to myself. I rang the buzzer another time or two, not wanting to admit defeat.

Jen texted me again. She'd called Iris yet again and still no answer. Did I want to move on to the alternate? I looked at my watch. The time was now 9:23 a.m. The interview was scheduled to start at 9:00. Where was Iris? I was getting ready to call it a loss and go to the alternate's home across town.

Suddenly, we heard the tumbling of door locks and the twist of the doorknob. The door released from its snug frame and began to open. The shadow of the carport and the diffusion of the screen door prevented me from seeing who was standing there until the screen door was cracked open. Emerging from that darkness, Iris stood before us. She was young and tall, with creamy white skin, a dewy complexion, and a face framed by long damp hair, soft coral pink in color.

Taking her in, I realized I was able to see both of her bare shoulders and arms—a lot more skin than I usually see on a respondent. As I began to gaze downward, I saw that she only had a towel wrapped around her. Her skin was glistening with moisture. Legs bare. No shoes, socks, or slippers. Looking for rational explanations as to what was going on, I thought to myself, *She must have been in the shower*. I continued to process the thought. *But for twenty-five minutes? That's a long shower when you know you have people coming over.* It didn't make sense.

"I'm sorry. I overslept," Iris said casually to us, more than twenty minutes after we had first started ringing her buzzer. Instead of having a tone of mortified embarrassment, she was more matter-of-fact, as though this happened all the time.

Iris was an attractive twenty-four-year-old. And it was her hair that stood out in particular. Swept back, off her face, it was damp, like she had been towel drying it, then ran a comb through it. The coral color, a pink faded over a couple months with soft, natural blond roots blending in, struck me most. Her hair continued down to about the middle of her back. In that moment, the image that popped into my head was Botticelli's *The Birth of Venus*. Iris's skin was that same alabaster cream color of the goddess Venus arriving on the shore; both had coral hair flowing down around their bodies. Venus brought physical beauty and the recognition of spiritual beauty with her. Completed toward the end of the great awakening during the Renaissance period, *The Birth of Venus* symbolizes the arrival of love for physical as well as spiritual beauty.

"C'mon in while I get dressed," Iris said to the three men, the female client, and the female videographer, all standing in her carport.

"No, that's okay," I quickly insisted, "you get dressed first. Take your time." I wasn't afraid of what we would do if we went inside; I knew the team with me quite well, but I was more sensitive to what could be *claimed* to have happened if we were all in this young woman's home while she was getting dressed. Even though she invited us in, I didn't want to risk making anyone, the clients or Iris, uncomfortable in any way. We spent a few more minutes on the porch while she got dressed. What had taken her so long to answer the door was still a mystery. I was concerned that either I, the clients, or all of us would end up stuck in judgment of Iris for being so egregiously late. She practically had flaked on us. I'd have to explore what had happened a little more. Since it's a delicate balancing act of inquiring to understand what happened versus making her feel shame about her tardiness, I would need to find good open questions to ask.

She returned to the door a few minutes later and let us in. She had put on olive-green shorts and a black T-shirt. Her damp hair was now pulled back and up in a loose bun. While we were getting set up, I had her sign our consent form and made some small talk. I was sitting directly across from Iris, and as I was getting my voice recorder and paperwork out, I noticed her T-shirt. It said the name of a high school and "Science Olympiad." It was the type of swag shirt that you would only have if you were the participant in the Science Olympiad or you regularly hunted for finds at Goodwill. I asked Iris about the T-shirt, and she admitted that she was a nerd in high school and that this was, in fact, her participant T-shirt. Impressive! She might run really late for an interview, but she must be smart if she was in a Science Olympiad.

The clients were all lined up on an old, tattered sofa that was across from the counter Iris and I were sitting at. They all had their notebooks out, pens in hand, ready to actively listen and jot down notes and observations. The room was a kind of living room/sunroom, and it seemed to have been created by closing in the original exterior of the house and combining it with the patio. The house wasn't exactly tidy, nor was it filthy. Let's say it looked "highly lived-in."

I got the signal that we were "at speed" (meaning we were recording). The topic of this project was sweet cereal and getting to know the people who love it. I prepared to start, as I do every interview, with general, broad, open questions.

Since we had such a late start, my usual list of good questions that was in the discussion guide flew out the window. I improvised by starting with a broad exploratory question about her background. "Tell me about yourself." She'd grown up in the upper Midwest, went to college there, then decided she didn't like the cold, so she moved someplace warmer. She found work first as an executive assistant. It didn't last too long, as she came to despise the executive, so she found work in customer service, working second shift for a tech company.

We actively listened, paying attention to the nuances, what hadn't been said compared to what was being said, and what we were sensing might lie beneath the surface.

This type of attention paid to the early open questions gives you rich context as to who a person is, what brings them joy in their life, and what their possible trials and tribulations might be. With Emmajean, I had started with "how are you?" and it all rolled from there. The listening is just as important as the questioning when trying to build empathy. It takes listening in order to hear someone else's perspective. The challenge is to be "headphones off," tuned in, paying attention, and looking for it. Otherwise you'll miss their perspective, just like with the noise-canceling headphones, or in the way someone walking down the street with their head looking down at their phone misses the scenery passing them by. In this interview, I was listening for anything that would give me perspective on how Iris managed to oversleep through doorbells, ringing phones, and barking dogs.

Me: What do you do for fun?

Iris: Mm, that's a good question. So, I actually have a sleep disorder, so I spend a lot of time sleeping, which doesn't leave a whole lot of room for hobbies. My hobby is napping, basically.

We were six minutes into a conversation that had started thirty-five minutes late, and a big influence on her life had just become apparent. Clearly this was why she had overslept that morning. By actively listening to her and noticing—the T-shirt, her choice of words—I could tell there was a lot more to Iris than the first impression of an irresponsible, oversleeping young woman. I decided that I needed to dig deeper than usual into her life, to find out more about who she was and what was going on with that sleep disorder. If I didn't, then I ran the risk that the clients would not be able to really connect with her. She'd become a war story told on future projects— "that girl that overslept"—rather than visible as the complex woman she appeared to be in only a few minutes of conversation. I needed to use my own empathy-building skills to help the clients get past their own judgment. I needed to get past *my* judgment to actively listen to Iris. That meant picking up and exploring the nuances and details to paint a picture of Iris that my clients could relate to empathetically. Otherwise, whatever she had to say on the topic of sweet cereal would be diminished in value. They might feel that it had been a waste of their time, or their money, or both.

From the Science Olympiad T-shirt to how she spoke with us, I could tell from the beginning of the conversation that Iris was really bright and seemed self-aware. She also had thoughtful, well-articulated answers to my questions, better than most other respondents. I didn't want her responses to be minimized by the clients because of this sleep disorder. I probed to learn more.

Me: If I can ask, what's the sleep disorder?

Iris: Essentially, I have narcolepsy. Technically, I have a much longer diagnosis with a whole lot of words in it, but yeah.

Me: So, how does that play out for you? What happens?

Iris: Pretty much if you leave me alone in a room for twenty minutes and you come back, I'll probably be asleep. I don't fall asleep unexpectedly when I'm doing things very much, but I get, like, overwhelmingly tired at times, and it's like I am going to fall asleep in five minutes regardless of where I am, so I need to be somewhere that's okay.

Me: Do you get, like, a kind of five-minute warning, so to speak?

Iris: Yeah. I get more tired, but unlike, I think, a regular person, I can't snap myself out of it. I can't be like, "Okay, I'm going to stand up and walk around, and then I won't be tired anymore." I'll stand up and walk around and I'll, like, lose memory. Like, my last memory that I have will be *I'm really tired*, and then I'll wake up three hours later.

Me: Wow. So, do I need to be concerned? Is that going to happen?

Iris: No, not during this.

Me: What tends to go on when you do, like...

Iris: It's usually when I've been awake for more than a couple hours. Like, it doesn't usually happen immediately after I wake up, and it definitely doesn't happen while I'm talking to people, that kind of thing. It's more just like ... It's like a normal person, like you feel tired sometimes, except for when I feel tired, I go to sleep.

Me: You completely go to sleep.

Iris: Yeah.

Me: You mentioned, like, three hours. Do you end up sleeping for that long usually?

Iris: Yeah. It's actually really hard to wake me up. I had an alarm set, but then you guys ended up actually waking me up. Well, more accurately, the dog alarm woke me up. They're useful for that.

Me: Yeah, definitely. So, how long have you had this?

Iris: Since I was about seventeen. At first, I really thought it was—I mean, everybody thought it was just, like, being a teenager. I would come from high school and just fall asleep until my parents got home at, like, eight o'clock every day. And I don't know, none of us were particularly concerned at that point. But then when I got into college, it didn't really go away, and by my junior year of college, it was a problem.

Me: How so?

Iris: Basically, [...] it got worse over time, and that was the year that I started falling asleep in public places and doing things and then not having any memory of doing it because I was tired at the time and, like, sleeping seventeen hours a day. Yeah, that's when we started to kind of suspect that there was something unusual. So then I went and got a sleep study, and they attach like a million electrodes to your head and a bunch to the rest of your body and put a tube in your nose to measure your throat pressure, just not the world's most comfortable thing.

Me: Yeah, but I'm guessing you were probably able to fall asleep.

Iris: Yes. I would immediately pass out.

Me: And did they know right away what was going on?

Iris: Well, they knew that I was an abnormally tired person because I fell asleep instantly, which doesn't happen very often in a sleep lab because of all the things attached to you. And then because mine was being overtired, I had to stay for the night and then the next day, and during the day they had, like, five periods where they're like, "Okay, now lay down on the bed and try to go to sleep." And I fell asleep within minutes for every single one. They were like, "That's unusual."

Me: So, do a lot of people have this?

Iris: Not a whole lot. Mine's kind of weird in that I just barely missed the qualifications for narcolepsy. Like, I probably have narcolepsy; it's just I fell asleep thirty seconds too late. They measure how fast you drop into REM when you fall asleep, basically, and I took very, very slightly longer than the guidelines for narcolepsy. So they were like, "Yeah, you have idiopathic hypersomnia with delayed sleep phase and long sleep phase disorder; treat it like narcolepsy." I was like, "Okay." And then yeah, they put me on medication, and now I'm significantly more functional. The less stressed out I am, the easier it is for me, and the more stressed out, the easier it is for me to fall asleep.

Me: So the more stressed out, the easier it is to fall asleep.

Iris: Yeah, and the less stressed out, it's easier just to stay awake.

I was curious to know more about what her life was like, living with this condition. How did she adapt? A glance over at my clients on the sofa revealed that they were now engrossed in Iris's story. They were getting beyond their own judgment, possibly to a place of sympathy and feeling bad for her. My goal was to get them to a place of empathy—seeing her as a person, and valuing what she had to say when we finally got to the conversation about cereal. So I continued to explore.

Iris worked the second shift since those hours aligned more closely to her natural schedule. She relied on alarms—many of them, it sounded like. She didn't have much time for hobbies in her personal time, as she spent a lot of it asleep. "Yeah, and I sleep at work on my lunch break. Like every day, I don't take lunch; I take a nap," she said. The alarm on her phone, placed right under her ear, helped her make sure she didn't sleep for more than her hour lunch break. On the executive assistant job she'd detested, she'd regularly end up napping for three to four hours, which probably didn't help relations with the executive she was assisting.

What I was having difficulty reconciling (aka Step 4: Integrate into Understanding) at this point in the conversation was how smart and well-educated Iris appeared to be compared with how she described her life. She just seemed scary smart. I went to a place of judgment, based on my own stereotypes. Iris came across as so smart and articulate and poised that I would have expected she'd be on her way in a career in some advanced-degree field. Instead of holding on to my stereotype-based judgment, I set that aside and decided to ask a good (although close-ended) question.

Me: Wow. I'm curious: is this what you imagined life would be like if we'd talked to you seven years ago, before diagnosis?

Iris: No, not at all. I think in a lot of ways it's limited my ability to kind of progress with my life. I think I probably would've chosen a more difficult or extensive career path if it wasn't for having to sleep so much. [But] I really enjoy customer service because I'm weird and broken that way.

Me: What do you mean?

Iris: Like, how many people really enjoy being in customer service? I know a lot of people that work in customer service, and there's an unfortunately high percentage of people that actually just hate customers.

Me: Which is probably why the customer service is so bad in so many places.

Iris: In a lot of places, yeah.

Me: What is it that you like about customer service, though?

Iris: I enjoy solving problems and sort of connecting with different people. A lot of it is just that people throw a problem at you. Like, person after person after person, it's a different problem almost every time; there's just different nuances to it. You know, you see some of the same stuff, but there's always something new, and it just gives you an opportunity to kind of figure out how things work, and with our software figure out how our structures are put together and how things, like, what information is important and what's not, and that kind of thing.

Me: And what did you want to . . . You said this has altered your kind of career choices.

Iris: Before the sleep disorder, I wanted to go into medicine. I wanted to be a doctor, and, basically, if you go pre-med in college, then you don't sleep that much. You're very busy, and definitely so if you're a doctor. Like, during residency and whatnot, it's not really, it doesn't really work very well if you sleep all the time.

Me: How do you feel about having to . . .

Iris: I mean, it's sad, but it's not really, you know, I don't know that I would have been successful in that direction anyway, so it's kind of like this is what my life is, so figure it out.

Me: Yeah, definitely. Well, thank you. That gives us a lot of context for my next question, which is what's a typical day like for you?

And just like that, the conversation transitioned to her day-to-day comings and goings.

Later on, Iris took us to her bedroom to let us look around. She was really hesitant to take us in there, citing that it was a mess. I reassured her that I had seen messy before, always thinking about Bailey's house in Atlanta years earlier. Then we went into the bedroom, which lived up to her claims of it being messy. It resembled a stereotypically messy college sophomore's dorm room. As I first gazed around the room, I was eyes wide open, taking it all in. There was a ton of stuff lying about—on the floor, in and on the cabinets and countertops. Most every horizontal surface area seemed to have things on it—books, half-emptied packages of food, electronics, cosmetics, toys, clothes, accessories. If her possessions represented her life, it was far from tidy. It was splayed out on display, just begging for organization. Maybe even for meaning?

Makeup completely covered one table. Clothes were spread out everywhere. She knew where things were and was able to point stuff out to us, but to a first-time visitor, it was intense. We had to step gingerly to find clear spots on the carpet to stand without crushing a lipstick or stepping on underwear or a T-shirt. She also had boxes of cereal (something very relevant to our project yet tucked away in a room we might not have gone into, which made me glad we did!). And there was an empty carton of ice cream on her nightstand. She said she managed to finish that one before nodding off. Otherwise, she'd eat only "dry" snacks, like chips or cookies or even dry cereal. Falling asleep mid-munch with those snacks wasn't nearly as disastrous for her as waking up to discover she'd slept in a puddle of Chubby Hubby, which she said had happened more than once.

Often while touring parts of the house, I am looking for consistencies with and contradictions to the stories people had told us earlier in the interview. So, the ice cream, the cereal, the cookies, all made sense. I could see the evidence right in front of me. And there was the TV she watched, right at the foot of the bed.

Iris: I live a lot of my life in bed.

Me: Yeah, it sounds like it.

Iris: But I have a very comfortable bed. I love that. You spend a long time in it, you care about your mattress.

Iris went on to explain her preference for memory foam as well as a waterproof cover on her mattress. Her medication for the sleep disorder produced "profuse night sweats" as a side effect, and she would "literally soak [her] mattress." She told us, "People don't believe how much I sweat at night until they see it, and then they're like, 'Oh my god, it looks like you peed the bed.' And I'm like, 'I know, I'm aware.'"

And suddenly I was able to connect more dots. Her glistening skin and damp hair at the front door—she hadn't showered; she had just woken up, soaking wet from her own sweat.

And then something else I had picked up on when Iris had first answered the door—with her damp pink hair and wrapped only in a towel—revealed itself to me as I looked around her room.

Me: What's that poster?

Iris: Oh, *The Birth of Venus*. I went to art school, actually, so theoretically I'm an art-type person. I have a little bit of art around, but not a ton because I want to move. I never fully unpacked while I was here.

I didn't want to mention to her about how I'd had a mental flash of that Botticelli painting when she'd first greeted us, but holy cow! In my mind I had a sense of her as Venus, and there was Venus, right in her home! Clearly, she had been inspired by this piece of art and adapted her appearance to reflect the inspiration. This was a case of active listening with my intuition and sensing, starting when Iris answered the door, and I picked up on the vibe she was transmitting about herself. I took the poster to be a statement about Iris and where she was in her life—arriving to an awareness of her inner and outer beauty and working with the hand she'd been dealt.

I couldn't get over how much this sleep disorder had changed the course of her life. Look beyond the coral hair, the piercings, the second-shift customer service job, the messy bedroom, and the fact that she'd overslept and was late to an appointment in her own home. Put the judgment aside—the real Iris was becoming visible to us. I'd had a glimmer of her when the interview first started, how articulate she was, how thoughtful and intelligent her responses were. But I'd underestimated her. She was the real deal. A smart, smart, smart woman. She was a Science Olympian for her school! She'd wanted to be a doctor! Except she wasn't able to become a doctor due to her condition.

For me, Iris was an example of how events in our life—whether big or small; intentional or unintentional; incidents, accidents, or serendipity—can have long-term implications, not just for ourselves but for others too.

Iris was never going to be a doctor. There was a different path for her. I believe each one of us has a purpose as to what we are to achieve in this lifetime. I was torn up for years after meeting Iris that she wasn't going to be the one to cure cancer or AIDS or Alzheimer's. That life had been cruel and steered her life off course. I would tear up when I shared her story during lectures and presentations—that she wasn't able to fulfill what I saw as her potential.

Now I wonder, *Was that really the course she was supposed to be on?* Perhaps there was another purpose waiting for her. Something other than medicine, more relevant to what she needed to tackle in this lifetime. Iris was figuring herself out, like so many twentysomethings. Her decision to physically resemble Botticelli's Venus may have been accidental, or it may have been intentional. Nevertheless, Iris, like the goddess, was arriving. The side door of a Texas carport is hardly a mystical clamshell, but it can be a symbolic one. Iris was in the process of arriving on the shores of her own being.

She'd be greeted by an adulation so complete and fulfilling because it is the adulation of self-love. Acceptance of oneself and a deeper knowing of your being, which in turn allows people to adore and love the real you.

I no longer pretend to know the purpose of Iris's life or shed a tear over what her life could have been. I know she inspired me, and, in turn, by sharing her story, I've been able to inspire others. I'm reminded of Iris every time I interact with someone in customer service. You won't know the story of that person until you ask. And truly listen. It's a lesson for any interaction we have with an employee, a colleague, or someone else in our life. We have to ask the questions and listen to the answers. We have all been Iris at some point in our lives, traveling on our mystic clamshell toward the meaning of our life and what we have to offer, which is the real beauty that lies within each one of us.

EMPATHETIC REFLECTIONS

- How would you have responded if you were me in this situation? Would you have left before Iris answered the door? How would you have approached the conversation? What would it take for you to have kept listening?

- When have you had on the "noise-canceling headphones" of judgment? How did you take them off? What were you able to notice once they were gone?

- When has active listening served you and you noticed something that gave you insight into the person you were talking to?

13

The Ghost
in the Room

*You must train your intuition—you must trust the small voice
inside you which tells you exactly what to say, what to decide.*

INGRID BERGMAN

SOMETIMES I HAVE to make a snap decision to change direction in a conversation based on something that I can sense but can't quite put my finger on. Perhaps you've had this happen before. You are having an external conversation, and suddenly a little voice inside you that isn't your brain but something else, speaks up and guides you to take the conversation in a new direction. For me, this happens when I'm present and actively listening to the person I'm talking to—picking up on what's not being said, the non-verbal cues as well as what they are saying. And then there's what I'm sensing, my intuition, which I've also learned to listen to.

The word *sensing* gets confusing. I use it to refer to my intuition, but it's also associated with the tangible five senses. In the Myers-Briggs personality test, S is for "sensing," but a person with an S is about what they have in front of them, whereas the N is the person who is more intuitive and "sensing" what might be going on.

(I'm an ENFP, in case you are wondering.) And because I believe intuition is a sixth sense, it can get confusing. I rely on all six of my senses, especially when I'm trying to build empathy and compassion. Everyone readily knows five of the senses: sight, touch, taste, smell, and hearing. The sixth sense is the one that's more elusive, and I find people tend to ignore it. It has several names, including intuition and gut feeling. I describe it as that sensing of what lies just beyond what I am seeing, hearing, or comprehending with my other senses. It shows up as the little voice inside my head, or sometimes it also manifests as a feeling in my heart center or my gut. Again, it's harder for the S person to tap into their intuition, which can create barriers when trying to actively listen with six senses as well as integrate into understanding. My guidance is to have awareness of this difference and see if you can catch yourself sticking to the five senses so you can move beyond them. Then, actively listen a little deeper to a voice that might be coming from inside you. What is it saying? For many, that's intuition.

The example of intuition that I find people can relate to is that well-known situation where we ignore our intuition and step into danger. It's the dark-alley scenario. Do you go down a dark alley alone at night to save a few minutes? It seems empty and quiet according to your five senses. But is it really? At a base level, intuition is what helps you sense the danger signals so you can go into "fight or flight" mode. The alley may seem safe. However, the hairs on the back of your neck are standing up. Maybe you feel a sort of tingle in your body or a knot in the pit of your stomach. Or a voice inside your head warns you that this isn't the best idea. All of those are forms of intuition. What would you do? Trust your intuition? Or tune out your intuition and head down the dark alley?

Unfortunately, intuition is the one sense we humans often ignore. It's pretty incredible when you think about it. We trust our other senses. But intuition, because it isn't as easily understood, and there aren't visible body parts acting as receptors, and it's just a little too woo-woo for some people, gets ignored. We downplay it when others share their instincts and even ignore our own. That's how we end up making a judgment to ignore those bad vibes and go off down the dark alley, even though we "know" better, hoping for the best.

Knowing this, I try to listen to my own intuition when I hear it. When I have, it's been profoundly impactful, like on one project in Boston.

It was mid-October, and the fall foliage was breathtaking. It was also the start of soup season, which meant it was the perfect time for a project to find out why and how people eat canned soup.

ONE AFTERNOON we were scheduled to meet with Jonathan, a mid-fifties, married father of two girls. After we got there, the videographer and the clients hopped out of the car and headed to the door. I was late leaving the car, rapidly tapping out one last email on my phone before I turned my attention to the interview.

My clients on this project, Krista and Roger, were no strangers to in-homes. They proceeded to go to the door and knock. I heard a very joyful, "Hello, come on in," greeting from a man who I guessed must be Jonathan. It was the type of welcome that immediately puts you at ease and makes you feel at home. Something inside me, my intuition, told me this was going to be a great interview.

Jonathan lived in a modest two-level house on a relatively busy street. He and his wife were now empty nesters, and their home had the signs of the comfortable wear from daily life where you want to just sink into the overstuffed sofa, cradle a cup of coffee in your hands, and have a chat. Or maybe cuddle up with a bowl of soup. Jonathan had a small business that he ran out of his house, which is what gave him the flexibility to meet with us on a sunny October afternoon while his wife worked at her office job.

During those minutes of getting the paperwork signed and the camera set up, we made small talk with Jonathan, who continued to be warm and effusive. He was putting us at ease more than the other way around. Finally, it was time for us to sit down and officially start the interview. I usually open the interview with a softball question: "Please introduce yourself. Tell us your name, age, and the names and ages of the other people in the house." On this occasion, I tried something a little different since he worked in sales, was very open, and I thought it might elicit an interesting answer. I asked him, "So, just kind of introduce yourself. What's the elevator pitch?"

His reply was hardly an elevator pitch, nor was it what I expected.

Jonathan: There may be tears involved just because my life, as I was telling [the videographer] a bit, is in a major point of transition. Because the guy on the radiator over there to the left, *[indicating a photo]* standing against the Wailing Wall in Jerusalem, is my nephew, and he just died two months ago.

Me: I'm sorry.

Jonathan: Thank you. So am I.

Me: So tell me about him. What happened?

Jonathan: He had cancer. A Ewing's sarcoma. They actually found it in his leg when he was thirteen, and that was over thirteen years ago. He started chemo three days later and had four recurrences. He fought extremely hard and was a miracle because nobody had ever, in the world, survived two recurrences. Let alone three. Let alone four.

Me: And it's called a Ewing's sarcoma? I haven't heard of that.

Jonathan: It's not actually very prevalent in males to a large degree. Ted Kennedy's son lost his leg from it.

Me: Okay.

Jonathan: And Daniel lost his fibula and part of his lung, and then another part of his lung because it metastasized to that. The two girls *[pointing at the photos]* are my daughters, and Daniel and [his brother] are my boys. They lived five miles from here. I'm very relationship oriented and connected to people and my family. The loss of him has changed me and is going to be part of the continuing change, as I am on the first stages of a rather profound spiritual quest, vision journey, whatever it might be. My family means everything to me, and my friends.

His eyes were welling up with tears as we sat together on the sofa. Some people are able to access and express their emotions readily, while others have them buried deep down. From the hard wiring we are born with to the experiences life deals us and the role models that shape us as we grow, we all approach sharing our feelings differently. I tend to wear my feelings on my sleeve. It makes me terrible at poker and terrific at spreading happiness. For some people and in some cultures, emotions are often considered too taboo to share. Which is really a loss for all of us, since emotions provide a richness, like color in our lives. Without emotion, without expressing emotion, you are keeping yourself bottled up and limiting others from seeing you fully as a human being. And when you are trying to get to know someone or connect with them, emotions are part of the connection.

The emotions in storytelling are often the texture that gives a story depth or heart. And it's not just the telling of a story—the emotions need to be present in the person, just beneath the surface, in order for them to come through. When you ask questions of someone, some people are able to give you emotion right away, and that helps you connect. As a friend or colleague, you shouldn't try to dig to get emotion out of someone; accept that they either can give it to you or they can't. As a moderator, in the quest for the truth, sometimes I tap into the emotions of the respondent with an innocent question about a memory, and that can bring tears; other times I have to really dig and dig to get them to access their emotions. And it isn't about getting someone to cry; I just want to hear some degree of happiness or disappointment when they are relaying how a product or service makes them feel. That adds texture and depth to our learning, and we can pass that on. With a topic as upsetting as the death of a young loved one, the emotions will usually be right there, ready to come forward. Jonathan was no exception.

He detailed how his nephew had gone to Boston University after getting accepted into a prestigious graduate-level theater program, in spite of the cancer.

> **Jonathan:** It's been nuts *[lots of changes with work and moving his company]*, and then in the middle of that, Daniel was going through what we believed was another successful fight until they could find the ultimate cure. Instead it turned out to be his final death struggle. But it wasn't his death struggle until just the last three weeks because that's not who he was. He just lived.

I sensed something, even from those opening minutes. Nothing physical, but there was definitely a presence in the room. An energy. I can only describe it as a hazy white aura that I couldn't see with my eyes but that I could sense was there. I didn't feel uncomfortable with its presence. It wasn't creepy or anything, but it was definitely there in the room with us. It was evident that it was also pulling on Jonathan's mental bandwidth, as though Daniel was in the room with us. In my "mind's eye," it seemed like he was floating about three feet above Jonathan. He spoke more about his nephew than himself, but it was also his way of telling us about himself and his family. If it was Daniel's "ghost" in the room, then it is understandable how it would be distracting for Jonathan.

It was hard to imagine how we were going to have a deep, productive conversation about soup when Jonathan was in so much pain. Who can possibly care about soup when you are questioning the meaning of your life? Soup is not nearly as important, and yet soup was vitally important to this project that I was getting paid to do.

Unless someone is truly despondent, it's likely that an individual grieving a loss is still able to find focus and get through the daily motions of life. That explained how Jonathan had made it through our screening to qualify for the session. He was highly articulate and in touch with his feelings, and, even though he was grieving, he may still have cared about what he was eating. At the precise moment in time when we were in his home with him, Jonathan's bigger life quest occupied a lot of mental and emotional energy. I knew, partly from intuition, partly from experience, that I'd need to unpack the loss of Daniel in order to bring Jonathan to a place where he could focus on what we needed to hear about. No matter if it's a loved one, a direct report, a friend, or a respondent, when someone is upset or has something on their mind, the best thing to do is to give them space to share. That space isn't physical; it's mental and emotional space, created by asking a good question and then actively listening. Ignoring what is going on will only twist and convolute the conversation you finally do have based on your initial questions. Instead of going around whatever is there, you have to go through it. The only way for us to learn about soup from Jonathan was going to be letting him talk out the loss of Daniel and what was happening to him as a result. That was what he needed to do at that moment. My job in that moment was just to be there to actively listen.

> **Me:** Tell me a little more about this sort of transition that you're on. You talked about a spiritual transition.

> **Jonathan:** I haven't voiced an answer to that question very much. I'm trying to figure it out. Many times, actually several times in my life, I've had the experience where I felt that spiritually I saw an opportunity in front of me to learn or to gain some insights. It was scary and also, I didn't know if I could do that and live the life that I was leading with my family and profession.

And so, I kind of saw a window opening and I'm like, *No, okay, I'm going to close that window, but I know it's there.* At the same time, I always knew there was more there. I feel very strongly that Daniel has given me some missions. One of them is to open my heart and feel what I feel and experience what I experience. Not close it off because I'm afraid or I'm worried about where it might lead me. Ten months ago, I put this [Boston Strong] hat on, which meant a lot to me ever since the marathon bombings. But I thought after he was re-diagnosed last fall, I just said [to myself], *Well, this is* my *Boston strong; this is my Daniel strong hat. My Be Strong hat*, and it's been pretty much on my head or near me ever since. It's not that I believed it was magical or anything, but it was representative for my belief.

But my belief has been shaken rather profoundly because he died when I believed he was going to be healed. So I'm trying to figure that out—what my belief system is going to be and how it shifted and how I can trust myself when I believe in something. And I think he's right here. He's going to be part of that. I'm really looking forward to it. I don't know what that journey is, but it's about opening my heart and just going with what happens and trying to make a difference.

I've started acknowledging people when I see someone, when I see that they're one of us, and communicating with them that it's a unique and special experience to recognize and acknowledge someone else. And that we can change the world by doing that more and encouraging others to do more of that. Because something he and I talked about is we believe we are defined by our choices and that every moment is a choice. Therefore, every moment is defining us, ourselves and others, and a lot of people don't understand that. They don't even have the remotest clue of that. But each moment is a choice; every moment we're interacting, even with just ourselves, we're changing the world because we're different. The five of us here [in the room for the interview] are different for this interaction.

Me: Absolutely.

Jonathan: We all have such power and opportunity to impact. I want to honor that and learn so much more about that and about spirit and energy and life.

Jonathan went on to tell us how incredibly supportive his wife was being.

Jonathan: She's like, "I know this has happened. I want you to do what you need to do. And if that's a year-long walkabout in Australia or a vision quest or whatever you want to call it, do it. I'm with you. Let's go. You can do it yourself, we'll do it together, whatever," which is so mind-boggling to hear.

Me: Did you not expect that from her?

Jonathan: I didn't expect to hear it, but I wasn't surprised to hear it. That's like so many things recently. For Daniel to go into what turned into a two-and-a-half-week span from literally standing up and kicking his brother's butt in a Ping-Pong game to dying, was horrifically shocking but not all surprising. Because he'd been sick, and he'd been dealing with this for thirteen years. Also, he was in the middle of, at that point, a nine-month fight with the last diagnosis. It's the same thing with my wife. I was shocked that she said that, but I wasn't surprised because I know who she is. That's why she's my wife.

Me: I'm sure it's a relief to hear her say it.

Jonathan: Oh, relief and terror, too. Because at some point you'd say, "Wait. No, no, slow me down. Hold me back, please!"

Me: To articulate that as well. And to understand that and what it means and where it might take you. You don't know.

Jonathan: Of course not. It could take me out of this relationship. It could take me to another side of the world.

Me: It could strengthen your relationship.

Jonathan: Oh, absolutely. But you go to the fear side.

He told us how his mom had taught him that the difference between fear and excitement is just a matter of letting go of control or understanding. "If you get a little too excited, it can be fear. Frightening. But if you can understand or accept or control the fear, it can be really exhilarating and exciting," he said. He told us that his wife was very anxious and worried a lot. He described her willingness to be supportive as "breathtaking." Jonathan also acknowledged that "so many people that I love and love me were so worried about me. Because I'm the rock. I'm the one to say, 'Come on, I got it. How can I help you? What's going on? Let's do this. Let's get it done.' For my sister and Daniel and for the family."

I could see that about Jonathan. It was what had put us all at ease upon arrival. You could tell he was normally a grounded person, a rock, even though he was currently going through some intense experiences.

Me: Have you started to kind of explore or travel?

Jonathan: Yeah, for sure. Well, it's just crazy. I am so in touch with Daniel. I am so connected to him. He is so frequently with me in a way that I've never experienced before. It's awesome and it's mind-boggling and, again, it's worry-evoking. Is that the right word? It engenders worry in some of the people who love me, a little bit. It's funny because your eyes right now, they're like, *Hmm, this is very interesting. I don't really understand this.* You take that from someone who loves me, and they're like, *Okay, this is scary. Is Johnny losing it? Is he cracking up? Is he just going to go over the deep end into the deep zone?*

Me: Yes, I have that look on my face because I'm trying—

Jonathan: Trying to understand.

Me: Yeah. So, my next question for you is how does that manifest itself for you?

Jonathan: Gotcha.

Me: Because I will tell you, I live in San Francisco. So you want to go "woo-woo," I am like all in and right there with you, and I've done some stuff that we can talk about at another time.

A little more than a week after Daniel died, the family had gone ahead with a planned trip to visit relatives in the Bay Area and then go to Yosemite. Jonathan felt that connection to Daniel in the national park.

Jonathan: I was standing on the top of Sentinel Dome, looking at one of the most beautiful places that I've been in my life, as close to the center of the powers of the universe that I've ever experienced. The other was right on that lake.

He showed us photos from a house on a lake in New Hampshire that the family had rented for more than twenty years. It was beloved by all, including Daniel. When it looked like Daniel was going to make a recovery, Jonathan had gone up to the lake house at Daniel's urging. Then, when things took what turned out to be a final turn for the worse, Jonathan drove back to Boston in half the time it had taken to drive up. A couple weeks after Daniel had passed, and after the trip to California, Jonathan returned with a close friend to close up the lake house. It was there that the first of two "manifestations" occurred.

Jonathan: For the twenty-four hours we'd been there, I'd been talking with Daniel. I was like, "Holy shit, don't think I'm crazy, man." To other people it's like, "Whatever. I don't care." But I kept literally talking with him; he grew up there, so he was there with me.

Me: His energy was there.

Jonathan: As we drove a boat down the lake, from just this one loop around the lake, we both came right around that island, and I was driving and my friend went, "Oh my God, is that what I think it is?" I went, "What? What's up?" I saw him looking up, and in the tallest tree on that island, you can see there's one taller tree, was a bald eagle. I just stopped the boat. There were three other boats looking, and we were just watching and went, "Oh my God! I've been coming here for twenty years. I've never seen an eagle on this lake, let alone... that is the island of my life. My ashes are going onto that island," or half of them; the others are going off the Monster at Fenway. They're still trying to figure out the logistics of that. During a game or not? On a play or not? But the bald eagle was there, and we were just watching. I said, "I just can't believe this," and my friend goes, "Well, if that's not a sign, I don't know what is." And I said, "Absolutely!" I stood up in this small boat and I just went, "Daniel, I love you so much." Like this! I didn't think about it or mean to, but the freakin' eagle just took off and flew right over us. He was about thirty feet up but an eight-feet wing span, white tail, feathers like this long, and the eagle just flew; we watched him for fifteen minutes. We could see him; he just flew off into the horizon, literally right down that way. I just said, "My boy's all right."

The second experience had been at a Chinese restaurant in San Francisco just a few weeks before our visit. Jonathan said he was reuniting with one of his oldest friends that he hadn't seen in over twenty-five years. Like many long-time close friends, their reunion felt like no time had passed, except for the need to catch up. Then, at one point...

Jonathan: My friend stopped for a second and she went, "Oh my God, I'm so sorry. We haven't talked about Daniel. I'm so sorry about your loss. He means so much to you, I know." I said,

"Yeah, I appreciate that. It's really hard, but it's all right. I'm okay."
Then she went, like, "Do you . . . do you feel like Daniel's with you
much?" I went, "Oh yeah. All the time. So often." And she went,
"How about right now?" I went, "Oh, absolutely. Yeah, sure, he's
right here." She said, "I thought so. I thought so." She kind of put
her head back, and she went, "Yeah. Yeah." It was really outrageous. I just went, "Daniel, this is my dear friend." And she's like,
"Hello, Daniel." We both just had goosebumps on us the size of
Mount Everest. I went, "Okay, let's get back to lunch here." We
got back, and we started talking about that, and she's like, "I'm
not really so connected. But my dad died three years ago," as
we'd already talked about, "and I've had the opportunity to talk
with him." I said, "What do you mean?" She goes, "I don't know.
At first I thought I was just hearing his words in my subconscious, but then I realized he was talking to me. Then what's
crazy is I was able to talk back, and we had like three or four
conversations." I'm like, "Okay, that's awesome. So, you *are* that
connected kind of person." She said, "Well, so are you."

During their reunion lunch, his friend described working with an
intuitive psychic in Monterey named Diane and recommended that
he contact her. Jonathan had a little more time left on this trip to
Northern California, so he decided to try to connect with Diane.
"You know, I may hear from her but if not, screw it. I'm going to
go see my boy, talk to him, connect with him in Big Sur by myself,"
he told us.

When he got down to Monterey, all the lodging was booked,
but Jonathan talked with a waiter at a local restaurant who told him
about a beach south of Monterey, because "I just needed to get
down by the water." He did the drive, walked down to the beach,
and slept on the rocks on the beach. "I was in this little nook that
I found that was just like a couch, and I was just surrounded by my
boy. I talked with him, again just me, just me and him. The next
morning when I woke up—because I kept falling asleep, woke up,

fall asleep—I woke up and there were like eighty sea otters in the water and all around me. It was like, "Okay, this is where I'm supposed to be. This is it. Final stage of that story was I hadn't even thought about this woman Diane in five days, because I was flying out west and working. And she called, and we talked. I was by myself, and we just started talking. I said, 'This is why I was calling; I lost my nephew and my friend, and I connected with him. I feel like he's often with me.' She goes, 'Well, he's right behind you right now.' I went, 'Yeah, sort of feels like it.' She goes, 'He is.' And so we talked."

According to Jonathan, without any information, she "nailed so many things. She's obviously connected with the spirit world, whatever that is." She was able to intuit they'd had another death in their family—his wife's father had died ten days before Daniel.

> **Jonathan:** Even in me telling her why I wanted to talk to her, I didn't mention anything about my father-in-law dying. Then she said a couple of things that Daniel was telling her, and one was, "Oh, he really wants you to say hello to his brother. He wants you to punch him on the shoulder?" I went, "Yeah. Yeah, he does." Because that's the kind of relationship, not a hard punch, just a tap. I wish I'd asked her, "Was it punch him on the shoulder or gnaw on the shoulder?" So that's how it manifested itself.
>
> **Me:** Wow. Wow.

We had been talking about Daniel for over thirty minutes. Jonathan was becoming much more relaxed as he shared these stories of his experiences. In some small way it must have been therapeutic for him to get this off his chest, to have us listen to him and what he was going through. During the entire conversation, Krista and Roger paid complete attention, engaged in active listening to what he was saying, as though it was what we had come here to learn about.

In this situation, my intuition, coupled with my experience that I had built up as a moderator, told me that I needed to let him share and we needed to listen. Clearing the air by actively listening to him freed Jonathan to focus on what we needed to ask him about. The real benefit was that taking the time to listen to him gave us a much more complete picture of who Jonathan was and what he was going through. This was real life. Death happens, and people have to cope with it. It's part of the human condition.

While he was telling his story, and we listened to him, the energy in the room began to feel lighter and freer. I didn't have the sense that Daniel was hovering over Jonathan anymore. That meant we could talk about soup. But we had just been talking about intuitive psychics and spirits and communicating with the dead, about as far away from canned soup as you can get (unless you're channeling Andy Warhol, perhaps). I had to figure out, on the fly, how to sensitively steer us in the direction of canned soup. I had been thinking about this while listening to the last part of his conversation with Diane. From psychics to soup. A real journey filled with lots of possible changes. *Aha! Changes.* That gave me an idea. This is what I said next:

> **Me:** All right, you've got, obviously, as you've been talking about, major change happening, in transition. Kind of from the spiritual side, emotions, lots of stuff going on. Talk to us about, through all of those changes happening—this gets down into some more physical stuff, but are you noticing any changes in the way you're eating or the foods you're eating or your approach to food? What's going on?

That really brought us down to earth from the astral realm. I probably went too fast going immediately to food. I could have asked about any physical changes he was experiencing, and food would certainly have been included in the answer, but I was concerned with time, so I went ahead and took us directly to food. His reply:

> **Jonathan:** Yeah. Absolutely. I'm much more conscious of what I'm eating. I'm feeling that I need to significantly change the way I'm eating by eating healthier. I want to have my body be in

a lot better shape than it is. I feel that's important for me and important for this journey as well.

We made it! The rest of the session was on topic and went really well. Jonathan had great observations for us about soup and the brands and styles he chose and why. Had I pushed forward in the beginning of the interview with my scripted questions about his philosophy toward food and the role soup played in his life, it would have ended up being one of the worst interviews ever. He would have given us answers that would have been all functional and surface level. And he would have been preoccupied by the energetic "elephant in the room." I needed him to have a clear path to sharing with us, absent of all obstacles. The way to do that in conversation is to actively listen. Explore what is coming up; let your intuition guide you even if it seemingly goes "off-topic." Get to know a person's whole story. Then respond accordingly. It's worth it.

EMPATHETIC REFLECTIONS

- When has your intuition told you there was something else going on in a conversation? How did you respond? How did that contribute to achieving empathy?

- What would it take for you to ask and then actively listen to a colleague or direct report share stories from their personal life? How would having that knowledge help in the workplace?

- Try an experiment with someone you know. Tell a story while your friend has headphones on and can't hear you. Ask what nonverbal cues they picked up about the story. Repeat the exercise with roles reversed.

INTEGRATE INTO UNDERSTANDING

This is when it all starts to come together. Making space in your head for someone else's point of view doesn't mean abandoning your own perspective on the topic; it just means recognizing that yes, there's another way of looking at this issue. You can still prefer chocolate ice cream, but just acknowledge that other people might prefer vanilla. You're entitled to your own opinion and so is the other person, even when it's more complicated than the best flavor of ice cream. Once space has been made, synthesize what has been heard, seen, and experienced to form insight into the person or topic. Make sure you've kept judgment out of it; you want your understanding to be a true reflection of the other person's point of view.

14

Altering Perceptions

If you change the way you look at things,
the things you look at change.

DR. WAYNE DYER

I T'S AN ABSOLUTELY false notion that to understand someone's point of view means you agree with them or approve of
that point of view or give up your own. Understanding does
not equate to approval. What integrating into understanding does
is ask you to make room in your mind to accept that a different perspective exists. That's what Step 4, Integrate into Understanding,
is all about. Making meaning out of all the information that you are
taking in. As with every step in the path to empathy, judgment has
to be kept in check lest it become an obstacle. I find that judgment
prevents people from even making room in their mind to accept
that, yes, there is another way of looking at a situation. Our frenemy,
judgment, is forming that block preventing you from accepting that
someone else might have a different point of view.

You may or may not approve of another's perspective, and
that's your prerogative, but hopefully you are able to hold space,

using your newfound understanding, to help drive an empathetic conversation in Step 5, Use Solution Imagination, that leads to collaboration, consensus, and maybe decision-making.

It is important to recognize, in the process of integrating into understanding, what barriers are coming up for you in trying to understand. I've found it's resistance due to my own lived experience or values. That can create a lot of dissonance and bring up our frenemy, judgment.

Try to step into the perspective of a person that you have been judgmental toward. Often, they are looking for tolerance, acceptance, or validation—all of which come from being understood. Fear of being misunderstood and therefore not being accepted is what keeps people "in the closet" on any number of personal situations—from sexuality and gender identity to religion, politics, recreational drug and alcohol use, and more. Hearing new information about someone, we may want to be accepting, but it can be hard to integrate into understanding in that moment, particularly if you have to suddenly rewire your own programming to the contrary.

I saw it firsthand as I was coming out as a gay man in the early to mid-nineties. After I'd say the words, "I'm gay," many people, including my parents, had a moment of silence while they were processing (integrating into their understanding) what I had just revealed to them. Whether they realized it or not, the next words they spoke were critical to how our relationship would evolve. I'm fortunate that everyone was very accepting, including my parents. "We still love you. You're still our son, no matter what," were the first words I heard from my parents after I told them. They were able to at least understand that I was gay even though they still had some judgment about what it meant to be gay, which we worked on dismantling in the subsequent days, weeks, and months. In the lead-up to coming out to my parents, I realized that they had always taught me to be accepting of others, despite differences. It would have been hypocritical of them not to accept me. If they taught me one thing but did another, that would have led me to question who they really were. I'm fortunate that, at the end of the day, they were true to themselves and able to overcome their own judgment and integrate into understanding. They even asked good questions and actively listened to me along the way to empathy. I'm lucky. Not every LGBTQ+ person has had the same experience.

Beyond sexuality, there are other taboo topics that society looks down upon but are more common than we realize, which means we may run into them more than we'd expect. In particular I'm thinking of drug use. Finding out someone is using drugs, either for recreation or due to an addiction, can come as a shock and create cognitive dissonance (a form of judgment), which gets in the way of understanding.

Depending on your relationship with the person admitting their drug use, and your own preconceived notions, your reaction can range from understanding to confusion to rejection. It can be easier to accept a stranger's behavior than a loved one's, and it can be easier to cast aspersion on a stranger as well. But what happens when you find out a stranger you hold in high esteem uses drugs?

On a project in Denver, Ignite 360's COO, Lisa Osborne, had this experience with clients while on an in-home. Our clients were from out of town, and the project was to understand the "brand champion" of their super-healthy snack brand. A brand champion is a consumer who uses or buys a product regularly and has loyalty to that product or brand over the competition. This person might even "champion" or advocate for your brand to others, which can help sales. It's critical that businesses understand their brand champions, who they are and what motivates them. Keep your loyals loyal, and you'll have a steady business.

On this in-home, the clients were suddenly confronted with a truth about their brand champion respondent, and that forced them to re-evaluate their own perceptions. Sitting in the corner on the floor of the respondent's living room was a tall glass tube with a lighter next to it. Lisa recognized it as a bong and realized that this consumer, or someone in their house, used marijuana. That's not a big deal in Colorado, since recreational marijuana use has been legal for several years. And Lisa, who lived in Washington state, where it's also legal, wasn't surprised either. The clients from the Midwest, on the other hand...

A discovery like this isn't always easy to absorb and integrate into understanding. Like when we discovered that Ryan was an online sex worker, some of the clients had judgment. I had to work to dismantle it by asking good questions that would allow Ryan to explain his career decision, making it easier for the clients to integrate into their understanding.

How you respond depends on experience, beliefs, and your own point of view. Perhaps you've had exposure, or engagement, with marijuana in college or young adulthood. But that might have been a long time ago. Or, as a parent, trying to keep your kids away from drugs of any kind becomes an overriding consideration, regardless of your own past personal behavior. That can turn into judgment toward others rather than allowing integration into understanding.

For our clients, who lived in a state where recreational marijuana use was not yet legal, seeing a bong and other paraphernalia in the corner of the living room of their brand champion caused a cognitive dissonance. This was not what they'd expected from the virtuous, all-healthy-all-the-time image they had of their brand champion, someone they'd been prepared to revere.

This discovery became the first point of discussion after the session was over. It wasn't what the clients had expected, and it went against how they thought about the stereotype of their brand champion. It was like a "coming out" moment, revealing information that goes against what they'd thought about a person.

It's not easy to get to Step 5, Use Solution Imagination, to put on the shoes of the other person. My past experience and current career have helped me work on my own internal clash of judgment versus understanding. It remains an ongoing struggle for me. And our clients were certainly having to come to terms with their own judgment clashing with the need to integrate this behavior into understanding.

One key I've found helpful to achieving understanding of this different perspective is recalling and acting upon the thought, *It's not about me*. It's so hard to remember that sometimes. I've found myself in interview situations where I've felt judgment getting in the way of understanding, and I've had to repeat this mantra to myself over and over. *This conversation is not about me; it's about the respondent.* Understanding who they are, what makes them tick. I have to put myself aside. No judgment, just intake. Listen to them. Hear their story. Then, synthesize it into my understanding. Consider what is happening, what might be motivating their behavior. Where are they coming from?

After the buzzy excitement passed, Lisa was able to help the clients understand that they were in Colorado, where recreational marijuana use is legal, so what they were seeing wasn't illicit. To our clients' credit, they integrated what they saw into their understanding; it was just beyond the norm in their home state. Fortunately, they didn't invalidate the respondent because of what they found. They were able to understand that this was simply an alternative to their own lifestyle. *It's not about me; it's about the respondent.*

Keeping that perspective and integrating that into their understanding, the clients didn't follow an instinct to reject the learning from the session. The fact that the brand champion had a bong and used it did not make the respondent any more or less important to the project. The clients embraced the voice of the consumer, "warts" and all. There was acceptance that differences exist. What makes us distinct as humans are the nuances in our lives, not the broad brushstrokes. Understanding the nuances, building empathy, leads to stronger relationships and connections. In business it allows for better marketing and innovation based on human truths, which drives business growth.

As Lisa was telling me about her experience, it took me back thirty years to my own "just say no" attitudes toward pot and harder substances.

"I've never smoked pot!" I proudly declared in 1988, just at the start of my sophomore year of college. I was at the New York City apartment of the mom of my roommate and good friend, Justin. Isabel was a free-spirited artist the likes of which I had never met before. That night she needed help moving furniture around. I'm not sure anymore how the topic came up, but in my memory, we were moving some gigantic potted plant. And that's where the "pot" reference came from (such sophomoric humor) and my announcement that I had never touched the stuff.

"Well, that's too bad," Isabel replied.

That was not what I expected to hear from a parent, certainly not the ones that I had been exposed to growing up in Indiana. I was expecting to hear verbal applause at my holding out on temptation. I wasn't wasting my time getting high. No sir. Not me. I thought that behavior would earn me praise for being a "good boy." But I wasn't getting praise from this independent woman. The way Isabel replied to me, it had a certain tone and quality to it; it was laced with a touch of pity that made me wonder if I was actually missing out on something.

While that was the extent of the exchange, those few words stuck with me. I began to wonder, *Why haven't I tried it? What's holding me back?* I had already started drinking alcohol at college when it was available to my underage self, but I had avoided marijuana my entire freshman year. My own stereotypes of potheads probably didn't help. If someone in my high school regularly smoked pot, they were seen by me and others as stoners, druggies, or "hoods." That was not a group I aspired to be in, even though, as part of my own survival technique, I'd talked to them and everyone else in high school. Deep down, though, I was pretty square and harbored judgment about their drug use.

Isabel's words continued to echo in my head. For me to have tried drugs while living at home would have rocked the boat, jeopardizing the safety and security of my home life. That was unthinkable. The world outside my house had cruel parts to it, and I had to constantly be on my guard to keep the gay rumors under control. That kept me on the pseudo "straight" (pun intended) and narrow. Now, at college, I had the opportunity to open up a bit more. Pot was available and some of my friends smoked. Some of the people in my dorm smoked it a lot. But I hadn't taken a puff, let alone inhaled. Why hadn't I tried it yet? I was afraid. If pot helps you relax and lose your inhibitions, would my gay secret come out? At this point in college I had a pretty good idea I might be gay, but I wasn't yet ready to deal with it; I was clinging to the fantasy that it might still just be a "phase."

I turned Isabel's words over in my head. I had felt a little foolish after our exchange. Who was I? Some big, proud, Indiana-raised straitlaced kid who stuck to the straight and narrow? That's not who I wanted to be. I wanted to experience all that life has to offer. Auntie Mame's famous call to action—"You've got to live! Life is a banquet, and most poor suckers are starving to death!"—spoke to my true self, but in that moment, I realized I wasn't really living its meaning: live life to the fullest! Now that I was in college, I had more freedom and flexibility to explore life. I could start to do that. I *should* start to do that.

Back at Syracuse University a few weeks later, I was doubled over on the floor, laughing hysterically at something that struck me as incredibly funny but probably wasn't to someone who wasn't under the influence. I was stoned! And a few weeks after that, I got so stoned that I declared, "I can feel the presence of Canada," which I think is only possible when a) you actually are in Upstate New York near the Canadian border; b) the clouds are really low—which I associated, in that moment, to being lower to the ground because we were so far north; therefore, we had to be near Canada; and

c) you're really stoned. Since that one incident in 1988, I can't say that I've felt the presence of another country without actually being in that country, but on that night, I would have sworn to you I did.

My personal recreational use of marijuana during college was short-lived, however, due to a tragedy. Having completed my finals at the end of the first semester of sophomore year, I decided to celebrate by getting stoned. It was December 21, 1988. Shortly after my last exam finished, I took some hits from a bong. It was the middle of the afternoon. As I was feeling the haze of the pot take me to a point of relaxation, word started getting around about the bombing of Pan Am flight 103 over Lockerbie, Scotland. This was particularly newsworthy in Syracuse because thirty-five Syracuse students were on board. They were returning home from London after a semester on the Syracuse University study-abroad program.

That news reverberated across campus like shockwaves. The school was large enough that I didn't know any of the students on the flight. That didn't matter. We had lost thirty-five of our classmates to a terrorist attack. That news was upsetting to everyone in the student body, but I was also the station manager of the campus radio station, WJPZ-FM, conveniently located in the basement of my dorm, three floors down. I was second in command, and this tragedy was a crisis moment for all of us. The station, as a news broadcaster, had to get the word out and let people know the latest information. The station interrupted its Top 40 programming, and the news team went on-air with continuous updates. Our reporters were talking to the airline, the university, aviation experts, anyone with credible information, all out of a little basement studio facility. The Z89 news team was sourcing and delivering so much news that ABC's *Nightline* crew stopped by and told them that they, ABC News, were listening to Z89 because our news team had the most up-to-date information. It was an all-hands-on-deck moment. It was the "out of crisis comes opportunity" defining moment for the station, and where was I? Experiencing couch lock on my sofa. I was too stoned to be of any help.

The general manager and I finally talked around 6:00 p.m. Scott had called me, hoping I could come in and help out. It was an easy trip downstairs when I was sober, but I was not in a place to do anything. I confessed to my altered state and said that, as soon as I sobered up, I'd come in and help out. Even at age twenty, I knew it wouldn't be appropriate for me to show up baked out of my mind during such a solemn moment requiring focus and peak performance.

Several hours later I had returned to lucidity enough that I could go downstairs. I found the team had everything covered for that night, so I volunteered to take the early morning news shift and provide on-air updates. I was so proud of everyone at the station; we were just college students, but we were helping keep people informed and up-to-date, even the professional journalists. And I was frustrated with myself that I couldn't have helped more. But we had a plan for the next day, and that was my chance to do my part.

I returned to my dorm room and packed up my suitcases, since I was getting on a plane the next evening to go to my parents' house in the DC suburbs, where they had moved after I graduated high school. I wanted to be ready so I could give it my all on-air as long as I was needed. I started my first broadcast at 6:00 a.m. and helped deliver news updates the rest of the day. There was a rotation of who went on-air, who monitored the AP wire, who wrote copy, and who took in reports from our team "in the field" on campus. Throughout it all, I put what I had learned in journalism class to work, diligently taking down information, confirming it, and putting it into copy that read well on-air. There was so much going on, and so much emergency station business to attend to, that I stayed in a pretty functional space, not really feeling the emotional weight of what had happened, even though I had to recite the facts over and over again on the air.

My shift ended just before 3:00 p.m. The station had been on all-news for twenty-four hours at that point. It was now time to return to its regular mix of music and news. I remember that last update I delivered. Scott was in the DJ booth, which was on the other side of the glass window from the news booth. I shared my final update, concluding with a recap of what had happened, announcing once again that thirty-five of our classmates, returning from a semester abroad, had lost their lives high in the sky above a small Scottish town. And while delivering that update, I thought of their lives cut short, after having what must have been some incredible, "life is a banquet" type of experiences in Europe. That finally got to me. I choked back a sob, the emotion of the past twenty-four hours having caught up with me. I held my quivering voice steady enough to sign off, "tossing" it back to Scott, who introduced our first song back, U2's "Angel of Harlem." The emotion of the experience, the thought of all those lives lost, caught up with me, and I let the tears flow once I was off-air.

After that experience I realized that, if I was going to be in a role where I had responsibility and might need to respond at a moment's notice, I would need to be more mindful of how I might drink or use drugs. So that curbed my pot usage to the occasional weekend here and there the rest of college and even less frequently in my adult life.

Later that night, when my plane touched down at National Airport in DC, my dad picked me up. I was exhausted. He consoled me on the drive and counseled me not to let the Lockerbie bombing end my own dream of doing Syracuse's study-abroad program in London the following fall. I had been torn, as I had fallen in love with my work at the station, and I expressed that. My dad reminded me that studying in London was a once-in-a-lifetime chance and I should at least apply, and then decide if I got accepted. I went for it and got in. That following school year in London was the biggest banquet of my life, and I feasted on life to the fullest.

SO, YES, I've inhaled more than once in my life. Having tried it, I was able to understand the appeal of it and why college students would want to use it. Integrating into understanding is usually a mental exercise rather than a physical one. What remained for me to understand was why adults would want to regularly use marijuana.

Inspired by the client's brand-champion bong experience, Lisa and I decided to do our own project to look further into who the consumer is that uses legalized marijuana. It's a fascinating stereotype to explore—do the people who use fit the image that many of us have? I was also really curious about what this subculture was all about, since I pretty much hadn't used marijuana for twenty-five years, so I had my own stereotypes to break down.

A few months later, we were back in Colorado for the start of our new project. We went into people's homes for sit-down interviews and also talked to managers of dispensaries. The people we talked to ranged from scientists to teachers, IT consultants to medical technicians and assistants. All of them were using legalized marijuana.

One of the first people I met was Tim, a late-twentysomething scientist. Really bright, handsome, recently married, a homeowner, thinking of starting a family. Not unlike many other American males of the same age and place in life.

We were at his dining table, which I remember being high up, so we were in tall chairs with our legs perched on a crossbar for support. Tim was a little uncomfortable at first, questioning what we were doing and how this interview was going to be used. After I reassured him that we wouldn't use his real name, "Tim" finally began to open up. I started by asking him to describe the stage of life he was in right then. "Happy, and kind of just trying to live in the moment and enjoy what, you know, what's happening right now, because I think kids might be in the picture sometime soon, and the spontaneity will probably be gone at that point. Where I can pick up and go to Las Vegas, like I am this weekend, and do stuff like that."

I followed that by asking about what goals he had for himself right then. Student loan and credit card debt weighed on his mind, but he expressed surprise at how fast he was able to hit the other goals— he was married, owned a house, had a dog and a yard with a fence. "I can't really complain. I mean, I find things to complain about because, you know, first-world problems, but life is pretty good."

Me: Okay. What do you guys do to relax?

Tim: Um, like, the obvious, or?

Me: Why, I don't know; what is the obvious?

I was being a little coy, but I don't want to make assumptions in conversations. Again, it's about asking good open, exploratory questions. His understanding of the "obvious" might have been different from mine. In this case, we were talking about the same thing.

Tim: Uh, I mean, I consume cannabis in my spare time. Sometimes to relax, not all the time. I mean, I don't know; we go hiking, and we just chill out on most weeknights, really.

Me: Okay, so first of all, how do you refer to it: cannabis, pot, marijuana? I want to use the language you use; I don't want to put words in your mouth.

Tim: Around friends and family, probably just weed. You know.

Me: Alright, so tell me about weed. Like, what role would you say, how would you describe the role weed plays in your life?

Tim: Um, I don't know. I'd say it's very similar to, you know, like, alcohol. As far as, you know, it's just something that can enhance a relaxation, and add to a good time, when the time is right. Um, you know, it kinda just goes hand and hand if you're up skiing or snowboarding or camping or something; if you're having a couple beers, then there's probably weed around at the same time.

Tim said he preferred weed because it didn't involve a hangover. "I guess some people can occasionally get anxiety attacks, but mostly it's just, you know, you get sleepy and tired. And you wake up the next day and you're good to go."

One of my biggest surprises from this study was how far marijuana has come. It's gone from a random guy delivering whatever he had on hand to now being an "industry" with manufacturing and distribution, product and package design. In the states where it's legal, you can have very involved conversations at the dispensaries with the "budtenders" to help you make your purchase decision, starting with the type of high you want to have—head or body. (In college I wasn't thinking about the type of high I wanted; it was just about getting high.) Then you choose how you want to consume—smoke it, vape it, eat it, drink it. In many dispensaries you can buy everything from the flower or a pre-rolled joint, to concentrates that you vape, to edibles and tinctures and full-on beverages. It's like a whole new world. A "wild west" of start-up companies with varying degrees of quality and marketing finesse. This is not to mention the CBD industry, which has also grown like a, ahem, weed.

Isabel would be so proud of how much I was learning! Tim explained that the "flower" is the bud of the plant as opposed to a leaf. He also had specific reasons for when he would use the different methods of consuming. Bongs and bubblers were for home use and delivered a smoother inhale, while joints were the granola bar of marijuana—"Good for, like, on the go." Joints also offered Tim a sense of throwback, "You feel like your parents back in the '70s," he told me.

Edibles were also in his repertoire, but only for certain occasions "because they last for so long, and sometimes they can be way stronger" due to inconsistencies in measurements of THC levels that vary across manufacturer. That kept edibles to "more of a weekend thing for me," when he was really able to commit to the experience, like on the past New Year's Day.

Tim: My best friend and his fiancée and my wife, we all, you know, just had an edible and hung out and played some video games because we had nothing better to do. So it's kinda just like you're committing to wasting the day, I think, when you eat an edible. It's not just, like, coming home and taking a hit of weed and going out and mowing your lawn. Maybe you can compare an edible to, like, taking shots versus having a beer. Like, you wouldn't come home on a Tuesday night and have six shots of whiskey unless you're an alcoholic. You would come home and just have a beer while you mow your lawn or something, and that's, like, the equivalent of taking a bong hit, I guess.

Me: Okay. So, um, we've heard a lot of different reasons why people are using weed. For you, what are the reasons why you use weed?

Tim: There's probably a few. I mean, obviously to relax and have a good time, like I said. I compared it to, very similar to alcohol, so you know, whenever you have a time that alcohol would be appropriate, whether it's a sporting event or, I don't know, family get-togethers, depending on what family is there. It's just a way to have a good time. But I also actually have my medical card, and I'll use it medicinally for my TMD [temporomandibular disorder] I was diagnosed with, because I don't like pharmaceutical drugs at all. I don't know if I'm sensitive, but I get really bad side effects from everything I ever take, so, um, I don't like what they gave me for that, and it can be bad sometimes, the TMD.

Those strong side effects left him questioning the value of pharmaceutical drugs. Tim told me he'd first received a medical marijuana card while he was in college and found that he achieved the same relief from the TMD with a daily hit of marijuana, usually from a bong that he kept in his living room.

Tim showed us a collection of eight to ten different varieties of marijuana he had on hand that he enjoyed using at different times depending on what type of high he was looking for. Typically, he'd take a hit when he got home from work. He kept likening it to having a beer at the end of the day. That notion of marijuana as a way to unwind, just like having a beer or a glass of wine, was a consistent theme across all of our interviews. And they weren't trying to get "stoned," just relaxed. Similar to how you want to unwind with a glass of red wine, feel the relaxing effects, but not get drunk. That was a new understanding for me, as my experiences in college were to get stoned. The analogy to alcohol made it easier for me to integrate his usage into my understanding.

AFTER DENVER, our project continued to Washington state. We met Shane. Late thirties, recently married, and a stepfather to two kids in the early stages of teen-dom. For Shane, marijuana was a preferred way to unwind.

> **Shane:** I worked in bars for a decade, so I just did that lifestyle for a long time. And I got to the point, and I saw enough, um, that I got to a point where I preferred weed to alcohol. I still love Scotch and whiskey and beer. I'm a fan of all that, but I think in order to unwind and relax and whatnot, I definitely would prefer just having weed.

> **Me:** Can you elaborate on that? What is it about weed that's preferable over having alcohol?

> **Shane:** I would say that the vast majority of different types of weed just, they just calm me down and allow you to focus or just, just relax. I mean, if your goal is relaxation, then there you go. And with alcohol, you know, you have a few more. Then a couple more, then after a few drinks, you're not relaxing. As a matter of fact, you might end up doing something really stupid. And that just, that doesn't happen with weed.

I was surprised this kept coming up, as it contradicted my preconceived judgments that I would find a collection of Jeff Spicoli–style potheads (see *Fast Times at Ridgemont High* if you don't get that reference) looking to just get really baked. Instead, I was beginning to integrate into understanding that people that had rational reasons to prefer pot over alcohol as a tool to help unwind at the end of the day. It wasn't about getting stoned to the point of "couch lock," like I had on that day of the Lockerbie bombing. And these people felt it was a safer way since they weren't going to "do anything foolish" if they smoked too much. It wasn't that one was better than the other, but it was about what was right for them. *It's not about me; it's about them.* (Note: I'm sure there are plenty of examples of foolish things people have done while high, but these people I talked to felt that wouldn't happen to them, and they were using it in smaller amounts. No matter the substance, please use responsibly, and be aware of how much is too much for you and when use may turn into abuse and addiction.)

Another Washington resident, Mike, liked the relaxation from marijuana as well as how it enhanced certain experiences.

> **Mike:** So, I didn't really drink at all growing up, so alcohol just always tasted really bad to me. Even, like, the hangover and just the feeling the day after drinking, it was never for me. But when I would have cannabis, like, the first initial draw, I really liked where my train of thought would go. Like, it was a very novel way of thinking [compared] to how I would normally think, and some of the things I like to do, like listening to music or watching movies, it seemed to, like, enhance it, make it more interesting. You ever noticed how when you listen to something through just, like, stereo speakers versus listening with headphones? And you notice a lot more with the headphones? Well, like, the marijuana is a step above the headphones, where there's so much more; there's all these different layers and things you suddenly notice. I think they're there; I don't think it's making me hallucinate, but there's definitely more, then. I'll notice things that I didn't before.

Mike also used cannabis to help with keratoconus. Apparently, it helped reduce the pressure in his eyes, which relieved discomfort from the hard contacts he had to wear due to the keratoconus. "And then the next day my eyes are not red when I wake up, so I can wear the contacts again, so it's like a reset button for me," he told us.

SUSAN WORKED in the education system in Washington state and used cannabis primarily to manage the pain she told us she'd had at that time for more than twelve years. "I've had chronic pain since 2003 and very severe. Bad to the point that I've had opioids prescribed to me. My primary physician is opposed to marijuana usage, which is funny. But she's more than happy to write me a prescription for opioids. For Oxycodone, specifically. Yeah. This is what's funny; I can actually work (in education) with opioids in my system and that's legal."

Like Susan, Tina in Denver had also faced the stigma of marijuana from her doctor, who wanted her off cannabis before he would prescribe Adderall to help her manage her ADHD. Marijuana and its consumers have been stigmatized for decades. From the *Reefer Madness* culture in the twentieth century to pop culture representations in films, users of marijuana have been depicted as stoners, not like the people that I'd been meeting. The stigma kept them in the closet, afraid to "come out" and acknowledge that they used. Tina was really mindful of how people perceived her.

> **Tina:** It's like there's a [pot] smoking community and there's a nonsmoking community. And then there's the kind of people that want to reserve the right to give you shit when they feel like it. Like when it's convenient for them to say that pot smokers are this or pot smokers are that. You know? I'm uncomfortable smoking on my porch, even though people are comfortable drinking beer on their porch. It's my neighbor that lives across the street, you know? She's—they're just not that

type of people. I guess there's still a lot of people that think you're either not smart or you're lazy or you're trashy or, or, or—there's just a whole lot of, I don't know. If you see a guy walking down the street holding a beer or sitting on his porch holding a beer, and you see another guy sitting on his porch holding a bong, people just look at him differently. Because it's not accepted everywhere.

The stigma that exists, for all the reasons that it exists, makes those who are smoking uncomfortable. Shane told me you couldn't talk freely at work about using marijuana, while it was perfectly acceptable to tell stories about drinking benders. The cannabis consumers don't feel that's right.

> **Tina:** I just don't think it should be frowned upon. It does more good than people think it does. It's helped me medically; it's helped me mentally and physically. Like, I think people think that you're just sitting around just getting high, like they portray on TV. It's not like that. It's not *Fast Times at Ridgemont High*; nobody's doing that. Like, I smoked a big old fat bong and went in the kitchen and just turned on the music and was painting away, you know? I'm just painting. I'm not being lazy.

Susan had similar feelings to Tina.

> **Susan:** Well, for one thing, it's a personal choice. I don't feel that people should be . . . I don't want to say persecuted; that's a little strong. But there is definitely . . . certain people in my circles do not know that I smoke or take edibles. Some people do, but very few; most don't. And it's mainly because I don't want people having that kind of "look down their nose" at me or, you know, think somehow I'm a lesser person, strength-wise. I'm not looking to escape—yes, I am. I'm escaping pain, but I'm not wanting an emotional or mental escape. Not all people that

smoke it are potheads. People think that I'm just going to sit around and have the munchies, which is funny. I don't get the munchies.

Tim put it all in perspective. "I don't want to hear other people's judgment against me. I just feel like people should keep that to themselves, and the world doesn't need hate. That sounds really hippy-like, but I mean honestly, why can't you just be nice to people and let them do what they're gonna do? You just see, like, the people that are assholes out there usually don't smoke weed. They're so uptight, and they feel like they're owed everything."

Like most societal issues, there's a lot of judgment to dismantle before we can ask the questions, listen, and begin to understand another's point of view. We can choose to live in a pit of judgment or we can commit to elevating ourselves to greater acceptance by understanding our differences. Marijuana use wasn't as difficult for me to integrate as gun ownership because I had personal experience. Regardless, the steps are the same; it's the issue, the individuals, and our perspective that differ. And how we choose to respond.

Having empathy doesn't mean giving up your own beliefs and values, just like "integrate into understanding" doesn't mean you condone or approve of others' behavior. For a less-polarizing example than cannabis, let's say your absolute favorite flavor of ice cream is chocolate. Others prefer vanilla. You don't agree, but can you let down your guard (judgment) and find the mental space to see that someone might like a different flavor of ice cream? Be okay with that knowledge. Remember: it's not about you. To integrate another person's perspective into your own understanding is a much more productive response than to maintain segregation through judgment. It is a step toward empathy—assembling the pieces that you've learned, observed, and listened to in order to step into the shoes of someone else in Step 5. It can be difficult. Judgment is a beast that comes back in many forms on the way to empathy, including making you rigid and set in your beliefs. With empathy we are trying to get to a place of understanding, which leads to conversations that help with many things, including conflict resolution, collaboration, idea generation, decision-making, even forgiveness. If we can't get beyond our own hang-ups, then we will be stuck, unable to advance out of fear, misinformation, and prejudice. And in my mind, as Isabel once told me and helped broaden my understanding: "Well, that's too bad."

EMPATHETIC REFLECTIONS

- What was something you had difficulty integrating into your understanding because of your judgment? How have you overcome that? What do you understand about it now that you didn't before? How would you apply that going forward?

- Ask a friend what flavor of ice cream they like. If it's different from yours, be aware of what it's like integrating into understanding as you ask them good questions about what they like about that flavor. Can you hold your personal preference and theirs together side by side in your mind? Share your feelings about your favorite flavor. Try the same exercise with movies, music, and books.

15

The Language of Home

Home is not where you live but where they understand you.
CHRISTIAN MORGENSTERN

CLOSE YOUR EYES for a moment and focus on the word *home*. What image or images come to your mind? What are the sights, sounds, and smells you associate with home? The first image that comes to my mind is the house I currently live in. I think about our living room, the blues and browns and chartreuse of furniture, and art popping off the white walls. Three cats, each black and white, curled up, resting as they do most of the time, waiting to snag space on a human lap for a nap.

I'm guessing you probably think of your own house when you think of the word *home*. Maybe it's the one you occupy now; maybe it's the one you grew up in, or perhaps a grandparent's. You know the language of that house or apartment building—the rhythms of the day, the sounds created with every step, the objects in the rooms, the emotions and relationships of the people inside, the scent of a thousand meals cooked over the stove. It's your home, where you can let your hair down and be you. You don't have to put on airs or worry about being an imposter. In a place where you can be you, there's no pretense required.

Expand from that image of home. Go broader now to consider the homes of close family members or friends that you might have visited. As you think about these homes, consider the similarities and differences. Think about how different the languages are in each one of them. Now, expand the number of these other homes into a multitude where there are more than 128 million homes. That's how many homes (defined as "households") were in the United States as of 2020, according to the US Census Bureau. Imagine that: 128 million. Take that in for a moment. Now, let your mind drift down your own block, and cross over to the rest of your street. Elevate your perspective so you can have a bird's-eye view of your neighborhood, your town or city. Now, soar high and see the broad swath of houses across America. From apartments to mansions, trailers to condos, sprawling ranches to suburban two-levels and duplexes, from the Atlantic to the Pacific, Mexico to Canada. Imagine you can peek inside these households and see what they look like. Each and every one of them is nuanced and slightly different from the other, like a dialect of the language you speak in your home. Some will be quite different.

Imagine one home and tour around it a bit more. Consider the smells in this home. What might be the occupants' favorite dish; is the scent still lingering in the air? What do their wall decorations look like? Do they have any at all? Are there pets? What type and how many? What type of carpet or flooring might be there?

Gently come back now to your reality. To your home. As you were imagining visiting that one home, did you envision a house similar to your own or something altogether different? It was probably similar to your own, wasn't it? Not surprising, since we have a predisposition to see things that are familiar to ourselves and support our worldview. We seek language that's comfortable.

It's a cognitive bias that we have to consciously overcome when we are in a home with a language that's not exactly like ours. That bias must be overcome in order to integrate into understanding because all of those 128 million homes and the people who live inside them have a language with much in common and much that's different. To integrate into understanding, you have to recognize what is similar or familiar to you in order to see clearly that which is different. And when you find something that is different, in order to integrate it, you need to lay out all the things that are different and try to derive meaning from it. What do these things have to do with a behavior or attitude you are trying to have empathy with? Or is it your bias against a different way of doing things—and can that be okay?

While nothing beats the feeling of home, it is made up of both the physical space (the house) and the emotional space (the home) in order to achieve it. Home is *your* house and the tangible and intangible elements that make it yours and where you, hopefully, feel safe and secure. That's what you are attached to. Objects, sights, sounds, smells, and emotions all combine to create the syntax that makes your home yours. That syntax is very specific and tailored just for you. Any other home just won't do. It's because the language in another home is unfamiliar, and that makes people uncomfortable.

Remember the times when you went on a sleepover, either as a kid or as an adult? As a kid, you may have felt "comfortable" because you were close with your friend, but maybe their house didn't seem like *home*. Recall that first "grown-up sleepover" you might have had? After the fun was done, did you find it hard to settle in? In both situations, what parts of the language of this other person's home made you feel uncomfortable? Was it the strange patterns cast on the walls by the voyeuristic streetlights? The firmness of the mattress, the lumpiness of the pillows, the linens, the decorations in the home, the sounds in the dark, the foreignness of it all? Did that contribute to the feeling of being out of place?

Whether as a kid or an adult, the home presented the syntax of a language you weren't familiar with. This language of home isn't about whether the chair you sit in or the bed you sleep on is comfortable. It's about how comfortable you *feel* in that environment. It's an emotional state.

As I work to "integrate into understanding" on an individual level just like the societal issues like marijuana, I keep in mind that I am visiting *their* home—with a language all its own, which is native to the other person. Despite the surface similarities, there can be quite a few differences and that's okay. Just like with the big values issues, I have to remind myself, *It's not about me.*

The family unit and what constitutes the family in these 128 million households also differs incredibly. How you view it depends on your perspective. In my own life, I grew up in what would appear on the surface to be the classic "nuclear family" of two white parents, two kids—a boy and a girl—and two cats. Picture-perfect, right? On the surface, as a broad brush stroke, maybe. Pictures snapped of us over the years probably do look pretty nuclear and "perfect," but that's the problem with a picture; it's only a frozen moment in time. Life is fluid and keeps meandering onward. So who we are as a family continues to morph as we age. Depending on who you talk to, and which picture they looked at, there are many things about my family that might not be deemed "perfect" in the eyes of another. We have an Italian last name and identify with some parts of Italian American culture. That was really strange in smaller small-town Indiana. As was the son being gay. When the daughter married, she moved overseas for years-long assignments, creating a painful distance between the parents and their grandchildren. Both parents faced battles with cancer (remission for both, fortunately), and the cats in the picture can only live for so long. The dialect of the language in our home was uniquely ours.

Viewed from the perspective of dog lovers, homophobes, and even people of color, my family doesn't resemble theirs in many ways. Therefore, they can't speak the dialect or maybe even the language, but if they can understand that every family is different and that's okay, since *it's not about them*, then empathy can still be achieved.

Getting to visit so many people in their homes, I've seen count-less makeups and compositions of the American home. My job is to explore how the various elements, or syntax, make this home similar to or different from others. And then how these beliefs and behaviors might inform the way my client's products are considered and used. Sometimes I walk into a home that feels very comfortable because it is more familiar to what I know. Or, in the case of Frank, I wanted it to be familiar because I sensed we were both gay. Or in a house like Emelia's, I discovered a penis mirror. No matter how different, many homes have the same human values at the base of it. Parents are protective of their kids. Powerful emotions, like love, are behind most actions, although that can take different shapes by way of expression due to the different people in the home and their own lived experiences. No matter, the foundation and base of the words in the language are the same; they just get put together in different ways, and that's where the fascinating parts to integrate into understanding exist. Making room in our heads that there are different ways of doing things and looking at the world, it becomes clear that these differences aren't wrong, they are just different. And different can be good. Different can teach you a thing or two.

I VISITED one home with a different, distinct syntax on a cold December morning in Philadelphia, and was quickly immersed in the language as the action pulled me in. It was a row house like so many other row houses in Northeast Philadelphia. Old brick build-ings lined the block, well-worn over time, with creaking floors and maintenance that might have made sense fifty years ago but felt impractical and unattractive now. It was just after seven o'clock on this December morning, and it was bitterly cold out. We were there, ready to observe a little morning ritual in action and then talk about it.

"Welcome to chaos!" was the greeting Natalie gave us as she opened the door. The house was bustling with activity. Christmas was already up in the living room, telling us immediately that this was a house with Christmas as part of its language. The rooms were small and cramped with furniture, plus storage bins to hold the belongings of the people living in this house: Natalie; her wife, Tammy; Natalie's daughter, Kelli; and her daughter's three kids, ranging in age from twenty-one months to twelve years old—all were in the midst of their morning routine. Natalie referred to the house as a "village." A multigenerational, lesbian-led, interracial village living in raucous harmony.

Natalie: The biggest thing about our village is this is where it is real; this is where we love each other. Tammy and I been together since '96. Kelli is *our* daughter, these are *our* grandkids, and it has been a long time. This is where we finally get to be. This is it. This is where we are safe, this is where it is crazy, this is where the shoes come off. So anyway, I am Nat and my wife is Tammy. And the tall one walking around, Aliyah's mom, is Kelli. And so we are the village and now, since we have extended family that's outside, we are the in-house village.

Me: Excellent. And earlier you were starting to say that your name is Nat, and you are she who—

Natalie: Must be obeyed. *[Laughter]* It is kind of the ongoing joke around here. When we got together years ago, we negotiated our relationship, and what I said when Tammy said she wanted a relationship was, "Well, I am okay, I make a living wage, my mortgage is paid. I do not really need an addition to the house, so why should we do this, and what are we going to do, and how are we going to arrange it?" And, uh, we agreed that I would have 51 percent of the vote 90 percent of the time, so the ongoing joke is I am she who must be obeyed.

Me: *[Laughter]* Because of the 51/90 rule.

Natalie: Yeah, I have 51 percent of the vote 90 percent of the time. And I cannot have it 100 percent of the time because 90 percent keeps me honest. You know.

And then, like a sudden clap of thunder over our heads, the conversation was interrupted.

"Fuck me!" came the yell from upstairs. "Shit! No. Goddammit," the cries of frustration continued. I was startled at such vivid language so early in the morning and when there were guests in the house. Not syntax I'd experienced in many homes.

"Tammy!" Natalie broke out of concentration on our interview and yelled toward the stairs in a scolding tone.

"No, we—I need you. Now!" yelled the same voice in reply.

"Oh, I'm sorry," Natalie said to us as she jumped up.

"The microphone!" Sergei, the videographer, and I yelled out in unison. The mic pack, resting on her lap, connected by a wire to the tiny lavalier mic clipped onto her collar, was about to go flying.

"Now!" Tammy insisted, as we fumbled to free the wire and mic pack from her wife.

"Okay!" Nat yelled back, somewhat defensively, as we got her out from our technology so she could go and investigate what was happening. As she started to climb the stairs, every step creaked under her feet. Once she was able to see the situation, she explained back to us, "Oh my gosh, I'm sorry. Apparently when Aliyah was in the bathroom this morning, she sat on the pipe or something."

The result of that "something" was going on in the upstairs bathroom, and from the sound of splashing water, that "something" sounded serious. It certainly gave me context to understand the language Tammy had used. It was about 7:40 a.m. This was looking to become the shortest early-morning interview of my life.

Sitting in the living room at the base of the stairs, we could hear their conversation.

"Get off the pipe!" Tammy yelled again. Then, in a still frazzled but gentler voice, she said to Natalie, "Sorry, I was goddamn lucky I was in the other room. Pipe busted. I need you to go downstairs, and there's a shutoff valve, and I need you to turn it off."

All you can do in such a moment, when trouble erupts and you are in a respondent's home, is sit there quietly and wait until you have more information before deciding on a course of action. I turned to the clients who were with me, shrugged my shoulders, and made a "who knows?" face, marveling at this first in my career. One of them asked, "Is this going to make the highlight reel?"

"It might," I replied.

Tammy told Natalie to go try the shutoff valves that she was aware of in the house—one above the washer and one above the garage. This must have been an example of the 10 percent of the time when Tammy got the majority vote. Natalie recalled that the garage door was locked and stuck, and she didn't have the key. Tammy told Natalie to stay there because she had a key to the garage. At the top of the stairs, she announced, "I need a guy." Natalie must have volunteered us four men sitting in her living room, because when Tammy got to the bottom of the stairs, she looked at me, then the rest of the group. "Um, any of you guys got muscles?"

"Kind of," I replied, thinking that, while I'm strong, I'm not a stereotypical "muscle guy" from the gym.

"No, seriously, I need help. A pipe just busted in my bathroom. My garage door will not open, and I need help."

"Okay!" we all agreed without hesitation, and three of us took off after Tammy toward the garage out back while Sergei, the videographer, stayed in the house to help, if he could.

We moved so quickly that I left my voice recorder in the living room, recording the rest of the sounds in the house, including Nat instructing her granddaughter to go down to the basement to get a bigger bucket while she sat there and held the one in her hand in the bathroom. What the recorder didn't pick up was what we went through trying to turn the water off.

The garage was detached, behind the house, facing an alley that ran between the backs of the houses on the block. We'd moved so quickly that we left our coats. I had a sweater on, but it was well below freezing, and it was still early; dawn was just giving way to morning. We got to the garage door, and Tammy showed us the lock and explained that they hadn't been able to get the garage door open for a month.

As the bitter cold started to prick its way through my sweater, I wondered what I was doing and why I'd agreed to try to speak the language of this home and be part of the "muscle" Tammy recruited to pry open their broken garage door. What else were we going to do? Say "no" and the interview would be over. Say "yes" and we'd have a great opportunity to help and be part of their village for a few minutes. Besides, I could tell Nat was a great storyteller, so once we did get back to the interview itself, it was going to be an A+ conversation.

The three of us examined the garage door. There was a handle one of us could pull on, maybe while the other two pushed up? The garage door was heavy. And more than a bit dirty. In my nice sweater, I was dressed to visit someone, not to be doing manual labor. So, I was mindful of brushing up against anything like a filthy garage door, as I didn't want to get my clothes dirty. It was only our first session, and we had a lot more to do later in the day. But if we didn't get that water turned off, we were going to have our morning suddenly free in search of an alternate interview.

The guys and I gave it an "on three" heave and a push, and the stubborn door let go and slid on up. Tammy said she was amazed we got it open. She ran back into the house and up the stairs. My voice recorder picked it up. It was less than a minute later, although when I was standing outside, it felt like five minutes had already gone by. "Alright! Natalie! They got it open! Quickly, I need you to go down there and shut it off, please."

Natalie headed down the stairs, ran into Sergei, laughed, and said, "Um, didn't we start out with 'welcome to chaos'?" Yes, we did.

Meanwhile, in the garage, the three of us were looking around for pipes, preferably a pipe with a shutoff valve. We spotted a thin pipe leading to a tiny twist faucet valve. But this didn't look right for the main water into the house. The pipe was really thin, too thin to supply the household water. And the outgoing wastewater wasn't there either. Having just had to turn off the main water at my grandma's house six weeks earlier, to clear air in the pipes of the sprinkler system, I knew that we should see two large pipes near a larger shutoff handle. I looked at the pipe again and followed it to see where it led. Just beyond where we found it, it dove through the wall and out the other side to the outlet for a garden hose. Definitely not right. I explained to Natalie, who had joined us in the garage, that this wasn't the shutoff to the water in the house. At least we got the garage door open for them.

We returned to the welcoming warmth of the house. I asked Tammy if they had a basement; perhaps the shutoff was down there. She led me down into their finished basement and showed me the first of two possibilities. Nope, another standard pipe. Then she brought me over to the basement bathroom, which was about the size of an airplane lavatory. Just enough room for a toilet and a sink. Natalie had joined us, and she sat on the toilet, reached down to her left, and removed a piece of wood paneling about the size of a piece of printer paper. Behind that paneling I saw the familiar big water pipes coming in from the foundation of the house. And on top of the incoming pipe was a handle, just like what I'd seen at my grandma's house. "That's it!" I exclaimed. "That red valve is what needs to be turned."

The handle was covered in what looked like a hundred years of dust. Tammy reached in, tried to give it a turn. No luck. I offered to try. I felt a crumbly texture of dirt and coagulated dust press into my hand as I gripped the valve and tried to turn it. Still nothing. It was stuck. "Do you have any WD-40?" I asked. Tammy said yes and stepped out to get it. *This is definitely a first for me*, I reflected while perched on the toilet seat lid, waiting.

Tammy reappeared with the WD-40. I sprayed it on. Not knowing where the valve was stuck, I sprayed all around the base of the valve. Then I reached in and gave it a turn. That coagulated dust and gritty dirt was now mixing with the oily lubricant. I put some force into it and the valve started to move. The water main closed.

Aliyah, handling the bucket brigade from upstairs, yelled that the water was off. I pulled my hand away from the pipes. It was covered in a gooey paste made of dust and WD-40. Yuck.

I stood up and stepped over to the sink to wash my hands. Then it hit me. *Oh yeah, I turned the water off. This won't work.* My hand was dirty and now it smelled like WD-40. Being creative, I asked if they had any Handi Wipes or anything like that. Tammy returned with baby wipes that they used on her granddaughter. Again, a syntax unfamiliar to me.

A couple of wipes later and the soot and lubricant were off my hands. Back upstairs, Tammy announced to Nat that "he's wonderful!" and we got ourselves resettled to continue our conversation about morning routines. As the interview continued, I kept noticing this odd smell. It was like the pungency of industrial lubricant infused with the oily "fresh" scent of a baby's bottom. After I asked Nat a question, I casually brought my hand up to my face near my upper lip. The smell got stronger. My hand may have been "clean," but it was now scented with a distinct blend of WD-40 and baby oil. With no running water in the house, I was kind of stuck like that until we could get to a bathroom where I could wash my hands. Repeatedly. *It's not about me*, I remind myself as I continued the conversation.

NAT AND TAMMY'S home was a far cry from what I think of when I think of home. The language was so different, but what I was able to ground myself with and use as a base for the integration into my understanding was the family structure and the abundance of love that was evident. Even though the house was old, creaky, and chaotic, it was filled with love, and it made a nest for this village where the residents could feel safe, secure, and taken care of. I could relate to that and understand it. That made understanding and accepting the differences much easier.

From my home to Natalie's to others I've visited during my work, each home and family looks different on the surface. Beneath the surface, relatable commonalities exist. When you integrate into understanding, start with what you have in common. You'll be able to relate and start to engage in a conversation, exploring the differences together. You'll reach understanding when you bring the two languages together, with a little translation and interpretation, to see the perspective of others and their life. Regardless of the structure of the home—a suburban five-bedroom, an aging inner-city row house in need of some TLC, or a hipster commune in the big city—in each of these homes is a place where people can feel comfortable to be real and be themselves. Home is always the place where the shoes can come off.

EMPATHETIC REFLECTIONS

- Think about the language of another home. What "syntax" in that house have you had to stay open to in order to integrate into your understanding? Or did judgment get the best of you? What could you do differently to better integrate into understanding?

- Think of other times you've had difficulty integrating into your understanding another person's opinions, beliefs, attitudes, or behaviors. What got in your way? How might you overcome that to accept there are different points of view and each one has validity for that person?

- What is part of your life that others may have difficulty integrating into understanding? What would you like them to understand about you? How might you express it to them to help them understand your perspective?

STEP 5

USE SOLUTION IMAGINATION

You've arrived! It's time to step into the shoes of another person and see the world from their point of view. Can you do it? Are you able to say, "I can see your point of view; tell me more about that?" Be sure you have taken off your own shoes so you can slide into theirs, which is what solution imagination is all about. Be careful—the dark storm clouds of judgment continue to loom on the horizon and threaten to muddy the path.

16

What Are You Willing to Sacrifice?

---

*Give me your tired, your poor, / Your huddled masses
yearning to breathe free, / The wretched refuse of your
teeming shore. / Send these, the homeless, tempest-tost
to me, / I lift my lamp beside the golden door!*
EMMA LAZARUS

COGNITIVE EMPATHY IS *the* tool to use to get to know people who might be "other." Whether it's based on race, ethnicity, sexual identity, gender identity, religion, political affiliation, or any of the other traits that divide society, using solution imagination—getting to a point of seeing the perspective of someone else—can foster conversation, understanding, and tolerance and even bring people together. Empathy can also lead you to take action. Some call that *radical empathy*, which I believe comes from either cognitive or emotional empathy, when the connection you are feeling is powerful enough that it motivates you to action, usually out of compassion.

Using solution imagination is that moment when you move beyond, say, recognizing that other people like vanilla ice cream and get to the point of "getting it." You can see their point of view that they like vanilla because it's got gentle, warm, floral notes that don't overpower the tastebuds. You will have reached that when you've successfully dismantled judgment ("Vanilla? Ew!"), asked good questions ("What do you like about vanilla?"), actively listened (noticed how their eyes lit up while they described their favorite flavor), and integrated into your understanding (there's more to the world than chocolate, as heavenly as it may be).

Of course, we all know that the bigger issues that divide us don't have to do with dessert.

Immigration is one of the great divides in our society. It touches on several perceived threats of the "other" that can trigger us: an immigrant might be from a different ethnicity or race; they probably have different customs and rituals, maybe a different religious orientation; and the immigrant may be seen by some to take work from the people already living in a country, which is a direct threat to someone's personal economy. While immigration is currently a polarizing topic in the United States, it's been a point of contention for people around the world for centuries—typically, with the people who have already arrived, seeking to keep out the newcomers that follow. Immigration really is the story of being "other."

In 2013 a client reached out wanting to build empathy with the immigrant experience in Canada; specifically, what happens right after they arrive in Canada? What sort of support do immigrants have? How do they adjust? How do they acclimate to Canadian traditions and customs, including the food?

This story takes place in Canada, but it is a universal tale that could just have easily been in the United States, Australia, Europe, or any country with immigrants. This is a universal tale of immigrants and the sacrifices they make when they come to a new country. The lesson is about using solution imagination to be in their shoes and imagine what their life is like.

Migration to North America is an issue fraught with both hope and terrible pain, particularly in the United States. European immigrants made the decision to come to North America in search of a better or different life. Yet Africans were brought over to the United States against their will on slave ships and forced into an existence that the European settlers would have considered inhuman if they'd had to endure it themselves. Over time, European migration gave way to immigrants coming from other parts of the world.

There are common themes of sacrifice in the immigrant experience, regardless of what century it took place or what country people emigrated from and immigrated to. Sacrifices are made in the hope of better opportunities for the immigrants and their descendants.

According to data from the Pew Research Center, in the United States the current leading immigrant population is Hispanic, with the highest concentration for country of origin coming from Mexico. In all, there are more than forty-four million immigrants living in the United States, accounting for 13.7 percent of the population. It's a large number, but the immigrant percentage of the total population was actually higher back in 1890, when 14.8 percent of the population was foreign-born. It may not surprise you that 25 percent of the US immigrant population comes from Mexico, given the proximity of Mexico and the long land border that the two countries share. Other Latin American countries and regions follow, including Puerto Rico, Dominican Republic, Honduras, Colombia, Venezuela, and Brazil. That's followed by Asians from various countries in northern and southeast Asia, as well as South Asians from countries including India, Pakistan, and Sri Lanka.

Because Canada shares a border with the United States, I think of them as a "connected" neighbor to the north, just like Mexico is "connected" to our south. Therefore, just as the United States has a large immigrant population from Mexico, I ignorantly expected a very similar immigrant makeup in Canada. I assumed that the largest percentage would be Hispanics followed by Asians and Africans. Wrong! The largest minority groups in Canada are not from Latin America. Instead, the immigrant community in Canada is composed mostly of people from South Asia (India, Sri Lanka, Pakistan,

Bangladesh) and China. Mexicans and Latinos were nowhere near the top of the list. I was surprised. My ignorance led me to assume that people from Latin America would start heading north and just keep going north if they didn't like what they found in the United States, rather than settling down. So, while the United States is a multicultural blend of Caucasian, Hispanic, and African influences, Canada, our neighbor to the north, separated only by a "line" in the dirt, is on a completely different trajectory when it comes to its population, cultural makeup, and resulting culinary preferences.

And while we are on separate paths, both countries' current populations were built on immigration. Based on that fact, the uproar over immigration that is occurring in the United States feels so hypocritical—especially when it's coming from the very people who were the descendants of immigrants themselves! How easily we forget our own history. I get the concern over illegal immigration, but it feels that we've just become anti-immigrant. Unless people are Native American, they are here because of immigration. My grandma, the child of immigrants herself, tells the stories of growing up in 1920s New York and how the Germans didn't like the Irish, who didn't like the Italians, and so on. They were all European, but they were so separated by language, mountain ranges, seas, and culture that they might as well have been from different continents. Each one of those immigrant groups was displaced over time by the subsequent group, which generated feelings of resentment, as it was perceived that opportunities were being taken away by the newcomers. Yet these European settlers were always positioned at a level above the African Americans, so it wasn't a true cycle of replenishment, only among the fairer skinned. (For more on the caste system in the United States, I highly recommend Isabel Wilkerson's eye-opening book, *Caste: The Origins of Our Discontent.*)

And it continued in New York, the animus shifting toward the Puerto Ricans as they began arriving in the city and joining the melting pot. And then the Dominicans arrived, and on and on. One immigrant class supplants the next and the next and the next.

After assimilation, each group seems to want to claim "ownership" of the country, behaving as though the gates to the country should be closed and locked forever after they arrive, freezing a country into a time capsule that can never be. And so we take for granted the tremendous courage and sacrifice it takes to emigrate to another country where the culture and customs, as well as the language and the food, can be completely opposite from your own.

Ah, the food. Just like in the United States, the influences in Canadian cuisine are being informed by its immigrant population. Restaurants open to serve the immigrant communities. Food markets start to dot the landscape, offering the ingredients and packaged products of home that are hard to find in the new country. Over time, popular dishes and flavors start to seep into the popular culture, creating a sort of "reverse acculturation" as the country's palate expands to include the immigrants' countries of origin. For example, imagine what eating food in the United States would be like without Mexican cuisine? Or Thai or Chinese. Or Italian, another immigrant specialty. And most of those dishes are "peasant foods" in their native country—starches, carbs, and cheap cuts of meat like hamburger that fill without costing a lot.

Now think about immigrants. They are searching for the life that might allow them or their children to enjoy a better future filled with prime cuts of meat. In the meantime, they have their filling starch and carb dishes, and they bring those with them. As people immigrated to the United States, their foods and flavors infiltrated society and gradually made their way into the mainstream. The degree of authenticity of the dishes may be diluted, but there is at least some version of familiar flavors that becomes available.

Immigrants also get introduced to the foods of their new country. This project was about how acculturation begins and where new foods get introduced. For me, it was about so much more than just how the immigrants learned to make poutine (a specialty from Quebec—French fries, cheese curds, and gravy!). One couple in particular has stayed in my memory because of their sacrifices on arrival in Canada.

The house Suhasini lived in with her husband, Harish, was like many you'd find in neighborhoods across suburban North America. A basic two-story with siding, and a yard that was relatively well maintained, with a car parked in the driveway out front. Walk in the front door and you saw furniture that you might recognize, as well as other pieces of art and objects on display that brought in aesthetic elements of their home country. The house was fragrant from the aromatic spices and herbs used in cooking and felt like a home that was well lived-in.

Suhasini and Harish were from India, specifically, a province near Punjab. They'd lived near Mumbai for a time before coming to Canada. When I'm talking with people, I like to use "solution imagination" to imagine myself as them, in their situation, and to formulate questions based on what I'm intuitively sensing they might experience. Inevitably, some of the details in my mind will be fuzzy, so the questions help fill in the blanks. At times I will find myself having emotional, affective empathy, and in addition to reacting to what they are telling me, I'll feel the emotions they might have been feeling in the moment, based on what is happening in their story and how they are sharing.

This use of solution imagination is second nature to me now because I started putting myself in others' shoes very early on in my life. It may have been all the role-playing of Wonder Woman, Charlie's Angels, and Bionic Woman that I did in the backyard with my best friend, Joey, that first developed my ability to step into the shoes of someone else. Think about not only imagining what it's like to be a superhero or a private investigator, but to be of the opposite sex, so those shoes weren't just another pair of men's shoes. They were shoes with high heels. That requires some extra imagination!

As I thought about what it must have felt like to be an immigrant coming to Canada from another country, I imagined the feelings of anxiousness and loneliness on arrival steeped in a tea of adventure and new beginnings. Frightening yet exhilarating all at the same time. That informed one of the first questions I asked: "Take us back to when the plane touched down at Toronto Pearson International Airport. Then what happened?" Turns out it was usually a routine arrival at an airport, just like many of us regularly experience. Often they had a distant family member that they knew who would meet them at the airport and give them shelter while they got settled.

Suhasini told me that her openness to the idea of emigrating to Canada was one of the initial questions Harish had for her when they were first meeting to discuss their arranged marriage. For several years after the wedding, they didn't think much more about it, establishing their life as a married couple in Mumbai working. Then, as they started to plan to have a baby, Canada started to come back into the picture. "So we thought it's better to move to Canada, and for our kid it's going to be a better life. There's lots of struggle there [in Mumbai], lots of corruption and everything, so we planned the kid. He came and he arrived, so we thought it better for us to go to Canada. So then Harish applied, and after three years—it took that much time for the process—we came here," she said.

Me: Why Canada?

Harish: My dream was especially to go to a cold country. India, it's always above 45 degrees Celsius [113 degrees Fahrenheit] temperature. So here we meet our friends, so usually I say I'm coming here to get rid of sun, so I came in this country. I have been in civil engineering, so in the back room I used to stay, you know, on the site always under the sun, all day. I wanted to get rid of sun, so my plan was to move over here.

Suhasini: Cold country.

When I asked why not move to the UK, Harish said it was not as diversified a country as Canada. And then within all of Canada, I asked, why Toronto? He said that most of the population of Indian immigrants was settled in the GTA (Greater Toronto Area). It was all based on what people they knew had told them based on what they had, in turn, heard from others.

I could relate to the subjects and understood how much it meant to move somewhere together. When my husband, Charles, and I first met in New York City, a love of California was something we both had in common. Even then, we were together for more than two years before a work opportunity even raised the idea of relocating to the West Coast. And once the idea started to become a reality, it wasn't an easy decision for us. That made Suhasini's openness to moving thousands of miles away—to a completely foreign land, with someone who was a relative stranger she had just agreed to marry—a pretty remarkable act of bravery. Even though they didn't move until after the birth of their son, she remained willing to make a leap across continents. And in their case, they didn't have a close family member or friend waiting with open arms to greet them at Pearson Airport, save for one former classmate of Harish's.

When I think about moving to a new city, or contemplate moving to a new country, I think about what I might need to have at the ready in order to make a smooth transition. For me, it's the following things in order: 1) shelter; 2) a source of income; 3) friends or a community that will start to constitute my new "tribe" in this new home.

For the immigrants we spoke with, the extended family that came before them played a critical role by helping to provide the shelter and tribe. Harish's friend arranged for them to stay in a basement apartment when they first arrived. The other part, securing a job, while allowed on the immigration visa to enter Canada, isn't as simple as it sounds. It isn't "just" a matter of finding a job. The logical first step would be to look in whatever field you were working in your country of origin. Sounds easy, yes?

Suhasini: Lots of his friends told us the main thing was the working. If you are moving to some other place, working is the main concern; how we are going to earn bread, right? So his friend told us you have to go to factory jobs, and it was so depressing. Doing those things is something else. Like, I worked in a school. Teachers go to school, teach the kids, come back, nothing else. And then he was a civil engineer. He goes to the sites. He supervises all day. Like when he feels like it, all the guys would bring the tea and the coffee. So then he started working at the factory. The first day he got to use the broom. That was the first time in his life he ever touched a broom, so it's so depressing in the starting, because he never did it before.

How does a civil engineer end up pushing a broom around a factory floor?

Harish: They said to clean the floor all around the plant and everything, but they gave me the position of machine operator. But first of all, they said, "Okay, clean the floor." Back home we didn't even touch those things. So, even having an office with AC... we had a guy standing outside the office. So I used to ring the bell. He'd go, "Yes, sir?" "Okay, bring tea." Okay, he brings tea. So it was a different culture over there. Like, here it's physical working, and there, it's not physical. We used to just go to the office, go to the construction site, watch the laborers, how they're working, and just instruct them "do this, do this," so it's fun over there doing the job. But here, we found difficult, because it was physical work. We never did it back home, so it was totally different.

Imagine: you've got an advanced degree in your home country, supervising construction projects on a regular basis. You've never had to do manual labor in your life, and then you go to another country to live, and you have to start entry level. With manual labor. All of your years of hard work, knowledge, and experience are completely discounted. Here's a broom, now go sweep the floor. Suhasini said Harish was really upset after the first day. Then the second day he saw another guy sweeping, and it was the plant manager, which boosted Harish's morale that he could do the job. Suhasini had a different experience.

> **Suhasini:** I didn't work for one and a half years. My son was, like, two years old. It's too early for me to, because I brought him from the family, so here we are alone, so I thought it might be good to give him some time so that he doesn't feel depressed. It's a basement, of course. You can't even see outside, you know, that kind of culture. So after a while again I started working. I started working in the Burger King as a team member.

It felt like a cruel trick; here you've invested all this time and money to learn and practice a career or trade that can help you live comfortably, and then you arrive in the new country and are told your past life basically doesn't count, and so you have to sacrifice it in order to start over.

I can only imagine how the standards for teachers and civil engineers might be different in the two countries. But I was surprised. Are they *that* different? In the eyes of the Canadian government (and in other countries, I've since learned), they are. So if you want the immigrant opportunity, you really do have to give up your past in order to forge a new life.

Harish, in a quest to make a better future for his son, away from corruption and pollution, went from civil engineer to sweeping a factory floor. Is that sacrifice worth it? Sweeping in a factory, that's some hard work that often goes unappreciated. I wonder how many of us are willing to make that sacrifice for a chance at a better life? Can we even appreciate how good we have it compared to people who come to our country from many other nations?

Harish and Suhasini came to the Greater Toronto Area with the "Immigrant's Dream," to improve the opportunities for their son (and, as a bonus, escape the brutal heat of India). As their son went to school and excelled, he would step ahead of their place in society. And, most likely, their son's son (or daughter) would do the same as well. I imagine Harish would have had a reasonably comfortable life in India, by Indian standards. Yet he gave it up and took a chance in coming to Canada with his bride. All in order to create opportunity for his young son.

Harish wasn't the only one who sacrificed. In some ways, his wife, Suhasini, made even bigger sacrifices. Like him, she was unable to transfer her education and experience as a teacher in India into a similar position in Canada. She also struggled to find work and turned to her new friends in Toronto's South Asian community for guidance. She spent the first couple of years helping her son adjust and learning how to navigate this new culture and the cuisine.

I asked if there had been any foods in Canada where she felt, *No, not going to make that.* She said no, except, "It's just the beef that we don't eat."

> **Suhasini:** When I first put him in the daycare, they provide the food there, so they make the beef things, and he was only two or three years old, and he wants to try it, and we tried to make him understand that we don't eat beef. It's not for us. We do the prayer for the cows, and it was hard to make him understand. So it took us, like, some time to adopt it, to think it, like, *okay, we have to allow him to eat.* It was a hard decision for us to make.

> **Me:** Do you allow him to have meat?

> **Suhasini:** Yes, we did. Because of the daycare, he was going there. They are making it. They used to make the chicken or the vegetables too, but because his best friend was eating beef... it took some time for us to adopt it.

Suhasini recognized that her son would grow up and go out with his friends, and at that point he could eat whatever he wanted to. They knew they couldn't stop that, even though it would shock them.

Suhasini: So it's better to allow him, but meantime, we tried to make him understand too that it's not good to eat. So we allow him to eat beef at daycare, but then slowly we were telling him that, yes, we eat chicken, but we don't eat beef. And when he grows up, he watches the movies, and then he starts [watching as] we pray to the cow, and beef is a cow. Now he doesn't want to eat beef.

Me: So he's vegetarian now?

Suhasini: No. He eats chicken, but he doesn't eat beef now, but in the beginning, I allowed him to. It's hard for me to accept it, but I did for the meantime. And he came up like, *okay, this is what I'm not going to eat.* At least I know that he ate beef in the past, and if he eats it in the future, I told him you have to tell us before someone else does, you know, tell me that this is what he was eating. It's going to be hard.

As she was telling me all this, an empathetic realization popped into my head. She was Hindu. The cow is a sacred animal in her religion. She'd already told me that she'd worked at Burger King. That meant she was working at a place that serves flame-broiled meat from a sacred animal. I wondered, *What was that experience like for her?* There are no sacred animals in Judeo-Christian faith, so I didn't have an immediate point of comparison. I was trying to wrap my head around this, to integrate it into my understanding—how do you reconcile cooking the meat of a being that is sacred in your religion? Is it like the vegans I've met who hate handling meat? Or does it go deeper than compassion for the animal? What does it mean to flame-broil a sacred symbol? I had to ask her about her experience working at the Home of the Whopper.

Me: But you also worked at Burger King.

Suhasini: Yes, I did, but I never eat.

Me: But how did that feel?

Suhasini: In the starting, it was like—the first day I cried, really; I cried at home. That's what I did. Harish doesn't want me to go to the factory jobs, because he was doing it, so he knows how it was, and basically the factories, most of the people working there are the people who were not, like, educated people in the back room. They're just like ten or twelve people, and they were just working there, and when you go there to work, they discourage you a lot. They will tell you that you are so educated; you came here on a point basis, on your education basis. Why are you working here? So they give you more depression. Somebody was working in a Burger King, so they told Harish, like, they are hiring, so I went there. They hired me. So first day when I came back, I really cried; I cooked beef there. But then, you know, he made me understand it's hard to work in a factory, but, you know, the main thing was you know how to speak English, and basically from the back you're going to come to the front one day. You will handle the cash more than you will handle the food, and I said okay. So I tried to work more. I really worked hard. Like in seven, eight years I was assistant manager. It's not easy. I really worked hard for that.

I used my solution imagination next to be in her shoes, to imagine what it would be like to immigrate to a new country, get a job unlike anything I had studied, then have to do something that violates my religious beliefs, then to work my way over the years to become assistant manager. I offered her a statement of empathy:

Me: That's impressive. It must have been really difficult, those first days.

Suhasini: Sometimes the cooked meat, when you put them in the broiler pans and put them in the heaters, dig them out, all of a sudden, sometimes the oil from there, it comes out. It comes on your face, and it comes sometimes on your lips. It was really hard for us. It was.

Me: How do you kind of reconcile that in your mind? Because, yeah, the cow is sacred; it's a prayer animal, but here in the west it's a primary food?

Suhasini: It was really hard in the starting, as I'm telling you, but other Indians were working there too. It's not, like, only me there. You are not eating it, and so just make it in your mind that this is only a job you are doing. Don't consider it as a food. Don't consider it as beef. Just say you are working. You have to work eight hours here. You are going to take that money to your home to pay the bills and everything. Just take it that way. That's how the people teach. That's what I talk to other people too, the same thing.

In the starting, it was hard with the money too. Like we don't have dimes, nickels, pennies back home, you know. It was hard. You don't even know what the dime is, what the nickel is. So how am I going to do the cash? So Harish started teaching me at home more of the time; like this is dime, this is nickel, like a kid. So I thought my math was strong all the time. I don't need the calculator to do the small calculations, so I told my manager I want to move to the front, as my math is strong. That's why, I told him; I don't want to work with beef. So he said, "Okay, let's try it," and then I said, "Okay, just start with me and see." It's not like big, big deal, and it's small math. It's not like somebody's giving us hundred-dollar bill or something. People are just giving small change, and it's only five-dollar, six-dollar things. So I told him I can do it, and so he gave me the opportunity to go to the front. And within, like, six months I was a front manager, and then shift manager, and then assistant manager.

Suhasini made a true sacrifice. In order to provide for her family and help make their way in a new country, working their way through the Immigrant Dream, she and her husband had to do things that would have been beneath them in their country of origin or were truly against their religion. You've got to really want something to be able to dig in and separate your religious beliefs from what is being asked of you.

Harish faced more struggles at the factory once he advanced from brooming. He started to work the night-shift assembly line, making consoles for SUVs. He was tasked with having to install nine screws in thirty-eight seconds. The first time he tried it, he dropped the screws and brought the whole line to a halt. The supervisor wasn't happy and was about to disqualify him. Harish asked him to give him two hours, in which time he mastered securing the screws in the allotted time. A month later, he managed to improve his speed and got down to twenty-five seconds to assemble all nine screws. He worked until a repetitive stress injury took him out of manufacturing.

Harish then learned to be a plumber and got his license but couldn't find work because he didn't have experience in Canada as a plumber. When no one would hire him, he switched careers again. "So, then I did the real estate, and real estate, no one asked me for Canadian [experience]."

I could imagine what they were going through. I thought about the times when I wasn't given a chance at a job because I didn't have the right experience or schooling. I took the emotions of how those experiences made me feel and used it as a proxy for what Harish must have felt. That memory formed the basis of my solution imagination in this instance. They could only make career choices based on where they could get accepted, not based on skill or education. For Harish, his job in real estate seemed to be working out. And after a successful run at Burger King, working her way up to assistant manager, Suhasini was faced with another decision that could have long-reaching consequences.

Suhasini: My son asked me, on his last birthday, that he wants a lifetime gift from me—to quit the job. We don't understand kids' feelings. It means he really needs me. So I quit. Retirement. Because I thought about it, and I thought, if he's asking me now, like, "I need you, Mom," and I'm not there, and in my world [when I'm older] if I will ask him, "I need your help," he might say, "Where were you when I needed *you*?" And for me, I think it's for my only son. We need him around in our old age. And he [Harish] was doing good in the real estate, so it's not like we need [money for] shoes. So I thought, *It's good to give him what he wants*, so I give him that.

For Suhasini and Harish, it's working out. He's in real estate, and she is focused on raising their son. They are on their way to achieving the Immigrant Dream.

I stand in awe of the sacrifices of immigrants. Not just Harish and Suhasini, but immigrants everywhere. They toil for many long hours of hard work, often beneath the education they attained in their home country and in jobs many citizens don't want. All this sacrifice for the chance of a better future for their kids. So, when I hear non-immigrants complain about "hard work," I think about former civil engineer Harish brooming the factory floor. Or I think of Suhasini flipping burgers made from the flesh of her religion's sacred symbol. Doing what it takes to make their dream a reality. It makes me question just how much the people who complain about immigration are truly willing to sacrifice to achieve their dreams. What are they willing to do? And is it worth it in the end?

Toward the end of the interview, I circled back to the beginning, when Harish had told me that Canada was their preferred country because it was cold. I asked him if he still liked the snow.

Harish: We like it a lot.

Suhasini: We love snow.

Me: And the winter?

Harish: We love snow.

Suhasini: Lots of people say that you love snow.

Me: It's so hard to shovel.

Suhasini: It doesn't matter. We love it.

Harish: It's good exercise.

Whether you are in Canada or the United States, the Immigrant's Dream is what we used to call the American Dream, except it doesn't seem achievable for the US upper middle class anymore. Thirtysomethings aren't all earning more than their parents did at that age, like the children and grandchildren of immigrants did. The first-generation immigrants still move with the hopes and dreams of improving their lives and providing better opportunities for their kids. That will finally get measured by the relative success of the kids. Now, the second, third, and fourth generations, after immigration, collectively find themselves in this slightly rudderless state of uncertainty on where life is headed and what our purpose in life is. Perhaps it's time to take a fresh perspective like Suhasini and Harish, who can find beauty in the countless snows of a Canadian winter. Perhaps it's time for a new dream to be born.

EMPATHETIC REFLECTIONS

- What would you have done if you were in Suhasini's shoes? Or Harish's? What would you sacrifice for a better life?

- Remember the first time you met or had an interaction with someone from somewhere else and they had their own customs and traditions and were learning to adapt? How did that go? How could using solution imagination have helped you?

17

Leave Your Boots
at the Door

What counts in life is not the mere fact that we have lived.
It is what difference we have made to the lives of others
that will determine the significance of the life we lead.

NELSON MANDELA

T HE SCENE WAS the interior of a small, modest home in
suburban Minneapolis. In my memory, the living room was
unremarkably beige—furniture, carpet, walls, all shades of
putty. A large flat-screen TV occupied one wall. In this room were
six participants, several clients, and me. I sat on an ottoman pushed
against one wall so I could face all the participants, who were seated
in a line on the sofa, an armchair, and a folding chair. We were
packed in tight. This was where my existential crisis began.

Me: Would you want to be in the upper middle class?

Debbie: Yeah, it would be nice.

Kim: Oh yeah.

Debbie and Kim were part of a "friendship circle," a group of respondents who all know each other in some context. Having friends together for a session can bring out some of the other parts of a person's life. You hear more about what they like to do when they are together. And friends keep friends honest, making it a lot harder to bullshit the moderator.

This particular circle of friends was participating in a project to help our clients get to know the American working-class consumer. Working in corporate America, in many different careers, my clients are automatically earning enough to be in the upper middle class. They might also come from an upper-middle-class background themselves. That creates challenges when they need to have cognitive empathy with a consumer that isn't just like them. To find cognitive empathy with someone who is different from you, taking the time to read, watch, and listen to the stories without judgment is critical. It provides the knowledge that can be integrated into understanding so that solution imagination can be utilized to see life from this "other" perspective. The stories that we hear of others become the foundational fuel for our own imagination. This project was designed to give people that direct exposure to hear those stories and build the foundation for using solution imagination.

Without this perspective taking, unintentional "elitist" attitudes and behaviors can emerge that come across as tone-deaf, out of touch, and even insulting. This happens outside of corporate America as well, when the best recent example on a national scale occurred during the 2016 US presidential election: "liberal elites" on the coasts were accused of not understanding, and being dismissive of, "working-class" Americans in favor of their elitist, well-to-do, city views that didn't take into consideration the perspective of the heartland. Donald Trump was able to connect with these heartland constituents on a base level, fanning the embers of their deepest fears of economic instability, religious persecution, and the "stranger danger" they saw in the faces of immigrants who looked nothing like them. We all know the outcome of that election.

Four years later, Joe Biden, an outspoken proponent of empathy, won the 2020 election, yet it's unclear if most of the coastal "elites" have done the work to replace the biased narrative in their minds with a true perspective of those in the heartland or who are working class. Similarly, have those in the heartland done the reading, watching, listening, and integrating into understanding of the people who live in the cities or who are different from them due to race, ethnicity, sexual orientation, gender identity, ability status, political affiliation, religious beliefs, and so many more discriminating situations? Is either side using solution imagination?

Donald Trump was still doing *The Apprentice* when this project took place. We spoke with people in households where the income was below fifty thousand dollars, which was just below the US median income at the time. The households were still above the poverty level of a household income of twenty thousand dollars per year. My clients, all six-figure earners with advanced degrees, who may or may not be "liberal elites" but were certainly part of the upper middle class, wanted to get to know working-class Americans. What are the worries they face? Their dreams? How do they see life? Think about the future? And of course, we had to explore the more practical day-to-day topics, including how they managed their money, thought about brands, and made purchase decisions.

As the project progressed, I kept wondering how the participants felt about their current position in life. Would they want to join the upper middle class? What would that mean for them? How would they benefit? And what would they be willing to sacrifice in order to get there? So I asked the question. Debbie and Kim said yes. The others in their friendship circle nodded in agreement, so I explored a little more, asking, "What would you be gaining by being upper middle class?" The security of having money, what that could buy in terms of a bigger house, and "not having to worry month to month" was the group's consensus on the benefits of being in the upper middle class. Of course, life is a trade-off, so I was curious to get their perspective.

Me: And what would you have to sacrifice in order to be upper middle class?

Chelsea: Taxes. More taxes.

Kim: Probably your time.

Annie: Yeah, time and effort.

Chelsea: Stress, because your job's probably more stressful if you're making more money. Traveling, maybe away from your family.

Annie: Totally, less free time because a lot of time those people bring their work home a lot more.

Me: And what would that end up meaning, bringing their work home more?

Kim: Like, be on call or work on their computers at home even after they've come home after a long day.

Chelsea: Less free time.

Kim: Yeah, because sometimes I wonder like how some people, like, a lot of people don't clock in and clock out, like I clock in and clock out. Like, I'm done. That's what's the good thing, I guess.

Annie: You leave it there.

Chelsea: Yeah.

Kim: Well yeah, basically, like we were saying, a lot of people, we get to clock in and clock out. You know, a lot of people are either salary or they just are working; they have to work from home. They have it set up to work from home. And they're maybe required to do that. They just have to get that work done. Like with my job, yeah, I may feel like it's stressful in my situation, but I do get to just clock out.

Annie: And leave it.

Debbie: And not bring it home with you.

Kim: And you bring a tiny bit home, like, you think about your day, but it's not negative or stressing on your family life or your home life so much because you're not doing it . . . you know, you can still do your personal things.

They were right: There is no clock that my clients and I get to punch. We can work and work and work and never be done. I hadn't thought of it this way before. I have pulled more "all-nighters" or "near all-nighters" since I got into this business than I ever did in college. Even after this evening's interview was over, my work wasn't done. There was still a debrief conversation with the clients, then a drive back to my hotel, then I'd check and respond to email and finish editing documents for another project. I'd be working till midnight that night.

My "do what it takes" attitude and work ethic have certainly driven me. But to where? Hearing these friends talk made me wonder how well this "ethic"—dare I call it a true ethic?—has served me and others like me. What are we giving up in exchange for money and security? Is it really worth it?

Considering my own work/life balance, I had the needle buried fully in the margin on the "work" side. I love my work and have found something fascinating about every job and career I've had during my journey through life. When I was in the corporate America seat, I worked the expected nine-to-five but was often there later or worked in the evenings or on weekends. Being an entrepreneur and starting Ignite 360 in January 2011, I became all work all the time. Launching a business is all-consuming. It really felt like a 24/7 endeavor of being in constant motion, juggling multiple projects, overseeing employees and consultants, reviewing and providing input on work products, searching for that perfect turn of phrase that would make the insights feel so relevant, and inspiring clients to take action and travel here, there, and everywhere to make it all happen.

Yes, I was starting to have a "meaning of life" crisis in the middle of an ethnographic interview! By using solution imagination and achieving cognitive empathy with this friendship circle, I found that the empathy enabled reflection on my own life and decisions. Was what I had been chasing all these years really worth it? Was I missing out on something more meaningful? What was I actually chasing anyway? What did I really want out of life?

Growing up in the 1970s and '80s, I maybe didn't know with certainty what I wanted to be when I grew up, but there was never a question that I'd go to college and get a white-collar job. I don't remember ever having a conversation with my parents about it; I just knew it was expected of me because it was modeled for me by my parents.

Both of my parents had graduated college and went on to get MBAs, which they used to advance their careers. As a result, we lived comfortably and had great opportunities for a family living in small-town Indiana. We went to Hawaii for spring break my junior year of high school! We were the first in our town to do so, that I was aware of. I was privileged in not having to carry student loans to get through college, just working during breaks to have spending money. Of course I wanted to maintain this lifestyle, especially the ability to escape, jetting off and visiting far-flung exotic locations. That really appealed to me.

The type of career I might have had that would afford this lifestyle and satisfy my curiosities was less certain. I remember wanting to be an airline pilot—a dream that was dashed when my dad informed me that "there's a lot of math involved" in flying. Since math is not my favorite thing, I abandoned that aspiration.

Broadcast journalism was my next fixation. Linda Ellerbee, an NBC News correspondent and anchor in the eighties who went on to lead *Nick News*, was my inspiration. She had such a gift to turn a phrase that made a story better, and it had a real impact on me.

I got further on the track to being a journalist than I did an airline pilot. I became editor-in-chief of my high school yearbook. My coeditor and I chose the theme "Reading Between the Lines," inspired by the movie *The Breakfast Club*'s message of seeing people for who they really are, not just by the stereotype of their outward appearance. "Reading Between the Lines" was about tossing labels aside and learning to appreciate each other and see one another's point of view. Even back then I was starting to promote empathy.

In tribute to my journalist idol, I even signed off the yearbook with her trademark phrase and the title of her first memoir, "And so it goes..."

I pursued journalism in college and was accepted to Syracuse's Newhouse School and its broadcast journalism program. My work at the campus radio station, WJPZ-FM, started in the news department. My plans for a journalism degree got derailed in the middle of sophomore year, when I decided I wanted to go to London on the study-abroad program. The journalism program didn't offer its program overseas. I'd end up falling behind my classmates, which meant either extending to a fifth year of college (something that was not done back in the late '80s on the East Coast) or not going to London (also something that shouldn't be done). Faced with the two choices, I rationalized in my head that I didn't like the idea of having to chase a new story every single day and that I'd prefer something a bit more stable with more routine, so I changed my major. The great irony is that part of what I love most about what I do now in marketing research is the variety that comes along with this type of work. Every day I'm meeting new people and solving new problems for clients. Steady and predictable, it turns out, is not what I seek. More proof that you can rationalize almost anything away in your head when you have to.

Hollywood was my next fixation. I was intrigued by a job known as a network television programming executive. The path to that job wasn't clear, except for the fact that I'd have to live in Los Angeles, so that's where I moved shortly after graduating from Syracuse.

I decided to just get my foot in the door so I could work my way to where I wanted to be. Thanks to a typing class in high school and a great summer job in an office, I had the skills to land my first job as a legal secretary at a small but powerful entertainment law firm. To twenty-two-year-old me, the job was lucrative and glamorous (if you like answering the phone to find celebrities and power players on the other end, looking to speak to their lawyers). Ultimately, however, it was not what I wanted. I also lost interest in the network programming position over time and slowly realized that my passion was around motivating consumer behavior through marketing. I think my fascination in how people behave goes directly back to my experiences growing up when I was being teased and bullied. I didn't understand what had motivated that behavior. Why were they doing that to me? And what could I have said or done that would have changed their behavior? What could anyone have communicated that would have changed their behavior?

That realization started me off on the long and winding path through marketing services careers to where I am today, CEO and founder of Ignite 360, an insights and strategy firm that consults with some of the world's leading brands, helping them understand consumer thinking and behavior and how to build better products and services that meet consumer needs.

And now, looking back on it, was it all worth it? I remember crossing two million actual miles flown on United Airlines. That's what they call "butt in seat" miles, no bonuses or extras. Two million miles. That was a long distance in time and space. Time away from home, from family and friends and hobbies. I spend enough time flying around, it's like *it is* my hobby. Still, is it worth it? Two million miles and the work that prompted it has enabled lots of wonderful trips: numerous times to Hawaii, excursions to Nepal, Thailand (repeatedly), London, Tokyo, Paris, Vietnam, and more. Since I love travel and experiencing new places, I'm tempted to say that yes, it's been worth it. But then I reflect on the countless nights away from home, the friendships that could be richer than they are, the many social engagements missed because I was on an airplane somewhere. Not only was I taking work home, but I was also making my life my work, to the detriment of my personal time. Then to have the perspective of Kim, Annie, Debbie, Chelsea, and others, who declared that their personal time was more valuable than being successful—that made me step back and question it all.

Am I a success? Does that matter? Yes. No. Maybe. All of those answers are correct. I've decided it really depends on what you are comparing it to and how you define "success."

Nearly every family and friendship circle that I met on this project have brought me back to the same existential question: Is it better to chase success or to be happy where you are, living a life where you are more or less content with a job that makes less money but rewards you with more quality time with family, stress-free weekends, and peace of mind in the evenings? It's not balance between work and life; it's a real equilibrium. That equilibrium is achieved not as the result of a corporate initiative to give overworked and overstressed executives some relief. It's just how life is. Now, use your imagination to be in my and my clients' shoes. We've been on the hamster wheel of corporate America, chasing the success, trying to get ahead because that's what's expected of us, and then we have this alternate reality shown to us. Not once, not twice, but repeatedly, by nearly every respondent we've met on this single project. People who are happy without chasing that last bit of more money or the phantom illusion of success.

ONE FAMILY that we met on this project whose words stuck with me were Jack and Tina. They lived in a modest home in an older Pittsburgh neighborhood. Their house was a bit like a ranch in a middle-class neighborhood. Nicely maintained, definitely modest.

Up the street in this same neighborhood were a few homes that seemed more built up and elaborate. I'll admit, from my place of privilege, it's easier to go on an in-home inside one of those elaborate McMansions up the street from Jack and Tina, or perhaps a lovely, well-maintained home on a lake. While I do not have either of those living situations, that type of home is somehow more familiar and comfortable for me, more aligned to my own upper-middle-class upbringing. That means it's easier for me to get to a place of empathy with those people because the differences between us are fewer, and therefore there isn't as much judgment and it's easier to understand and put myself in their shoes. This is an example of sticking with the familiar over the foreign. But I'll tell you what. As lovely as those McMansion people may be, and no matter how valuable the information they provide, I've found that the people I learn more from—and connect with on a more deeply human level—are usually the ones where I wouldn't have ever met them in my day-to-day life in San Francisco.

It would be safe and secure and easy to stick to what I know and only interview upper-middle-class people. It would be like staying within my social media bubble or my San Francisco social circle. It'd also get boring. That comfort zone isn't where we find growth. Growth comes from pushing the margins, stepping into the unfamiliar, daring to use solution imagination to consider what it might be like to be someone else. Allowing myself to get to know others by dismantling my judgment pushes me outside my typical comfort zone. I have to walk in with an open mind, ready to actively listen. By seeing beyond the superficial "otherness" that their material goods declare, the shared values of the tribe called "human" begin to emerge. Love. Compassion. A desire to be safe, seen, and secure. These are all values that we each possess. We share them with others and seek to have them shared with us. I find that when I allow myself to approach others by using these values, I connect to those people on a much deeper level.

We were doing a "make-along" with Jack and Tina, similar to the session I had done with Frank. We wanted to see how Jack and Tina made dinner and then talk to them about their choices. Seeing what they did and the tools they used to help with meal preparation enabled us to better understand the trade-offs and other decisions they were making. It also served as a platform for Jack and Tina to easily open up about their cooking habits, which gave us entrée into their kitchen for an extended period of time so we could notice, observe, and question. Were they an oil, butter, or Crisco family? If oil, what type of oil and why?

The menu Jack and Tina had created for this make-along included pork chops on the grill, mashed potatoes, and green beans, with a large platter of fresh fruit for dessert. What we weren't expecting was that they had bought enough food to feed their family as well as the four of us coming to their house! We were touched; that was really generous of them! This was a family of four making less than fifty thousand dollars a year in total. They didn't need to spend the money making a full dinner for an extra four people. We made polite protestations, but they insisted. They wanted to do this for us. We were their guests, and "that's what you do," Jack told us as he insisted that we join them. Perhaps we shouldn't have been looking at it purely from a dollars-and-cents perspective and instead considered the polite human decency of the gesture.

Expressions of generosity like this turned out to be the norm on this project. In addition to Jack and Tina, every house we went to welcomed us into their home like friends of the family. We typically tell participants, "Don't feed us," in advance of our visit, so it's not expected, and there is no pressure on the host. (Imagine, some prospective participants must think, *I'll be evaluated on my answers as well as how moist my meat loaf is, and that will be compared to the meat loaf of others just like me across the country!* That's why we say, "Do not feed the researchers"—to take this pressure off the respondents.) Make of it what you will, but here is an observation: on other projects where we were doing a "make-along," it's been common for us not to be included in the meal, per our instructions, particularly among the McMansion set. On this working-class America project, however, we were fed on more than one occasion. To them we were guests, and, as Jack said, "It's what you do."

I remember standing with Jack by the grill; the smoke was rising up with the scent of at least a dozen searing pork chops, blowing this way and that, infusing us with a smoky flavor. Jack was telling me about his immigration to America from southern Italy as a child in the mid-'70s. He loved his adopted country, which he described as "the greatest country," and was proud to be an American. But he had noticed a different way of life back in Europe that appealed to him too.

> **Jack:** What they have there, as far as simplicity, the simple things in life are more important, to where we even notice when we would go there and they would say, "What do you want to do? Let's go take a walk." And you're walking, and you notice you're walking ahead of everybody. And they're like, "Where you going?" Because there, you walk around the town, and you catch yourself sort of doing everything fast. It's like, why? And I think what kind of caught me the most was, I was on the beach; I was looking at a family, a couple with two kids. And they were sitting down, having a cup of coffee, them two, and the kids were playing in the sand. And they just looked so simple but so warm. It's kind of really hard to explain. In other words, you don't need all that stuff to kind of—the simple things just seemed to be more exciting.

I don't know what "simple" really means, but I would say Jack's life was typical of what I'd come to find while visiting working-class families. They owned a modest home (not all of them, but Jack and Tina did), they had kids (two), both worked (warehouse supervisor and office aide at their church), they attended their kids' events, and they even had a dog. To me, in that moment with Jack and his family, it felt like a classic representation of America and Americana. Enjoying the backyard, the grill going, pork chops sizzling away, genuine neighborly hospitality being shown to us. The apple pie may have been physically missing from the menu, but it was present in spirit. Jack and Tina had a down-to-earth graciousness that those of us who live in the bigger cities don't always get to experience. That's because we're often in the tiny bubble of our daily lives. We "city folks" are still there for each other in a crisis, but otherwise we shut out most everyone but our colleagues, our friends, and the person bumping into us on the subway. As a result, this interaction and connection that we were experiencing with Jack and Tina felt so much more genuine.

I was curious about how Jack and Tina experienced stress and stress management. When I asked, he shook his head no, while Tina recognized what I was talking about. She admitted to bringing stress from work home—but not work itself. And similarly, she indicated that she brought the stress she felt from home back to work. Jack, however, behaved differently.

Jack: When I take off my work shoes, my day is done.

Me: Your day is done. And you're—

Jack: Miserable, and that doesn't matter. *[Laughs]* The way I am now is the way I'll be tomorrow morning, the way I am at work. You know, like everybody else, sometimes I get upset, whatever. But when I come in, if I yell at the kids, it ain't because I had a bad day at work; it's because, "Why are your shoes here?" or "Who left the ball in the middle of the...?"—you know? "Why did your mother call me three times today, bitching you didn't clean your room?" For that aspect, yes, but no—I won't be upset because of work. And I think once you're able to do that, it makes your day at work and at home more, you know, *[makes separating motion with his hands]* really. I mean, we work; I work twelve-hour shifts a lot of times, so the last thing I want to do is work twenty- or twenty-four-hour days. Basically, once you bring all your headaches home, that's like you're being at work. I tell those guys, once I leave, take off my shoes, I'm done working for that day.

I thought about my own work/life "balance" and how unsuccessful I was at leaving work at work. Not just the physical work to be done, but the emotions of it. Unlike Jack, I wore the same pair of shoes at work and inside my own house. When I debriefed with the clients later, they admitted to having similar thoughts, reflecting on their own situations and the choices that had created them.

Jack wasn't alone in terms of the idea of leaving work at work. That was exactly what Kim, Chelsea, Annie, and Debbie had told us in their session. In fact, it would become a sentiment echoed by many in our study. Work is work. Home is home. And the two should not intermingle. They don't want it to. No work/life balance programs needed here. They understood you are either at one or the other. I tried to use my solution imagination, put myself into that state, completely at peace at home, none of the work stress with me during dinner, hanging out, reading. When I imagined the feeling of having the two completely separated, it seemed like a dream, or a great vacation—the type you want to go on forever. For many people in traditional white-collar jobs, where being Type A and pursuing career advancement is encouraged and rewarded, this "leave your boots at the door" mentality seems unheard of. Nights and weekends are for writing PowerPoints, catching up on emails, or, in my case right now, squeezing in some time to work on this book. Yes, family and friends are there, but those activities are squeezed in, rather than the other way around.

From the way Jack and Tina talked about their life—about their after-work activities, which largely centered on their son or other family time—they weren't having to work at achieving a work/life balance. It just happened for them. An equilibrium that was natural, without it having to be taught or mandated through countless memos, signs, and books. Tina admitted she brought the stress home, but even for her, it wasn't manifesting in her parenting; she simply processed stress differently from her husband, carrying it around. What she definitely didn't do was literally bring work home with her.

Just because you may be having empathy with someone's way of life doesn't mean that you have to abandon your job or your own aspirations. Empathy lets you explore what it might be like to be someone other than you are, to see life from a different perspective. Using your solution imagination and achieving cognitive empathy doesn't mean abandoning your own way of seeing the world. It might broaden your perspective, though, so you can approach someone without coming across as a "liberal elite," and instead have a conversation where you come together to discover shared values and even discuss the benefits of the other's point of view.

As the interview drew to a close, I put the question to Jack and Tina, who, as I said, were not making more than fifty thousand dollars per year as a household: "What would the trade-off be to have a significantly higher household income?"

Jack: I worked at the hospital [prior to the warehouse], nurses, young girls, middle girls, older women working night shift, twelve hours. I'm thinking, *Man, what kind of life can that really be?* The money was great.

Tina: But sometimes you've got to think, *Is money really everything?*

Jack: Yes, so it's important, as, like, we financially think, *Okay, we're not... boy, it would be nice to make that extra five thousand, ten thousand.* I think we kind of realized that if we're kind of more together and even if it's less... we struggle financially, but it makes it up in other things. It's kind of, it's odd, a little bit, you know what I mean?

During Jack's answer, Tina had said something I couldn't quite hear, but I'd heard enough to know it was insightful. I asked her to repeat what she had said.

> **Tina:** You might struggle financially, but you're always rich in love.

> **Me:** What does that mean for you?

> **Tina:** It means you know you might not have a lot of money, but you have a nice life; you have a wonderful husband, wonderful kids, and they love each other. There's some people that are just married just for money. You see that all the time. I mean, I've seen it.

> **Jack:** If they offered me a job and said I'll double your salary but you're going to have to work different shifts or travel, I'd probably turn it down. I'm sure I would turn it down because okay, that'd be great; we'd be able to, oh boy, maybe pay off the car, pay off the house, who knows. But...

> **Me:** What would you be sacrificing?

> **Jack:** Everything, everything that kind of seems to matter. That's what's amazing. And after it's all said and done, you want more money so you can be more financially secure, and you can spend more time with your kids and this random BS— but there's no need. There has to be a happy medium, because just because you're making more money—we'd probably end up being very, very unhappy. Money-wise it'd be great, but...

But there'd be real sacrifices to make. Sacrifices that just aren't worth it to Jack, Tina, Debbie, Kim, and so many others. And now that I understand their point of view, I can't say that I blame them.

IN AMERICAN society, success is often measured by three criteria: how are we doing compared to our neighbors, how are we doing compared to our peers, and how are we doing compared to our parents. Typically the indicators of success are through material goods—the size of the house, the type of car, the bling, the vacation destinations. Is it what we really need? We've been trained to celebrate excess as a symbol of success—from "glamorous" fictional TV shows to the reality stars and influencers on social media. It's so easy to get caught up in someone else's measurement of success rather than your own.

Until that little virus infected the world and equalized so many things in our life that the only thing we could show off was how beautiful that week's loaf of sourdough bread was. The COVID-19 pandemic brought so much in everyone's lives to a screeching halt and left us looking in the mirror at our own reflection.

Having more than a year without many of the activities that let us show off our success—no parties; no fancy dinners out; no glamorous vacation destinations; nowhere to show off that expensive new bag, shoes, watch, or device—we're reflecting on who we are as people and where we want to go with our lives. In Ignite 360's study *Navigating to a New Normal*, we asked people if they want life to return to how it was before the pandemic or if they'd like a change. Consistently, over the course of the pandemic, our research (starting in April 2020) showed that 72 percent of people said they want some form of change in their lives instead of returning to how things were. The type of change people are wanting to make is focused on their personal connections and how they are showing up in their whole life. Gratitude and appreciating what they have in life is also high on people's lists. Spending on material goods and getting new jobs to make more money have become much lower priorities. While the crystal ball is perpetually fuzzy on what exactly will happen, it does appear that some values have been reset and redefined, including how we think about success and the trade-offs to get it.

The pandemic has affected everyone differently, based largely on socioeconomic status. The idea of stronger connections transcended most of the demographics in our study. Parents have appreciated the added time with their kids, despite the headaches of distance learning and lacking the built-in babysitter elements of school and after-school activities. The parents in the qualitative part of our study say they've valued this time with the kids and are looking to be less overscheduled in the future.

Similarly, the way we are looking at where we work is shifting. As the first year of the pandemic drew to a close, nearly half of our respondents who are working from home because of the pandemic say they want to work at home more in the future than they did pre-pandemic. Almost one-third indicate they want to go to the main office less in the future. People in this situation have found benefits of working from home: more time with family, more engagement with their community, the ability to better manage their health, flexibility with schedules, and the comfort of actually being at home.

The implications of these shifts have the potential to be huge, depending on how deep the commitment to change goes, how flexible corporations are willing to be, and how much empathy we have with one another.

Where did I end up after my experiences with Jack, Tina, Kim, and Debbie? I didn't give up my crazy hours, and I was traveling full tilt until the pandemic brought that to a halt. What this experience has done is given me greater understanding of the life and priorities of working-class Americans, while also helping me appreciate my own decisions and the trade-offs I've made in my own life. I can more easily identify what the "needs" are in my life instead of the "wants" that I yearn for, and I can be okay with having my needs met and pushing off the wants. The pandemic has also given me a wonderful chance to be home and in one place more than I've been in any one place in twenty years. Like so many of those working from home, it's felt good to reconnect with the language of my home.

Will these possible post-COVID-19 shifts give society the chance to redefine what real happiness and success in life is about? Can the white-collar workers exist more fully in their personal space in the future? What the pandemic has shown us is that what you achieve and accumulate materialistically isn't actually that important. Rather, it's about how you engage in the world and with the people around you. Using your empathy skills will be crucial to achieving this both at work and in your personal life. How we show up, how we engage, how we perceive one another, how we treat one another. What if, moving forward, being successful was measured differently? What if it was about leaving your boots at the door and enjoying your life? How would you move through the world differently? What if your contribution to society wasn't about making millions for yourself but helping and engaging with others? Being measured by a life of "significance" rather than a measure of success. How would you approach your own life differently?

EMPATHETIC REFLECTIONS

- Think of someone who is different from you demographically. Imagine what it would be like to live their life. Use solution imagination to put yourself in their shoes. How, if you were them, would you approach a day-to-day decision that you've recently made for yourself?

- What did you learn about yourself during the pandemic? How have you applied that learning? What were the challenges? What was easier than expected?

- What do you want to change in your life? How will you start to make that a reality? Share your ideas in a conversation with a friend or loved one. Use solution imagination to connect with them when they share with you.

18

The Trappings of Success

It is not the destiny of Black america to repeat white america's mistakes. But we will, if we mistake the trappings of success in a sick society for the signs of a meaningful life.

AUDRE LORDE

HUMANS HAVE ALWAYS desired showing off the visible signs of their status and power. Once upon a time, in the 1800s, those status symbols were conveyed by decorations on the bridle and saddle of a person's horse. These ornamentations were referred to as "trappings." When a person in that time saw those trappings, it conveyed the level of wealth of the owner, which translated to what status and power they held. The idea of these trappings conveying our wealth, status, and power holds true today. Consider what we covet to show that we've "made it." There's a range of products and experiences, but it's often expressed by the cars we drive, the designer clothes we wear, the house we own, the trips we take, and the accessories that complete our "look." These are the trappings of today's success. What it is supposed to reveal, without directly saying it, is how much money we make. And how much money we make is supposed to say something about our value within society.

Many of us allow ourselves to get distracted by these trappings. Celebrities and the "rich and famous" are adorned in these trappings. They sparkle off them. It's the glitz that goes with the glamour. And we risk becoming enamored of these trappings ourselves. They are shiny objects that pull our gaze away from pursuing a life of significance. Instead, they say that we are successful. And there is a perception in our society that being successful means that you are somebody. Being seen as successful is another form of validation. And if you are successful, that means you have money, which means you have the trappings that go along with it. And here comes that first pair of designer sunglasses, or the luxury vehicle. Then it's the luxury appliances in the house, the neighborhood you live in, the clothes your kids wear, the activities they participate in, where you go on vacation. Fortunately, for those of us who are chasing this sense of self-worth, upscale brands have made it easier for people to acquire products to show off their status and bask in the magic glow of the brand. And in that glow—which is really just the halo from the glitz and glamour—what was once a true trapping of success comes within reach for the mainstream consumers. Whether they need it or not. Many people in the United States have the ability to run around and look (somewhat) like they are "important," at least compared to their actual socioeconomic level. The fact that they can afford these designer goods telegraphs that they have a modicum of income and a sense of venality. Appearances can be deceiving, however. While people have the right to spend their money as they see fit, what these trappings do not say much about is who someone is as a human being.

By early 2009 the country was in an economic tailspin. The stock market had recently plummeted. The daily declines were jaw-dropping, even to the average consumer like me, who is not very engaged in investing. Banks were near bankruptcy, and the housing market collapsed. Millions of Americans were impacted by the Great Recession. Millions upon millions were displaced from jobs, lost homes, or had their savings disappear. The recession also changed our relationship to material goods. Like waking up with a sharp hangover, we collectively realized our lust for the trappings of success was sinking us. We were carrying too much credit card debt and didn't have any "rainy day funds" saved up, nor could we honestly afford the glamourous life we were trying to live.

One of our clients wanted to understand how current events were impacting people's spending habits—how they were thinking about grocery shopping and food purchases as well as the trappings in their lives. In addition to our usual pre-recruited in-homes, we decided to also get some "man on the street" perspective about how the recession was affecting them. To do that, we set up booths at a few events in the cities where we were doing our in-homes. One of those cities happened to be Indianapolis, not far from the smaller small town where I grew up and had my traumatic formative years.

Memorial Day weekend in Indiana, like the rest of the country, officially marks the unofficial start of summer. The first long holiday weekend in warm weather, Memorial Day weekend is also ground zero for one of the greatest "spectacles in racing," the Indianapolis 500. Growing up, I was never a fan of the motor speedway. A lot of people loved the event and its social aspects. It just didn't hold appeal to me. Perhaps if my parents were into it, that would have made a difference. So despite growing up so near, I've always felt far away from that big event and all the festivities during that weekend. The Indy 500 makes the streets of downtown Indianapolis a great place to find a lot of people to interview. Since it was getting into hot and humid season, we set up a table and chairs with plenty of signage in the blissful air-conditioning of the Circle Centre Mall in downtown Indianapolis.

Days when we have any sort of intercept-style, "man on the street" interviews are typically long and exhausting. Not only do they involve constant standing and sometimes being outside in the sun, but you also have to be ready at a moment's notice to pounce on the stranger walking near your booth to try to land the interview. You don't get the luxury of scheduled start and stop times, like in a focus group or an in-home. Anyone could walk by at any time. Even minutes after you finished your last session. And the interviews can have even more of a feeling of an improv session, as you are meeting whoever happens to walk by and says yes to an interview, instead of a narrow demographic subset that has been pre-recruited for in-homes and groups.

Our approach to attracting people was simple; we all wore T-shirts with the words "Tell Us Your Opinion" printed on them. We offered passersby a gift card in exchange for ten minutes of their time. You get pretty good at reading body language when you are doing intercepts. Some people ignore you totally, while others will sheepishly look at you, then look the other way as they walk by. Others make direct eye contact. Some will look at their watch as they pass. And others just project a warm energy that you can sense will convert into a good interview. Unless I'm getting total "don't bug me" vibes, I tend to ask as many people as possible, acting under the philosophy that you don't know until you try.

Toward the end of this particular day at the Circle Centre Mall, we had already had some good conversations with folks. It rounded out much of what we were learning on our in-homes and in the other markets. What other stories could we possibly hear? We'd heard about lost homes, lost jobs, working two jobs to make ends meet. Sacrifices made at home, at work, and by all members of the family. What remained a constant for everyone was the joy of family and loved ones being together. No matter how bad things got, they still had each other, and there were simple pleasures that they enjoyed.

As the afternoon wore on, we were starting to wonder if we should call it a day. Mall traffic was dropping off, and we'd definitely talked to enough people who echoed similar stories to what we had been hearing. I encouraged the team to stick it out this one last hour. And moments later, Gregory walked up. He was a mid-thirties, handsome Black man wearing a blue, short-sleeved polo shirt and jeans. He might have had on Top-Siders or maybe sneakers. Well-groomed and incredibly pleasant. He sat down across from me, and we started talking.

Just like everyone else, Gregory started to tell me how the recession had affected him. He used to be a mortgage broker in Indianapolis. A bright guy eager to succeed, he rose through the ranks very quickly at the brokerage he was working at. He and his wife had two kids who were "lovely," by his description. The family was able to buy a house with a four-car garage. I think he said it was on a golf course, or they had a membership at the country club. In other words, they acquired many of the trappings of success available as he moved up in the world.

In Gregory's case though, once the recession hit, the trappings were more like weights, dragging him and his life down underwater.

First, Gregory lost his job at the mortgage brokerage. And once that happened, his friends at the club started to shun him. His wife, who was enamored of the lifestyle and all the trappings, wasn't happy with this change. Their marriage started to dissolve, he said. He couldn't keep up on the house payments. Or the car payments. Before he knew it, Gregory had lost the car and the house. Shortly after that, his wife left with the kids. He lost everything. He was, he told us, homeless.

Wow. That piece of information I wasn't expecting. I'll admit, I was a little incredulous at first. Gregory didn't "look homeless" in the way that I encounter homeless people on the street. His clothes were clean. He was well-groomed and tidy. There was no evidence, visceral or olfactory, to indicate that this man was living on the street. But he was telling me that he was, and I couldn't imagine why someone would lie to me on a spontaneous intercept interview. So, I pressed on to find out more.

As Gregory unraveled the workings of his now homeless life, my client, Mandy, and I followed along as best we could. I was trying to use my solution imagination to understand what it would be like to lose my home and have to live on the street. I imagined what I might do if it happened to me and used that to form my follow-up questions. First, it was difficult for me to understand how someone didn't have friends that would help him out and give him a place to stay. Next, what type of spouse would kick him out and take the kids because he hit hard times? But that's what had happened. Gregory did tell us that one friend helped him out by letting him stay at their house shortly after he lost his wife and trappings. That friend let him stay in the garage.

Once the goodwill of friends wore off, Gregory went to his mom's house in downtown Indianapolis. Surely a thirtysomething man, down on his luck, could count on the support of his mom. But his mother had troubles of her own, and his pride was also getting in his way. So, Gregory told us, he stayed at his mom's house occasionally, but he was often on his own, out on the street.

I had all sorts of judgment going on in my head at this point, but none of it was blocking me from getting to empathy with Gregory. I was being judgmental toward the wife, the friend, even his mom a little bit. Who would abandon this nice man and let him live on the street?

But also, I was curious. What is life on the street like? Of course, my guard was still up, as this was just so mind-blowing. I tried to use solution imagination to see what this life must have been like, but I remained cautious, looking for holes in his story. Gregory had come upon us as he was walking the mall, dropping off applications to hopefully get hired at one of the stores. And then he laid out his story of being homeless. Throughout the interview, he was consistent. Each piece of his story made sense and fit into the next part or aligned to what he had told me earlier. And since this was a serendipitous meeting, not anything planned or prearranged, there was no way he could have practiced this. After a while, I decided to let go of my skepticism and go on the journey, no matter where he took me.

I started by asking more questions about what life was like on the street. As you can probably tell, my usual interview style is like

Oprah Winfrey or Diane Sawyer—chummy, like two friends talking over coffee. I find it helps respondents open up so I can get to the deep stuff with compassion, rather than cracking them open like a suspect in a criminal interrogation. I prefer this soft approach in my interactions with most people in my life, so it makes sense that I adapt it as part of my interviewing persona. With this interview, however, I was in full Lesley Stahl or Mike Wallace *60 Minutes* mode, challenging and playing devil's advocate to try to get to the bottom of Gregory's story.

On the topic of being homeless, Gregory shared that the greatest indignity he felt was when he was asking for money from people, and they wouldn't even make eye contact. He said it made him feel less than human when that happened. I immediately recalled the many times I hadn't acknowledged the panhandlers on the streets at home in San Francisco. Gregory's bringing that point up helped me use solution imagination to put myself in their shoes. I thought about the times when someone ignored me when I was asking for an intercept interview and how that rejection made me feel. Then I imagined what it would be like to be ignored repeatedly—to not be seen while asking for money or help, which you need to make it through the day. That ups the emotional stakes even further. That cognitive empathy made me realize that I could show a little more kindness and compassion; even if I had nothing to give, it didn't mean I had to ignore the homeless. I made a mental note to at least make eye contact with people asking for money, to help them remain feeling human.

An assumption I had about being homeless was that the money from panhandling was used toward food. Gregory said that was not the case. He told us it was relatively easy to get food when you are homeless; you just have to know where the good restaurants are. Apparently, steak houses throw out the overcooked cuts that are sent back to the kitchen. Unsaleable, out they go into the back with the trash, and into the waiting arms of the hungry. Gregory assured us that he ate quite well many nights, and that finding food was not the issue.

And I believed him. He didn't look malnourished. In fact, he looked relatively lean and fit.

The biggest fear, Gregory told us, was sleeping out on the street. "Rolling" is what can happen when you fall asleep outdoors. People, other homeless and those "up to no good," approach you while you sleep in your bag or on your piece of cardboard. Quietly, they grab the edge of your sleeping pad, whip-snap it, and roll you over. Disoriented from being asleep and suddenly tumbled, you aren't fully aware of what's going on. That's when they grab whatever valuables you have that they want for themselves. You are so discombobulated; you can't get your bearings in order to chase after the people who are making off with your stuff. In order to avoid "rolling," Gregory used the money he made each day to get a cheap hotel room where he could at least get a proper sleep and clean himself up in the morning. It seemed pretty smart and made sense. How can you get a job and change your situation if you aren't hygienic or at least clean-shaven? Staying in a cheap hotel let him do that.

Through this experience, Gregory said he reconnected with his faith so deeply that he had enrolled in a local theology program. And right there and then, Gregory reached into his backpack and showed us his textbooks, which he had just picked up earlier that day. His goal was to minister to the homeless, since he had such newfound appreciation for what people experience when they've lost everything. Seeing the textbooks gave me a deeper sense of trust in the story he was telling us. That was real.

When I'm presented with a respondent's information that doesn't add up or just seems incredible, I will circle back through the story over and over in my questions. What I'm doing is looking to poke holes in the story without saying, "I don't believe you; prove it." Circling back lets me ask a question from a different perspective. If I don't get an answer that aligns to the earlier one, then I'll know something is off and I can ask additional questions or try to clarify the discordant information.

With Gregory, there was no inconsistency. There wasn't any-thing that I could find that didn't line up, only sheer jaw-dropping "wow" at his situation. No job, no home, no car. Wife and kids moved out of state. Sees mom occasionally but she has her own problems. Shelters are limited in number of beds and aren't a desir-able option, as your stuff isn't secure. Sleeping on the streets isn't desirable, as you aren't safe. We kept the conversation with Greg-ory going for forty-five minutes, well over the ten-minute length of most conversations for this type of intercept. Mandy sat with me through the entire interview. She was just as stunned as I was, curi-ous to know more. And I could see, in her eyes and the expression on her face, the empathy she had developed with Gregory.

That final hour we had left at the mall went by quickly. We were still talking with Gregory while the other team was packing up. Finally, realizing how much time had gone by, I wound down the interview so we could let him go on his way and we could get back to the hotel. Mandy and I said goodbye to Gregory. I gave him his gift card and the little extra cash I had in my wallet to help him get a hotel room for the night. He was really appreciative. After he said goodbye and walked off, Mandy and I just looked at each other, stunned. What had we just experienced?

Gregory's interview was an intense moment of empathy with someone going through something we had never experienced or imagined before. This was already an intense project. We had heard so many stories of loss and concern about the future. The Great Recession impacted so many people in so many ways, but Gregory went through more than any of them in the study. The one-two punch of his work and home life falling apart was a lot for us to take in and integrate into our understanding, let alone put ourselves in his shoes. There was so much information that he shared with us, situations of life on the street—sleeping, finding food, panhandling, job hunting. Our brains were spinning, trying to process it all.

I find when I have intense interviews, like this one, that it can be difficult to stay in cognitive empathy, and I will drop into emotional empathy, dialing in on their situation and feeling what I imagine them to be feeling. I imagined what it would be like to be living his life. How would I handle being homeless? Could I face the constant rejection of panhandling? What would that feel like? What would I do to make sure I wasn't rolled while trying to catch some sleep? As we debriefed, we found all of those thoughts and feelings were running through my head and Mandy's—as well as our hearts. I had images of Gregory in various settings in my head. Mingling at the country club, driving the luxury car, the big house, the beautiful wife and kids, and now, nothing. And Gregory seemingly had made peace with it. In fact, he'd had an awakening from that experience in his decision to minister to the homeless.

WE MADE our way back to the Westin Indianapolis, wearing our "Tell Us Your Opinion" T-shirts and carrying our equipment and the scent of the day on us. As we entered the hotel, we encountered a well-dressed group of middle-aged Americans. They were gathering in the lobby of the hotel to head out to one of the gala events in honor of the race weekend. The men were in suits, women in dresses created by semi-reputable designers. Each and every woman was adorned with jewels as big as their hair was high, and the men sported belt buckles the size of dinner plates. Like the bridle and saddle of centuries ago, the trappings of their success were prominent.

My hands were completely full as we entered the hotel and worked our way through the crowded lobby. I was weighed down by my backpack, a long poster tube with our booth signage, and just the sheer enormity of what we had borne witness to in our interviews that day. Metaphorically it felt like I was dragging a cross through the town square. My emotions were right on the surface. I just wanted to get to my room and a hot shower that would allow my tears over Gregory's story to flow, blend in with the soap and water, and be washed away.

There were so many small clusters of gala attendees sipping on cocktails and engaging in lively conversation, it was hard for us to navigate through the lobby. It felt so surreal, having just heard of someone's fall from a life of comfort and luxury, to walk in and witness the Indy 500 version of glitz and glamour. I marched on, emotions in check. My eyes were focused on parting the crowd and leading our troop to the elevators without my "cross" knocking a vodka cranberry onto a pretty white dress.

With the end in sight, a woman in an off-the-shoulder dress with her hair sculpted high and stiff was all that stood between me and the elevator bank. A thick layer of makeup was painted on her face. It struck me as a type of mask projecting the illusion of success and, therefore, happiness. Of course, there were the jewels too. A necklace, diamond earrings, multiple rings. I don't remember every detail, but she seemed to me like she was from Texas. My suspicion was confirmed when she honey-drawled, "What do you want to know my opinion on?" *What? Why is she asking me?* I wondered. *Oh. These damn T-shirts are still on us. I don't want to talk to anyone. Not now.*

Not one to be rude, I told the woman that we had been interviewing people at the mall to find out how the recession had been affecting them.

There was some glint of humanity in her eyes as she pondered the question. Beneath the makeup, the hairspray, and the jewels, she was still a considerate being. Before she could reply to us and share her thoughts, an older man, who I imagined to be her husband, turned around toward us and took over the conversation. He was probably fifty-something but looked sixty-something, thanks to the effects of life and too much exposure to the sun. I clearly recall the oversized silver belt buckle he had on. In my mind, his name was Tex.

"What recession?" Tex scoffed at us. "There's no recession. It's just a made-up story from the media and the liberal elite."

Dumbstruck, I couldn't believe what I'd just heard. I think the wife sensed my shock. She certainly could have seen it on my face. My eyes were wide in disbelief. My mouth might have even opened. I couldn't believe what I was hearing. He actually doubted the recession was happening? By this point, banks had collapsed. The stock market had fallen. Millions were out of work and were losing their homes. It was real. And I knew it was real. I had spent the past three weeks interviewing people about the recession, only to have it capped off by one of the most traumatic stories I had ever heard as a moderator. And this guy was doubting the whole thing? Negating the empathy I had established? And he could say it out loud, in public? Painting it as a figment of the imagination of a liberal media? What the hell?

The audacity of his statement seemed completely outrageous in 2009. How could someone say something so preposterous and with such braggadocio? Over a decade later, with our descent into bubbles and self-assuring media, such talk isn't so surprising, but it still remains shocking to hear.

Unfortunately, I didn't have much of a snappy retort. I was beaten down from everything that I had heard and seen. Oh, how I wished I could have channeled Julia Sugarbaker from *Designing Women* and delivered a short but eviscerating monologue detailing the stories of the many people we had met who were truly suffering from the recession and weren't a figment of the imagination of the media or the liberal elite. It would be the type of monologue reserved for liberal TV shows and movies that would have torn him down while also opening his eyes to the errors of his way of thinking. But righteous indignation escaped me on that Saturday night in Indianapolis. "You're wrong!" was all I could mutter as I squinted at him in disbelief. I then shook my head in disgust, pushed passed the Texans, and finished the walk to the elevator.

Make no mistake. The Great Recession was real. From what I was witnessing, the guy at the hotel with the silver belt buckle was more concerned in that moment about the trappings of his own success than about other people. He chose to be blind to the stories of other people's suffering that were everywhere in the media in those months. He even chose to be dismissive of a crew of people (us) who bore witness to the recession. It's not dissimilar to how the liberal elite were dismissive of the working class in the 2016 election. They too chose to be blind to the struggles of a segment of society they didn't really understand or have empathy with. Years later, I remain unconvinced that either side "gets it."

Many words go through my mind when I think about that man. *Jerk*, *fool*, *idiot*, *pig* are just some of them. It's really difficult for me not to go to a place of judgment about him based on that experience. He was so dismissive of the recession—and of us, by extension—that I felt like he was minimizing us. That made me feel like he didn't feel we, or our work, had any value. In turn, my internal reaction went to a place where I felt like he was being an asshole for saying what he said rather than *asking questions, listening, and considering* what we had to say. We could have told him the story of Gregory or one of the many others we had heard but Tex showed no empathy with us or curiosity to learn our perspective on the topic. Only his opinion counted, which he had to state as a pompous declaration rather than ask us to tell him more about what we had learned. That would have threatened his worldview if he were to question how real the recession might be. So in that moment, I could have no empathy with him. Instead of compassion for his ignorance and arrogance, my immediate reaction was to be judgmental back toward him. I know I shouldn't have, but it was really insulting to be dismissed like that, and I was too drained to engage further in conversation, so I stayed in my place of judgment.

This is the challenge with empathy. It's a two-way street. One person has to be willing to share, while the other has to be willing to take the 5 Steps to get to a place of empathy. Gregory shared with me and I used the 5 Steps. When it was my turn to share, Tex wasn't able to get beyond Step 1 and so it shut me down. And just because you can build empathy with someone, such as Gregory, doesn't mean everyone else is capable of that same empathetic connection. My focus that day was to build empathy with Gregory and people like him. However, I still wanted someone to have empathy with me and my experiences. Tex could have had empathy with me or allowed me to have empathy with him. I needed the former in that moment in the lobby of the Westin. Because Tex had caught me off guard, the latter wasn't going to happen. I wasn't in a space to ask good questions and listen to him. I was so completely fried from our day in the field, my conversation with Gregory, and all the other people I had talked to. I just wanted a hot shower and a good cry. Had I met Tex in another circumstance, say he stopped by the booth in the mall, yes, I would have talked to him, dismantled my judgment, asked good questions, actively listened, integrated into understanding, and even used solution imagination to understand where he was coming from with his beliefs about the recession. But that's not where I was in that moment when he was dismissing me.

Because I didn't *have* to have empathy with Tex, nor was I in the mood to, I held my tongue and continued toward the elevator. I still don't know enough about Tex to get to empathy. I never gave him the chance. I only have my bias built up against him because of what he'd said and the way he presented himself. I will have to dismantle that bias at some point.

And then there was that belt buckle he was wearing. Big, silver, and gaudy, serving no real purpose other than decoration, it was a symbol of his perceived status. To me, that trapping of his success represented more than his rank in his community; it was emblematic of his blindness to the suffering of people outside his immediate life. The sparkle of the buckle, the shimmer of his wife's jewels, all glittering objects that distracted his vision and concentration. It kept him from focusing on what was really important.

Instead, he was just striving for that next trapping to adorn his saddle. Gregory had been chasing after a gaudy belt buckle of his own. The recession had thrown him off his saddle, though, and he'd found a new path where success is defined by service, not silver.

Gregory still comes to mind whenever I'm approached by a panhandler in San Francisco who doesn't appear to have mental health issues or pose a physical threat. I think about what Gregory said and try to look the other person in the eye, even if for just a moment. I don't know if it helps them retain a sense of dignity as Gregory said or if it just makes me feel better. I do know, though, for that quick flash of eye contact, we are seeing each other beyond the trappings of our lives. For that brief moment, I am seeing them with cognitive empathy, aware of the struggle they are facing. We are connecting, one human to another.

EMPATHETIC REFLECTIONS

- How do you interact with people in need? When have you been ignored or not seen? How did that make you feel?

- Think about a time when someone has suffered a loss. How did you reply to them? Were you able to be empathetic or did you default to sympathy? What could you have said that would have shown cognitive empathy? "I can see/imagine..."

- How would you have handled the interaction with Tex and his wife? What would help you get to a place of empathy with them?

- How have the pandemic and the events of 2020 changed you? What types of changes are you seeking to make and why? What do you notice about the changes others around you are trying to make?

PART 3

Embracing Empathy in Everyday Life

19

A Work in Progress

Stand in the middle, no matter what's around the wall.
Stand in the middle, 'cause that's where healing
happens. That's where conversation happens. That's
where change happens. It happens in the middle.
TYLER PERRY, accepting the Jean Hersholt
Humanitarian Award at the Academy Awards, April 2021

MPATHY IS ALSO useful in achieving forgiveness. As an
adult I've been able to return to the smaller small town
in Indiana, my "scene of the crime." With each visit—there
have been five since my parents moved to DC after my high school
graduation and I went off to college in Syracuse—I've been processing through my pain. One of the last visits was in 2002 with
my husband and a good friend. We sat in our rental car, parked in
front of the elementary school. I pointed out the top floor window
of the classroom where I was first called "gay" by another student.
The tears came, and I couldn't hold them back. Charles and Marla
comforted me as I released some of the pain of twenty-year-old
wounds. After that trip, Charles decided he'd seen enough of this
smaller small town and wasn't interested in returning.

I felt a mix of trepidation, curiosity, and dread when I got the message that my thirtieth high school reunion was on for August 2017. I had skipped the last few, not feeling a need to return after my tenth reunion. But thirty felt significant. A lot had changed. I was working on healing myself in therapy, so going to the reunion would help me move toward closure. I also had a greater understanding of empathy, having sketched out the 5 Steps by then, and I was well underway drafting an early manuscript for this book. I was much more aware of how the 5 Steps show up in my life and what I need to do to reach cognitive empathy, even in situations when I just wanted to be judgmental.

I checked with a few classmates who I was friends with to see who would be attending. Once I knew they were in, I felt more comfortable making the trip. I had let go of my revenge fantasies by the time of my tenth reunion, when I realized that most of my classmates' lives were on different trajectories from mine. I had also received some acknowledgment from some of them, recognizing that I had been mistreated by them when we were younger. Hearing that empathetic outreach did a lot to defuse my surface anger, but a lot of underlying mistrust and pain remained. I don't think I got to a place of real forgiveness until that particular summer visit on the occasion of our thirtieth graduation reunion.

It was August, which of course meant the weather in Indiana was hot and humid, like a swamp. (If you haven't realized it yet, I hate hot and humid weather. I'm a creature built for air-conditioning or at least temperate climates.) While the official reunion, a casual get-together at the local lodge, was on Saturday night, the events actually started on Friday at the local Italian restaurant. A sign of progress in this smaller small town—there was another Italian restaurant besides Pizza Hut. And on the other end of town, a Thai restaurant! Having Italian food beyond pizza would have made life more tolerable in the '80s, and a Thai restaurant would have been amazing. I actually ate with a friend at the Thai restaurant before the reunion. Dinner was great, but when it came to the reunion, I was nervous on arrival.

We were there on the early side and grabbed drinks as people started to show up. They were older-looking versions of their childhood selves, and I recognized almost all of them. But I soon realized I had been more nervous at the five- and ten-year reunions. Back then I didn't know as much about their lives. Now, social media had exposed a great deal about each of us, so we were able to move quickly past current events that we had already validated with "likes." That made room for us to dive into the past.

During the course of the reunion weekend, I sat and actively listened to my former classmates. The last time I had seen most of them, I wasn't cognizant of asking good questions or how to dismantle my judgment. Some of my classmates opened up about their own childhoods. Listening to each one of them, I started to recognize how different their childhood lives had been from my own. Where I'd had a "safe harbor" at home with my immediate family, it wasn't the same for everyone. Some had had lives that were more difficult than I'd realized, whether they were dealing with emotionally distant or divorced parents, alcohol or substance abuse, mental health issues, struggles with their own sexual identity, or other events that are not what stereotypically defines a "normal" childhood. And then, building on those revelations and further conversations (always ask good questions!), I could see how the events from childhood had played out in their adult lives. Some were enjoying more traditional adult lives with great or steady jobs, home ownership, spouses, kids, and grandkids(!), while others had a history of failed relationships, challenges with their own kids, trouble with the law, or early-onset health issues.

I could have felt bad for my classmates. However, that would have been sympathy—me feeling grateful that I didn't have their misfortune. I wouldn't have been seeing them on equal footing; I would have been in a superior position, looking down on them, almost from a place of judgment. Knowing the pain I had experienced, where I just wanted the other kids to *see* and *accept* me for who I was, on equal footing, it would have been hypocritical of me to have taken that posture. Instead, I tried to get to a place of empathy.

Moving past my pain-induced judgment toward my classmates, even those whose taunts I can still remember, I asked open questions, listened, held space in my mind for their experiences and how that had affected them, and, finally, moved into a place where I could imagine what it would have been like to be them when we were kids. In that place, using solution imagination—that was where I finally got to a place of cognitive empathy. I realized that all of us as kids were nothing more than wounded animals, on the defensive, bumping into each other and lashing out in order to protect ourselves from being wounded further.

That realization was it for me. We were all damaged in our own ways, through no fault of our own, just trying to make ourselves feel better, usually at the expense of another. Being able to take that perspective and see where each of my classmates was coming from based on their own life experiences gave me the understanding that I needed in order to forgive the behavior from our childhood that had caused my wounds. Empathy-led forgiveness doesn't make the original offending behavior acceptable, but it has enabled me to get some closure and heal myself more fully. I left the reunion weekend feeling more whole and healed than at any point in my life. Cognitive empathy helped me get there. I forgive them.

I MAY NOT have been born an empathy guru, but empathy has become my superpower. It started as a survival skill when I was growing up and trying to navigate those painful years. The ability to listen to people and connect with them helped me move across different cliques of students as a kid, and now it has helped me navigate my adult life more easily too.

As a society, we often move too fast to stop, be present, and truly listen to each other. To hear what people have to say and understand where they are coming from. It can feel safer to stay in our bubble, repeating what we want to hear, rather than face the people we pass every day on the street with grace and respect. Maybe you don't give them a second glance, but what are you missing out on as a result? Life is so much richer and more enjoyable when you can develop empathy with others and have them develop empathy with you in return.

I created the framework that became the 5 Steps to Empathy because I recognized that we—every one of us—need help strengthening our empathy muscle. The polarization of our society, fueled by many things, including social media, politicians, and our addiction to validation, has allowed our "frenemy"—judgment—to stand in the way of our ability to have empathy.

Each one of the 5 Steps is a skill to master all on its own. Like hurdles that a runner faces, each one needs to be cleared in order to reach the finish line: empathy. And once you reach a place of empathy, you can continue on to what empathy enables—collaboration, conversation, decision-making, leadership, forgiveness, compassion, and so much more.

Step 1: Dismantle Judgment. I've found that this first step is truly the hardest. Of all the people I've coached the 5 Steps to, this is the one that gets in the way and keeps coming up after they've completed training. Be aware of when you are being judgmental. Be mindful of what is causing the judgment. If there is a pattern, you may need to tend to that injury or bias.

Step 2: Ask Good Questions. Open questions that are exploratory in nature get better, deeper answers than questions that are closed or pointed in a particular direction. Start with something simple, like, "How are you?" And if you want to know more about a topic, just go with, "Tell me more about that."

Step 3: Active Listening. Be present. Listen with all of your senses. Remember that body language speaks volumes. And don't forget to look at the surroundings. Otherwise you might miss a find as awesome as the penis mirror!

Step 4: Integrate into Understanding. Make room in your head for what you've heard. You don't have to discard your own beliefs or values; just recognize intellectually that this other way of thinking or living is true and right for that individual, and that's okay. Watch out! Your "frenemy" judgment likes to sneak back in here.

Step 5: Use Solution Imagination. Now for the moment of truth. You've taken off your own shoes in Steps 1 to 4. Now step into the shoes of someone else. Try to say, "I can see your point of view," and then restate that point of view as that other person. Don't stop with just stating it. That's the previous step. Here you want to consider the *why* behind it and add that to the narrative. It's to know that this is true, to see or feel *with* them. Welcome to empathy.

The 5 Steps should go with you wherever you are and with whomever you are interacting. It can be a colleague, a friend, a family member, a neighbor, or a lover. Empathy is important, and it increases the quality of all of those relationships. Whether you apply it at work or in your personal life, cognitive empathy will make your world a better place.

For me, I continue to interview people for projects, in particular the *Navigating to a New Normal* study, which Ignite 360 launched in April 2020. What started as a short three-month project to understand how people were coping with the pandemic has morphed into a much more fascinating exploration following the societal changes in values, attitudes, and behaviors that began in 2020. The qualitative participants in that study (the people we have interviewed) include a diverse range of everyday Americans—from a Disney-loving right-wing anti-vaxxer to a progressive gay man in New York City; a retired priest to a newly released parolee; and a Jehovah's Witness to a Millennial mom of three with a shopping addiction, the range of voices and experiences is so broad and largely different from my own (except for the progressive gay) that I'm having to rely on the 5 Steps to get through the more difficult conversations about racism, prejudice, election results, and the January 6 Capitol insurrection. Getting myself to empathy with some of them on these topics can be challenging, but the result is a clearer understanding of who we are in America and where we are headed. I'm hopeful that we are changing for the better by the majority of American adults in our quantitative survey who said they want to make an effort to have empathy with others.

I'll be the first to admit that I'm not perfect. I'm human, just like everyone else. Even for someone who spends a significant amount of time thinking about the principles of empathy and how to create more empathy-building experiences with our clients, I still have to be vigilant and make sure I'm following the 5 Steps. Judgment gets in my way just like it does for most everyone else. What's important is that we continue to make the effort to try to have empathy with one another. The muscle may be atrophied, but it's still there—and with the 5 Steps, your empathy muscle can be made strong once again.

EMPATHETIC REFLECTIONS

- How might you use cognitive empathy to reach forgiveness with someone? What would you need to understand? How can the 5 Steps assist you?

- Which of the 5 Steps do you struggle with the most? What makes that one difficult for you?

- What's holding you back from using cognitive empathy more in your life?

Acknowledgments

T HANK YOU FOR taking the time to read this book. It wouldn't exist without the thousands of respondents I've had the good fortune of meeting and who have shared their stories with me.

Naomi Henderson of the RIVA Training Institute unlocked my gifts in moderating, teaching me how to "ask why, without using the word *why*"; to have "unconditional positive regard" for everyone, no matter how difficult; and to have some probes at the ready to get deeper, including "tell me more about that." Thank you, Naomi, for all you taught me and for being gracious when I asked to use the phrase you taught me as the title for this book.

None of these interviews would have happened if it weren't for the clients who hired us to understand *why*. I'm grateful for all the challenges they asked us to solve—in particular, the General Mills iSquad, a best-in-class team that embraced the importance of building empathy before most others did.

The 5 Steps to Empathy came about at Ignite 360 after we declared empathy as our "major." I cannot thank our COO, Lisa Osborne, enough for all of her amazing contributions to the company. Eric Snyder helped me work through the steps, particularly when I was trying to determine if there were four or five. He described the last step as "using solution imagination," and it stuck. I also want to thank everyone at Ignite 360 for all of their smart work, which has made the company what it is today, and particularly those who have led Empathy Camps.

I learned more about the psychological aspects of empathy from my therapist, Greg Millard, PhD. He's been invaluable as both a therapist and a resource for my own understanding.

There was an early, much longer draft of this book that several brave souls read and shared valuable feedback on: Lisa Osborne; Melissa Algaze; Iris Mansour; Greg Millard; my sister, Jen Herink; and Diane Leake, who made me so happy when she told me she "burned the greens to a crisp" because she was so engrossed reading that draft.

Thank you to James Stewart and James Turner for making their cottage in a lovely Welsh village available so I could write, edit, and think.

I owe a huge thank-you to my editor, Emily Schultz, who provided feedback and inspiration that led to the final structure of this book. She made me feel safe and secure in the process, a gift for a first-time author.

The entire team at Page Two has been wonderful and collaborative in making this vision a reality: Jesse, Elana, Chris, Jennifer, Peter, Christine, Lorraine, Rony, and the rest of the team. I'm grateful for the introduction (thanks, Dov Baron!) and the experience.

One of the hardest parts of this process has been deciding on the jacket design! Early on, Perteet Spencer, cofounder of AYO Foods, said, "Rob, you're a researcher; you need to research this." And so I did. More than 130 people responded to my personal request to complete a survey, and over thirty clients, colleagues, and friends agreed to one-on-one calls.

Thanks to everyone who shared their feedback: Vicky Mostovoy, Joe Lam, Katie Jensen, Kerry Juhl, Simon Hough, Kim Spaid, Molly Wright, Tisa Ford, Katy Steadman, Elizabeth Oates, Anna Estlund, Cory Lommel, Sarah Daniels, Julio Acosta, Sharon Hoeting, Renee Balliet, Julie Kurd, Susmita Burnett, Rachel Endress,

Kelly Kees, Tori Palmer-Kern, Claire Farber, Lisa Osborne, Kaylin Tucker, Joe Bagby, Kirsten Killean, Quincy Long, Jon Overlie, Sara Wight, Carol Kauder, Mark Elder, Stephanie Spencer, Robin Algaze, Becky Clontz, Nate Depies, Lori Lekfowitz, Lauren Collins, and Mark Achler—I'm grateful for you sharing your opinion.

Thanks to Ignite 360's intern, Simona Zhang, who built an understanding of who might be interested in this book and analyzed research on the jacket design. And thank you to my friends at our "sister agency," Delineate—notably, James Turner, Ben Leet, and Francisco De La Torre-Gutierrez, for their help with our data collection.

I consider myself incredibly lucky to have had both of my grandmothers, Mae Volpe and Sarah Sturm, alive well into my fifties. Love to both of you! More cookies are on their way.

I'm most grateful for my parents, Mike and Margaret Volpe, who have always supported me, no matter what it meant for them. They've always been there for me, and the same has been true with my writing this book; they read early drafts, took time to discuss specific chapters, and questioned and offered affirmation where needed. I love you both very much!

My heartfelt thanks to my husband, Charles, who always supported me and let me do what I needed to do when I was "writing." I love you!

Finally, empathy is a squishy subject for many people, and I thank you for your interest in the topic. Together we can help make the world a better place. It's not easy to take the time to understand others and reflect that understanding back as empathy, particularly to people with opposing viewpoints. Thank you for being courageous and taking the first step. It will be worth it in the end.

Glossary of Terms

being judgmental: Casting aspersion or looking down on someone in order to feel better about oneself or to one-up another person. Being judgmental is one of the biggest barriers to developing empathy.

cognitive empathy: Perspective taking; seeing a point of view; being able to say, "I can see where you are coming from." The 5 Steps to Empathy focus on achieving cognitive empathy.

compassion: Feeling moved to action as a result of having either form of empathy (cognitive or emotional) with or sympathy for someone.

emotional or affective empathy: Feeling what another person is feeling; being able to say, "I know how you feel" or "I can imagine how you feel." The 5 Steps to Empathy can be helpful in reaching emotional empathy, although it is harder for some people to reach down and access the emotions.

empathy: Being able to see another person's point of view or feel what they are feeling *with* them; stepping into the shoes of someone else.

ethnography: A qualitative approach to research that involves an in-context location, such as a person's home, a retail location, a workplace, or a venue where people gather.

focus group: A qualitative research approach where a small group of participants gather in a central location for a facilitated session led by a moderator.

FOMO: "Fear of missing out." A term coined by Dr. Dan Herman in 1996, FOMO (the acronym, now a recognized word, first used by Patrick McGinnis in 2004) is a phenomenon where people compare their regular life to the curated lives of others, often on social media, creating a feeling of discomfort, insignificance, or falling behind.

making a judgment: A decision-making process where you consider the situation or evidence and come to a conclusion or a course of action.

marketing research: Exploring people's perceptions, opinions, beliefs, attitudes, and behaviors in pursuit of creating better products and services to meet consumer needs.

moderator: A researcher trained in the art of asking questions and facilitating conversations in order to uncover the *why* of human behavior.

qualitative research: An approach to research that involves open-ended questions and exploration with a relatively small group of people in search of understanding *why*. Typically done in some form of conversation or written dialogue.

quantitative research: An approach to research that uses surveys and closed-ended questions with large groups of people in order to understand *what* people prefer, think, or feel.

respondent: A person who is recruited to participate in a research project and is compensated for their time and opinions. Also known as a "participant."

sympathy: Feeling *for* another person instead of *with* them as you would in empathy.

About the Author

 ROB VOLPE is an astute observer of life and a master storyteller who brings empathy and compassion to the human experience. As CEO of Ignite 360, he leads a team of insights, strategy, and creative professionals helping the world's leading brands across a range of industries release untapped potential.

As a thought leader in the role of empathy in marketing and the workplace, Rob frequently speaks on the topic at conferences, corporations, and colleges, and he has been quoted in *Adweek*, Mashable, *HuffPost*, *TheStreet*, *Gourmet Retailer*, and the *Chicago Tribune*, among others.

When he's not speaking at industry conferences, listening to consumers around the world share their stories, or adding to his two-million-plus miles flown, Rob can be found at home in San Francisco with his partner, Charles, and their three cats, reveling in the rare luxury of standing still. He is a graduate of Syracuse University's S.I. Newhouse School of Public Communications.

5STEPSTOEMPATHY.COM

CONTINUE YOUR EMPATHY JOURNEY

Learn More: More content, more information, engaging empathy training courses, and other empathy resources are available at 5stepstoempathy.com.

Spread the Word: It will take everyone strengthening their empathy muscles to bring about change. Please help get the word out by writing a review of this book on your favorite online book retailer's website or reading community. Buy or share a copy with a friend. Post a picture of yourself with the book and something you learned from it on social media with the hashtag #5StepstoEmpathy.

Book Clubs: Discussion guides are available for both personal and corporate book clubs at 5stepstoempathy.com. Email the team at speaking@5stepstoempathy.com to book Rob to join in your group's conversation!

Bulk Orders: Special orders at your fingertips! Working with Page Two we can accommodate bulk orders and special print runs of *Tell Me More About That* for your organization. Email us at order@5stepstoempathy.com.

Speaking and Presentations: Rob loves presenting to groups and can customize presentations for your organization and meeting needs—in-person or virtual. Send an email to speaking@5stepstoempathy.com for more information.

Reach Out:
📷 @empathy_activist
in linkedin.com/in/rmvolpe

LEARN MORE ABOUT IGNITE 360

For more information about how Ignite 360 can help your company elevate human understanding to unlock business growth through insights and strategy consulting, as well as our stand-out storytelling and empathy training programs, visit ignite-360.com or send an email to hello@ignite-360.com.

We look forward to hearing from you!